ethNYcity

The Nations, Tongues, and Faiths of Metropolitan New York

Chris Clayman and Meredith Lee

Metro New York Baptist Association
New York, NY

Baptist State Convention of North Carolina
Cary, NC

ethNYcity:
The Nations, Tongues, and Faiths of Metropolitan New York

ISBN 978-0-9826889-0-8

Cover design: Leslie Crane
Interior design: Heather Bowshier
Maps: Jonathan Blazs
Editors: Brittni Pueppke, Mike Pueppke, Tom Williams
Cover and interior photography credits listed under "photo credits" at the end of the book
Printed and bound by Sheridan Printing, Alpha, New Jersey

Published by
Metro New York Baptist Association
236 W 72nd Street
New York, NY 10023
http://www.mnyba.org
and
Baptist State Convention of North Carolina
205 Convention Drive
Cary, NC 27511
http://www.ncbaptist.org

For more information about *ethNYcity*, the research behind *ethNYcity*, or to contact Chris Clayman about a speaking engagement or something else, send an email to info@ethnycitybook.com or ethnycity@live.com, or visit http://www.ethnycitybook.com.

All proceeds from *ethNYcity: The Nations, Tongues, and Faiths of Metropolitan New York* will be used for starting new churches in Metro New York.

Endorsements

ethNYcity is a missiological gem. It is brilliantly compiled and magnificently written. It convicts the church of His global mission in our own backyard. And, its narratives are woven together so that the reader better understands the people groups in NYC, and also how to meet their physical and spiritual needs. This book will become a template for this type of inquiry in cities around the world. Chris, may your work multiply both in terms of new Christ followers in NYC, but also a mobilized church to reach the nations within our nation.

Phillip Connor
Department of Sociology, Princeton University

Chris Clayman has made a beautiful and important contribution to understanding how God has moved the nations into our neighborhoods in New York City. This is an important piece of research that can inform us how to love our neighbors in the most influential city on the planet.

Dr. Mac Pier
President, The NYC Leadership Center

I am deeply grateful for the many hours of insightful, hard work that Chris has put in on producing this book. It is a tremendous, long needed resource and not only for those in the greater New York City area. I see this book as the sounding of a Macedonian call to Christians in every major metropolitan setting of the world to "come over and help us"—the people of the nations of the world whom God has brought to neighborhoods just around the corner from them in the cities where they live. My prayer is that God will use this book not simply for the tremendous information resource that it is, but to give you, the reader, a vision of the doors he has opened for you to touch the world for Him.

Dr. Mark S. Snelling
President, Antioch Network

Too often, our study of cultures and mission is a purely informational endeavor. *ethNYcity* by Chris Clayman gives the church in one city what I would love to see in every city—a view of who lives here. It is well-researched, written with an engaging style and will surely benefit the work of the church in New York City. I hope many others will follow this pattern and learn about the mission field in their own cities.

Ed Stetzer
Author of *Breaking the Missional Code* and *Compelled by Love*

The New York Metropolitan area has experienced a radical influx of people groups. The necessity of reaching every people group with the message of Jesus Christ has escalated as well. *ethNYcity* is a valuable resource that opens the door for better understanding of the cultures, the mindsets, and the belief systems of the peoples God has entrusted into our care. The knowledge we gain will enhance the opportunity to greater impact the world as those who become believers return to their homelands as a springboard for the gospel. Chris Clayman has blazed the trail and provided the research to accomplish the task of making disciples of all nations.

Terry Robertson
Executive Director, Baptist Convention of New York

International missionaries have recognized that the world is not configured in homogenous countries but as a vast matrix of more than 11,000 ethnic and language people groups. When our Lord sent us to make disciples of all nations, the terminology He used was "panta ta ethne" or all the peoples of the world. Although Americans recognize a history of immigration has created a diversity of peoples in our own country, especially in major urban areas, no one has sought to systematically identify them, their location and cultural worldviews in an effort to reach them with the gospel. Chris Clayman has done a masterful job in identifying and profiling the numerous people groups found in Metro New York. This book, *ethNYcity*, will be a valuable resource for those called to reaching this populous, world-class city for Jesus Christ.

Jerry Rankin
President, International Mission Board, SBC

I have known Chris Clayman for years and can't think of anyone who better combines the intuitive insight of a strategist, the willingness to risk it all that characterizes a mission pioneer, and the humble reliance on God that directs his steps into the most fruitful paths. I am sure that the reader will find new motivation to pray and engage in ministry as they read the people group overviews in this volume.

Dan Morgan
National Missionary, North American Mission Board, SBC

If you are a Christian in the NYC Metro Area, part of a church planting team in North America or engaging in ministry to large urban centers anywhere... this book should be part of your reference library...even a model for making your own introductory work to the ethnic peoples of your own area of interest. For several years I have looked for a model that would guide me in identifying the ethnic people from other nations in the LA Area, know where they lived, who to contact and how to best relate to them as a Christian. On the whole, we know so much about the people groups in other nations but so little about those where we live. *ethNYcity* offers hope we can change this! This book is truly a step forward in facilitating urban outreach.

Craig Prest
Unreached Nations, Inc.

ethNYcity is full of encyclopedic pleasures about NYC ethnic and religious groups: intriguing photos; pithy facts; and entertaining and insightful anecdotes and spiritual commentary.

Tony Carnes
President, Values Research Institute

I love *ethNYcity* and Chris Clayman. The book is well written and provides terrific information on the immigrant groups of Metro New York, but much more than that it was created by an individual that I could not commend more highly. Chris has God's heart for the nations and he understands the call of believers to strategically and intentionally reach out to all peoples with the love, care, message and authenticity of Jesus. This book is equal parts research, education, love, art and passion. It will help you better understand the colorful tapestry of culture that each group brings to the city and it answers all of the normal questions that you and I would ask about each specific population. It is a book designed to be used. I wouldn't be surprised if people that buy the book and use it have to buy another one from wearing it out in the field!

Brian Audia
President and CEO, Surgance, Inc.

Though Ellis Island may be closed, New York City still receives many thousands of immigrants every year. *ethNYcity* is a can't-miss resource for those who want to learn about the people groups that have come to live in Metro New York! As the leader of a ministry to Muslims in NYC, I appreciate what *ethNYcity* provides in the way of prayer and missions information. Everyone will love this book's readability!

Rev. Fred Farrokh
Executive Director, Jesus for Muslims Network

If you have a heart and passion for reaching the people of Metro New York, this book is a must read! The result of years of thorough research, *ethNYcity: The Nations, Tongues and Faiths of Metropolitan New York*, offers keen insight into the various people groups of one of the world's most influential cities. Every missions strategist working in Metro New York needs this vital tool in their tool box.

Chuck Register
Executive Leader, Church Planting and Missions Development, Baptist State Convention of North Carolina

D.L. Moody once said, "Water runs downhill, and the highest hills are the great cities. If we can stir them we shall stir the whole country." In his book, *ethNYcity*, Chris Clayman makes a case for New York City being the highest "hill" in the world. New York City is a catalyst for the global spread of the gospel. If we reach it we will literally reach the world. I have used Chris' research extensively and highly recommend this work.

Aaron Coe
Executive Director, SendNYC

The book looks great! It will be a great asset to anyone wanting to know how to reach out with the love of Christ to the nations living among us. It is a valuable resource for anyone living in the US with a vision for reaching out to immigrants as the people groups mentioned represent most of the immigrants located in the rest of the country also.

Vance Nordman
The Peoples Connection, The JESUS Film Project

What happens in New York City will change the world! This book will serve as your guide to join God in writing redemptive history over this most influential city. *ethNYcity* will serve to raise awareness of the many immigrant groups within the Metro New York City region. It is my prayer that this book will lead to the increase in the population of heaven and the decrease in the population of hell!

Lamar Duke
Missions Team Leader, Baptist Convention of New York

Have you ever read a reference book that is interesting? It rarely happens. But here is a reference book that will hold your attention better than the sports page. Don't start reading it if you need to go somewhere in the next hour. I hope that Christ-followers will use this book to begin a new season of short-term mission efforts. Instead of going on trips around the world, it is very possible to begin strategic ministries with the "world" that is close at hand.

Keith Carey
Managing Editor, Global Prayer Digest

Chris Clayman has produced a significant and ground-breaking resource on people groups living in the New York City Metro area. *ethNYcity* combines accurate and insightful ethnographic research with artful photography and anecdotal commentary, all of which do great justice in putting a face on the world's most colorful conglomeration of peoples. This work will be a great resource, informing greater advocacy for gospel witness amongst the peoples of New York City.

Steven L. Allen
Tri-State Metro NYC Church Starting Team, Baptist Convention of New York

If a person wants to develop Great Commission eyes for the mission field of New York City, then *ethNYcity* is the book you must have! Chris' book is the best and most current research on many of the multiple cultures and peoples living side by side in Metro New York. The peoples of the world will open before your eyes in vivid color as you thumb through these pages. Use it is a prayer guide and use it as a guide to learning about the peoples in your own community. And be prepared for God to change you as you encounter the peoples of this book!

Dr. Van Sanders
People Groups Consultant, North American Mission Board, SBC

Contents

Forewords

When I first saw an early version of *ethNYcity*, my first thought was, "Wow! This is truly an amazing work!" Chris and Meredith have done an outstanding job assisting us in better understanding the ethnic mosaic comprising New York. What you hold in your hands is a visually stimulating, intellectually informing, and emotionally convicting book. This work will assist you in obtaining a better glimpse of the present realities facing the Church in this world-class city. You will come to know both history and contemporary facts about the people. But this is not simply a book to inform. Rather, the authors want this book to serve as a catalyst to move you to prayer and ministry.

The story of *ethNYcity*, however, is not just a story confined to one city. This is a story that is repeated in the urban contexts across the globe. It is my prayer that the example of Chris and Meredith will be an example to other evangelicals in the cities of the world. We need better research to better understand the peoples the Sovereign Lord has brought into our neighborhoods. We need more authors to write such outstanding works.

While the colorful palette in the metropolitan areas of the world is constantly changing, a helpful resource to assist us in knowing our contexts is needed. *ethNYcity* is that helpful resource. May the Lord use this book to assist you in multiplying disciples, leaders, and churches throughout New York and beyond!

J. D. Payne
National Missionary, North American Mission Board;
Associate Professor of Church Planting and Evangelism,
The Southern Baptist Theological Seminary

New York City is the most influential city in the history of the world. Since the nations of the world are in this city, when the church shares the gospel here, that gospel goes around the globe. The key to world evangelization could be the success of the church here in reaching these nations.

This is easier said than done! That success depends upon how well we understand the culture and worldview of the peoples around us. In his book, *ethNYcity*, Chris Clayman provides a snapshot of 82 people groups in Metro New York. Using the most current research and contextual photographs, Clayman shows where these people groups live, what they believe, and how the church can reach out to them in prayer and ministry.

I do not know of another resource like *ethNYcity*. As you read it, you will find your prayers reaching up to God and your heart reaching out to others. If you are a church pastor, church planter, or denominational leader, who prays for the glory of Christ to be praised among the nations, this is a book you will read over and over again.

George Russ
Executive Director,
Metropolitan New York Baptist Association

Acknowledgements

Only through God's grace has this book come into being. It started with the vision of Brad Veitch, who then worked for the Baptist Convention of New York (BCNY). He asked me to document the peoples of Metro New York because, as he put it, "No one has done it, and someone needs to." Brad envisioned this research as the first step in igniting strategic church planting among all peoples in Metro New York. This book is dedicated to Brad and the vision he established. Similarly, a deep gratitude must be given to BCNY for their financial support throughout the process, with special thanks to Lamar Duke and Steve Allen for their support.

When we moved from an idea to action, Van Sanders and Phillip Connor of the North American Mission Board (NAMB) helped tremendously to get us started. I am thankful for Tony Carnes, a well-known sociologist and religion expert in New York City, who early on in the process agreed to meet with me. This meeting turned into regular meetings working together on a religious census of the city. Tony has turned into a good friend, mentor, and excellent source for this project, and it was Tony who pushed me to put our research into book form.

I am thankful for all the people who worked tirelessly to obtain the information and photographs we needed for this project (names are listed in the credits at the end of the book). I am especially thankful for Alan McMahan of Biola University, who led dozens of students on multiple excursions to study the city with me. I am thankful for Kelly Rehm and Paul Pierce of Southwest Baptist University for doing the same. When photographers were desperately needed, Regina Fancher passed on the word to Brenda Sanders of Go Now Missions. I am very indebted to them for not only sending us photographers but also researchers! A debt of gratitude needs to also be expressed to NAMB for helping send researchers for two summers. I am thankful for Clark Frailey and the First Baptist Church of Tecumseh, Oklahoma, who sent out college students from their congregation to research with us. One of these, Jamy McMahan, spent two summers in New York City, bringing a slew of college friends with her the second time around.

Thanks to Meredith Lee who lessened my workload and made the completion of this project possible by writing thirty-six of the profiles. Thanks to Jonny Blazs (the map guy), Leslie Crane (the book cover lady), and Heather Bowshier, who worked hard in designing this book. Brittni and Mike Pueppke, as well as Tom Williams, were a great editorial team. All along we prayed for the right publisher, and when it seemed like the options were bleak to publish in full color, the best publishing scenario appeared right before my eyes—in my office! The Metro New York Baptist Association had just established a partnership with the Baptist Convention of North Carolina, who could not have showed more enthusiasm in providing the upfront money to bring this into print. Thanks to George Russ and Chuck Register for making this happen. Last, but certainly not least, I am thankful for my extended family for their support and certainly my wife and kids, who have persevered through much in order for this to come into being.

Introduction

Recently, my sister-in-law from Texas visited Harlem for my son's fourth birthday party. Around twenty friends and family piled into our sixth floor apartment for the celebration. Shortly after, she commented on something that has simply become commonplace for us (and many New Yorkers). "That was crazy," she said. "There were people here from all over the world, and we were the only white Americans in attendance!" As we recalled who was at the party, we realized this was true. The parents of my son's friends at the party are Algerian, Nigerian-American, Korean-American, Korean, Filipino-American, African-American, Japanese, and Venezuelan. And there were only six families there!

New York City is possibly the most diverse city, ethnically and religiously, in the world, yet no one has ever collected information and photographs to portray the breadth of this diversity in a single book. The book in your hands does just that! When the Hart-Celler Immigration and Nationality Act was adopted by the US in 1965—which abolished the previous policy favoring Western European immigrants—the ethnic landscape of America was forever changed through a new influx of immigrants from every region of the world. Up to sixty-five percent of New York City's population is now foreign-born or children of foreign-born. In the entire metropolitan area of New York (Metro New York), there are approximately two million Jews, 800 thousand Muslims, and 400 thousand Hindus, and Metro New York is the American hub for Russians, Chinese, South Asians, West Africans, Caribbeans, South Americans, and so on.

At the same time, American Christians continue to be the world's largest supporters of cross-cultural missions. A quick ride on a New York City subway emphatically displays the cross-cultural mission opportunities that exist in America's own backyard. Unfortunately, however, the same American Christians that travel two days on a plane to minister among "exotic ethnic groups" in a foreign land are often unaware that the same peoples have a significant population located in Metro New York. Although the paradigm shift is happening slowly, American Christians are beginning to realize that "foreign missions" does not have to be so foreign anymore. *ethNYcity: The Nations, Tongues, and Faiths of Metropolitan New York* helps solve this problem of unawareness, as it reveals the identities and lives of eighty-two of the largest and most significant peoples in Metro New York, encouraging people to pray, which will play a vital role in starting new ministries among the peoples described.

Evangelicals as the Intended Audience

While Christians and non-Christians alike would enjoy the content of *ethNYcity*, the book was written with an evangelical Christian audience in mind. So many evangelical denominations and ministries in the US are purely reactionary when it comes to cross-cultural ministry. The process usually begins with a strong immigrant Christian visiting a denomination or mission headquarters to ask for support in starting a church among his or her people—which usually means a group of people who are already Christian. The denomination or mission board desires to expand their "ethnic" ministries, so they support the new church and begin reporting that they are reaching that particular ethnic group for Christ. While this type of work is certainly necessary and good, it is rare for a denomination or mission board to proactively assess the peoples around them, see where the greatest spiritual needs are, and strategically pray and begin ministry in these areas. What if there are no strong Christians in a particular ethnic group to approach a denomination or mission board? How will that ethnic group hear the good news of Jesus Christ, especially in a way that the message will be understood and easily transmitted to others in their group? *ethNYcity* was written to say, "Hey! Here are the peoples of not only Metro New York but the US. Do something! Pray for them. Minister among them. Come alongside them. Partner with them. Start churches among them." No longer should an excuse be heard that says, "We didn't know they were here."

Evangelical Christians are usually described as people who emphasize that salvation from sin and its punishment comes by God's grace through faith in the death and resurrection of Jesus Christ. They also believe that the Bible is the authoritative Word of God and that personal faith and conversion are necessary. Evangelicals often refer to themselves as "born-again" believers. The evangelical community is very diverse, often diverging on doctrinal points, but they agree on the main tenets listed above. While evangelicals—such as Baptists and Pentecostals—are Protestants, not all Protestants are evangelicals. Most non-evangelical Protestants in the US are called "mainline Protestants," and they are more liberal in theology and politics than evangelicals. While strong evangelical movements exist within these denominations, most Presbyterians, Lutherans, and Episcopalians are mainline Protestants.

The Christian community is much broader than Protestants, however, and includes Catholics, Eastern Orthodox, and others. While certainly evangelical in perspective, I have tried to soften evangelical diatribes in the book against those Christian traditions that are "not like us," while still holding firm to the belief that the gospel of Jesus Christ does not include adopting traditions and customs that function as required add-ons to the Christian message. The gospel, at its simplest, is the good news that God has provided a way of salvation for all who believe Jesus died and rose again, taking the punishment of our sin upon Himself. As a result, the gospel is the grace of God, because we are not saved by our church traditions or good works but simply by the works of Christ. The gospel, then, encompasses the living out of this good news by allowing God's grace, forgiveness, and love to transform our own hearts, thoughts, and actions. Not all evangelicals "are saved," and some Catholic and Orthodox Christians have understood and accepted God's grace better than some evangelicals. It's a big kingdom! That being said, I believe that the evangelical stream of Christianity best reflects the teaching of the Bible, and the profiles in this book come from that perspective.

The Geographical Scope

While there are over eight million people living in New York City, there are over 22 million living in Metro New York, which extends beyond New York City to include northern New Jersey, Long Island, six counties in New York State north of the city, and the three closest counties in Connecticut. The US Office of Management and Budget describes this area as the New York-Newark-Bridgeport Combined Statistical Area. Depending on how people arrive at their numbers, Metro New York is usually listed as the third- or fourth-largest metropolitan area in the world. When many people think of Metro New York, they think of New York City and its suburbs. While certain aspects of that assessment are true, there are many areas throughout Metro New York that are urban, with high population density and ethnic diversity. Despite this fact, most books that discuss immigrants in Metro New York purely focus on New York City, even though there are many immigrant groups in the Metro area that brush past the five boroughs to centralize in places like Paterson, New Jersey, and Hempstead, Long Island. As a result, *ethNYcity* focuses on Metro New York as a whole.

The Complexities of Immigration

The immigration process is terribly complicated to understand. Sometimes people are fleeing from war, poverty, or persecution. Sometimes they are simply attracted to what Metro New York offers or seems to offer. Usually, it is a combination of several factors, and once immigrants arrive, they begin negotiating their own space within the city while establishing beliefs and attitudes that reflect their desired relationship to the home they left behind. Some immigrants say goodbye to their homeland forever. Some cannot wait to get back. Some will only go back if conditions change. Some come to New York in order to initiate that change. Some bring their families over. Some believe that bringing them over is the worst thing they could do. Some embrace America. Some use America. Some assimilate. Some integrate. Some become more religious. Some drop religion. Some send most of their money home. Some would not even have anyone to send it to. Furthermore, the very nature of immigration causes many immigrants to shift ethnic boundaries, which is usually much broader than it was back home. Therefore, the "people group" they are part of back home is not necessarily the "people group" they are part of in Metro New York. Nevertheless, it is not accurate to say that Metro New York is a melting pot. It is an ethnic stew, with ingredients that retain their distinctiveness within a larger whole. For reference purposes, in the quick facts section of each profile I have listed a standardized registry of peoples number from Harvest Information System to correspond peoples described with their most related group back home and those listed on websites such as joshuaproject.net and peoplegroups.org.

In this book, immigrants who come to the US are referred to as the "first generation." They often have culture wars with their children born in America, the "second generation." In between these groups is the "1.5 generation." These are immigrants who were born in another country but moved to America at an early age. As a result, they retain more of their parent's culture than the second generation while still adopting many American ways. The rate at which subsequent generations lose the culture of their parents and adopt a more general American identity depends a lot on the insularity of their ethnic group. Subsequent generations of some Jewish ethnic groups in Metro New York, for instance, have a more cohesive ethnic identity than their parents did upon arrival. By attending *yeshivas* instead of public schools, carrying on family businesses instead of going to college, and strictly marrying only those within the ethnic group, they have retained ethnic distinctiveness. More often than not, however, ethnic identity lessens with each new generation. Some of these become simply American, others become hyphenated Americans (e.g., Korean-American), while others become "closet ethnics" who have an American identity but retain some affinity for the land, food, and customs of their ancestors. When "total ancestry" is referred to in this book, it describes all people who list a certain group as part of their ancestry in a census, even though they might list other ancestry groups as well. When "single ancestry" is referred to, this number counts people who indicate only one group.

Methodology

Over the last four years, I have led over one hundred people to assist me in researching the ethnic groups of Metro New York. Many of these came from universities across the US and spent two weeks studying their assigned groups. I would often give them dozens of pages of notes I already had on the group from external sources along with maps of where they live and whatever contact information I had already obtained. For macro information such as statistics and immigration history, we interviewed government representatives, local or national association leaders, and religious leaders. To understand what everyday life was like for the group studied, we interviewed everyday people on the streets, in the parks, and in their ethnic community's hangout spots. To protect the identity of some interviewees quoted in the book, I have placed an "*" by their name to indicate a pseudonym has been used. Almost all personal interviews were conducted from 2007-2009. Furthermore, we had a small army of photographers that captured images of the ethnic groups featured in the book. Two of these photographers spent several months in Metro New York fully focused on this project. Others shot an assignment or two. Most photos were taken from 2008-2010.

Choosing which groups to study for the book was difficult. In short, I looked at American Community Survey information (ACS, the Census Bureau's work to collect and produce population numbers annually) for New York City and Metro New York and immediately chose to research the top forty foreign-born groups. Some of these nationality groups (e.g., Chinese) needed to be split into several ethnic groups. The remaining groups we chose to study were based on population numbers, sometimes coupled with the lack of Christian ministry among them. For population estimates in the book, I have used ACS information and, sometimes, the most-quoted or conservative community estimates for the group. ACS information is generally regarded as undercounted, while community estimates are usually inflated. The truth lies somewhere in between. Instead of organizing the book predictably by largest borough of concentration or world region of origin, the book progresses from one ethnic group to the next by some unique, insightful, and sometimes unlikely, connection. These connections display the fusion and paradoxical relationships in Metro New York's immigrant world, one in which Little Colombia and Little India are on the same block, and Orthodox Jewish and Pakistani Muslim ghettos amicably bleed into one another. There is nothing significant about the number of eighty-two groups. We simply had to stop at some point, as there are probably over five hundred ethnic groups in Metro New York with a significant enough population to study. Welcome to the world in our city!

Chris Clayman
New York City
March 2010

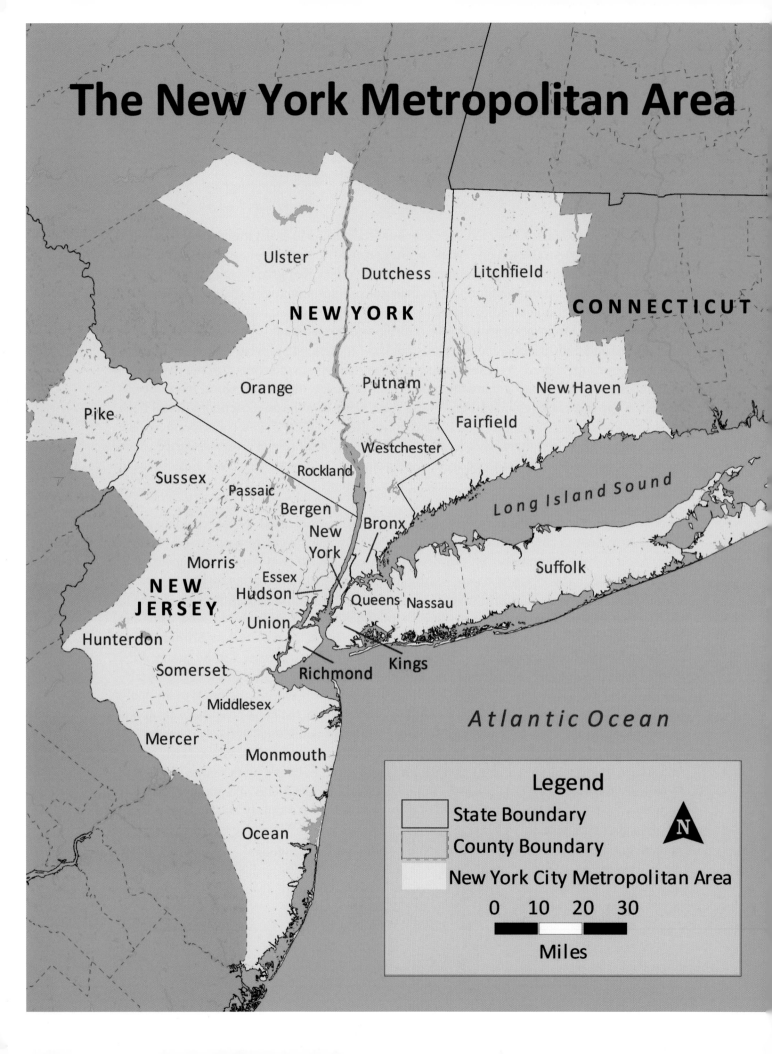

The New York Metropolitan Area

NEW YORK

CONNECTICUT

NEW JERSEY

Ulster
Dutchess
Litchfield
Orange
Putnam
New Haven
Pike
Fairfield
Westchester
Rockland
Sussex
Passaic
Bergen
Bronx
New York
Morris
Essex
Hudson
Queens
Nassau
Suffolk
Union
Hunterdon
Richmond
Kings
Somerset
Middlesex
Mercer
Monmouth
Ocean

Long Island Sound

Atlantic Ocean

Legend
State Boundary
County Boundary
New York City Metropolitan Area

N

0   10   20   30
Miles

The New York Metropolitan Area: Referenced Cities

Waterbury

West Haven

Connecticut

Bridgeport

Long Island Sound

Stamford

Larchmont

Brentwood

New York

White Plains

Hicksville

Great Neck.

Spring Valley

Yonkers

Hempstead

Monsey

Kiryas Joel

Hackensack

Mineola

Paterson

Garfield

Passaic

Jersey City

Stapleton

Clifton

New Jersey

Orange

Newark

Concord

Staten Island

Morristown

New Brighton

Atlantic Ocean

Edison

New Brunswick

South River

N

Miles

0   8   16

The Bronx

Manhattan and
New Jersey

Lincoln Mount Vernon
•Woodlawn
Eastchester•

Van Cortlandt Park

Bronx Zoo

Morris Park

Belmont

Parkchester

University Heights

Morris Heights

Highbridge

Morrisania

Mott Haven

Major Road
Miles
0   .6   1.2   1.8

Palisades Park
Fort Lee
Edgewater
Cliffside Park
Fairview
North Bergen
West New York
Union City

Washington Heights
Harlem
Spanish Harlem
Central Park
Upper East Side
Midtown
East Village
Lower East Side
Chinatown

Major Road
Miles
0   .9   1.8   2.7

Westchester
New Jersey
Manhattan
Long Island
Queens
Brooklyn
Staten Island

Bronx
Queens
New Jersey
Long Island
Staten Island
Brooklyn

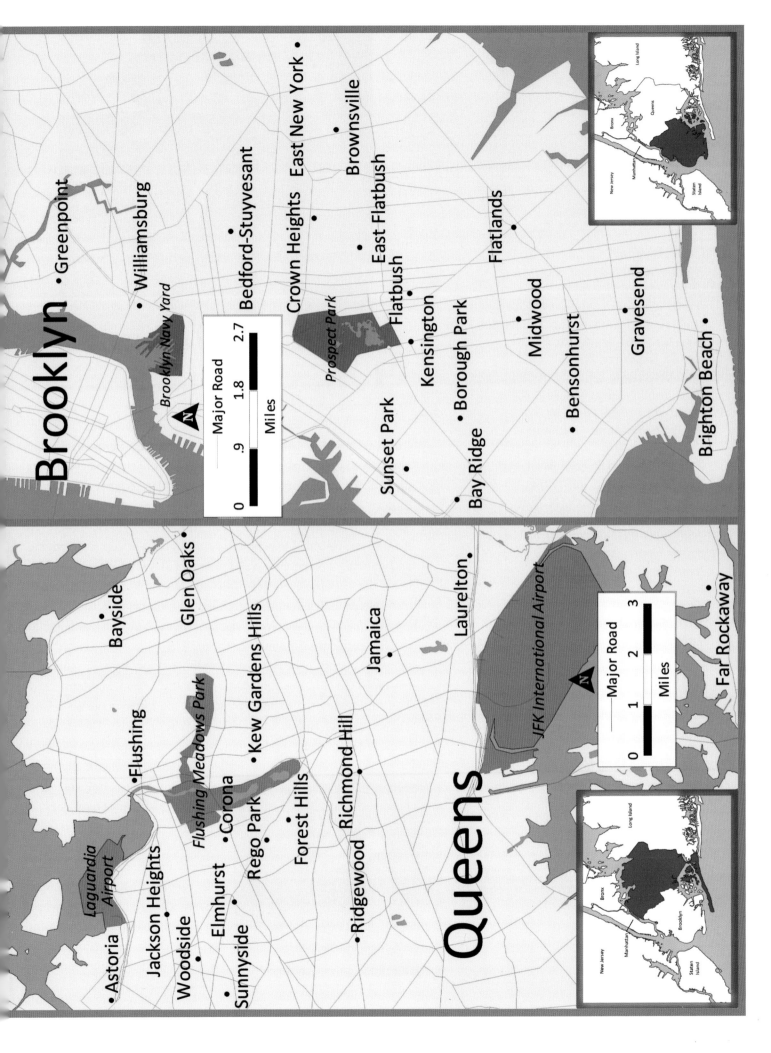

Brooklyn

- Greenpoint
- Williamsburg
- Brooklyn Navy Yard
- Bedford-Stuyvesant
- Crown Heights
- East New York
- Brownsville
- Prospect Park
- East Flatbush
- Flatbush
- Kensington
- Flatlands
- Borough Park
- Midwood
- Sunset Park
- Bensonhurst
- Bay Ridge
- Gravesend
- Brighton Beach

N

Major Road

Miles
0   .9   1.8   2.7

Queens

- Astoria
- Bayside
- Laguardia Airport
- Jackson Heights
- Flushing
- Glen Oaks
- Woodside
- Flushing Meadows Park
- Elmhurst
- Corona
- Kew Gardens Hills
- Sunnyside
- Rego Park
- Forest Hills
- Ridgewood
- Richmond Hill
- Jamaica
- Laurelton
- JFK International Airport
- Far Rockaway

N

Major Road

Miles
0   1   2   3

New Jersey
Bronx
Long Island
Manhattan
Queens
Brooklyn
Staten Island

Bobover Jews

QUICK FACTS:

Place of Origin:
Southern Poland (Galicia)

Significant Subgroups:
Those that follow Mordechai Dovid Unger as their rebbe and those that follow Ben Zion Aryeh Leibish Halberstam.

Location in Metro New York:
Brooklyn (Borough Park, Williamsburg); Rockland County (Monsey)

Population in Metro New York:
10,000 (Community Estimate)

Primary Religion:
Judaism (Bobover Hasidism)

Status of Christian Witness:
Less than 2% evangelical. Some evangelical resources available, but no active church planting within the past two years.

Primary Language:
Yiddish

Secondary Language:
English

Significant Notes:

※ Hasidic Jews will not take a census, citing God's judgment of King David for counting the Israelites in II Samuel 24.

※ Bobover Jews, like all Hasidim, maintain a distinctive appearance rooted in Eastern European tradition and biblical commands to the Israelites.

※ Men wear long black coats, black pants, and black hats—fur hats on Sabbath. Along their waists, they have a white belt with fringe called a *tzitzit*. Men also wear full beards and *peyos*, which are uncut, often curled sideburns.

※ Women dress modestly with arms and legs covered. Upon marriage, women cut their hair short and wear wigs or head coverings.

※ Hasidic Jews typically have large families—7.9 children on average.[3]

"**I**f I were a rich man [....] I'd discuss the holy books with the learned men, several hours every day. That would be the sweetest thing of all!" sang the character Tevye in *Fiddler on the Roof*. Tevye's song aptly illustrates a problem with Orthodox Judaism's emphasis on study of the Torah (Jewish Scriptures) as the best way to grow closer to God—most Jews did not have the means or time for such in-depth scholarship. In late eighteenth-century Eastern Europe, a movement called Hasidism arose to challenge this tradition. Hasidim, which means "pious ones" in Hebrew, teach that prayer, mystical experiences, and joyful worship with singing and dancing are equally valid ways of drawing closer to God. Over the centuries, Hasidic Judaism has broken into numerous movements called "courts," each led by a rebbe, a spiritual leader revered for his holiness and wisdom. Metro New York is home to the largest Hasidic population in the US with an estimated 165 thousand people.[1] The Bobover Hasidim, numbering approximately ten thousand, are the third-largest Hasidic group in Metro New York, following the Satmar (p. 46) and the Lubavitcher (p. 174).[2] The essence of Bobov teaching is *shalom* or peace. The Bobover are known for their moderation and tolerance, qualities modeled

by the first American Bobover rebbe, Shlomo Halberstamm. Sometimes tolerance only goes so far, however! The Bobover split in 2005 after the death of Rebbe Halberstamm's son, Naftali. One side claims Naftali's younger brother is the rightful rebbe, while the others champion his son-in-law. The Bobover maintain two rival synagogues while the matter is before a Jewish court.

When Did They Come To New York?

Hasidic Jews came late to America, opting to stay in Eastern Europe during the massive Jewish emigration from 1880-1920. Bobover Jews took their name from their hometown, Bobowa, in the region of Galicia in southern Poland. Ninety percent of Polish Jews perished in the Holocaust, including the Bobover rebbe. Among the survivors were his son Shlomo Halberstamm and grandson, who came to New York and rebuilt the community. Bobov has attracted other Jews with its moderate and peaceful ways. Today, very few Bobovers are descendents of Polish immigrants. Instead, most were drawn to Bobov from other Jewish communities.

Where Do They Live?

Observing the mass of Bobover families out for a Sabbath stroll, it is easy to see how 48th Street in Brooklyn's Borough Park received the name "Bobover Promenade." The Bobov left Crown Heights for Borough Park in the late 1960s to escape growing crime, settling along 48th Street between 14th and 15th Avenues. Their two rival synagogues are on 45th and 48th Streets. Because housing in Borough Park is expensive, some Bobovers live in other Hasidic enclaves, such as neighboring Williamsburg and Rockland County's Monsey in upstate New York.

What Do They Believe?

Like all Hasidim, the Bobover's beliefs are centered on studying the Torah and obeying the 613 *mitzvot* (commandments), laws that cover every aspect of life and include ethical, social, and ritual obligations. At the core of Hasidic belief is the power of prayer—especially the prayers of the rebbe—to obtain miracles typically related to health or business concerns. The Bobover tend to downplay tales of miracles performed by their rebbe, focusing instead on the rebbe's holiness and wisdom. Bobover Jews are friendly with all Hasids. They do not take a political stand on Israel, unlike the Lubavitch and Satmar, who disagree vehemently on the subject.

What Are Their Lives Like?

If a young Bobover man wants to pursue secular studies after the *yeshiva*, a religious school, the rebbe will not forbid him. This openness, uncommon among other Hasidic groups, has provided the Bobovers with a home-grown crop of professionals that serve the community. Like all Hasidim, Bobovers center their lives on family, community, and worship. They marry young, raise large families, and have defined roles. Women manage the home and children, and men have a few career options, such as rabbinical studies, teaching at the *yeshiva*, or entering a profession or family business.

How Can I Pray?

✳ The Bobover seek *shalom* in their lives, a word that signifies being "complete, perfect, and full." Pray that they would recognize Christ as Messiah and *Sar Shalom*, the Prince of Peace.

When West Indians, including Trinidadians, became a large presence in Crown Heights in the 1960s, the Lubavitch Jews decided to stay, but all of the Bobover Jews moved to Borough Park, Brooklyn.

Afro-Trinidadians

QUICK FACTS:

Place of Origin:
  Trinidad and Tobago

Location in Metro New York:
  Brooklyn (Flatbush, East Flatbush, Crown Heights, Flatlands, Canarsie); Queens (Cambria Heights)

Population in Metro New York:
  210,000 (Community Estimate); 116,316 (ACS 2008 Born in Trinidad and Tobago); 103,952 (ACS 2008 Total Ancestry Reported)

Population in New York City:
  91,495 (ACS 2008 Born in Trinidad and Tobago); 78,482 (ACS 2008 Total Ancestry Reported)

Primary Religion:
  Christianity (Roman Catholic, evangelical, mainline Protestant)

Secondary Religions:
  Islam, Shango, Spiritual Baptist, Rastafarianism

Status of Christian Witness:
  Greater than or equal to 10% evangelical.

Primary Languages:
  English, Trinidadian Creole

Registry of Peoples Code:
  110196

Significant Notes:
  ❉ Christopher Columbus discovered Trinidad and Tobago and named them. Trinidad is the larger and more populous island.
  ❉ The steel pan drum and calypso music were invented in Trinidad and Tobago.
  ❉ Basketball great Kareem Abdul-Jabbar's grandparents emigrated from Trinidad to New York City, where Abdul-Jabbar was born and raised.

There is no bigger annual party in New York City than Carnival, the weeklong festival of Caribbean concerts, costume pageants, steel drum music contests, and other cultural events that lead up to the wild West Indian-American Day Parade on Labor Day. Over three million people participate in the annual parade along Eastern Parkway in Brooklyn.[1] The celebration, held in many countries across the Caribbean, traces its roots to West Africa, where festivities performed for tribal deities were transported to the Caribbean as a result of the slave trade. In the Caribbean, the celebration has taken on a life of its own, and the island of Trinidad, just a few miles from Venezuela, is widely regarded as the original host and perpetual heart of the Caribbean Carnival. Trinis, as people from Trinidad are often called, brought the party to New York in the 1920s, and the event has continued to evolve, with people now wearing massive, colorful costumes that sometimes require the support of wheeled contraptions to wear! In the last US Census, close to seventy percent of immigrants from Trinidad and Tobago identified themselves as "Black or African-American." The rest are Indo-Caribbean (p. 74) or mixed race. While the Trinidad and Tobago Consulate and other community leaders believe there to be several hundred thousand Trinis in Metro New York, ACS 2008 estimated over 116 thousand Metro New Yorkers were born in Trinidad and Tobago.[2]

When Did They Come To New York City?

While smaller waves of migration from Trinidad and Tobago took place throughout the twentieth century, the only large wave started in the 1980s. Trinidad and Tobago's economy was largely dependent on oil. When oil prices plummeted in the late 1980s, the country went into a recession, and New York's Trini population subsequently increased by fifty-seven percent through the 1990s.[3] Recovery in the home country has taken place quickly, however, and Trinidad and Tobago now has one of the highest economic growth rates and per capita incomes in Latin America.[4] Consequently, migration has slowed down, and wealthier and older Trini New Yorkers are returning home to invest or retire.

Where Do They Live?

Eastern Parkway in Crown Heights, Brooklyn, is filled with sounds of calypso and smells of curry chicken and roti every day of the year, not just during the Carnival festivities. This neighborhood, along with neighboring East Flatbush and Flatbush, are the US centers of Caribbean life. Afro-Trinidadians in Metro New York prefer to live in the city, and the greatest concentration lives in these neighborhoods just east of Prospect Park in Brooklyn.

What Do They Believe?

Wharton Nicholson came to New York to attend school but saw a bigger need once he arrived. "Many Trinis had come to New York City, and once they arrived they forgot all about God," he said. "I felt called to stay and work with them, so I planted a church." While the small country of Trinidad and Tobago is very diverse religiously due to the Indo-Caribbean population, most Afro-Trinidadians claim to be Christian. Pastor Nicholson claimed that the population in New York is forty percent Catholic, forty percent evangelical, and twenty percent Anglican although other community leaders have claimed the Catholic population to be larger than the evangelical. Either way, Caribbean Baptist and Pentecostal churches abound in Brooklyn, with some having more of a Trini concentration than others. Although a small percentage of the population, some Afro-Trinidadians are Muslim or belong to Afro-centric religions such as Shango, Spiritual Baptist, and Rastafarianism.

What Are Their Lives Like?

"We didn't even know there were blacks, Indians, or Chinese in Trinidad until we all came to the US—they were just people," a Trini business owner claimed, referring to the race consciousness of Americans. This has been a struggle for Afro-Trinidadians, who feel they are misjudged and stereotyped regularly, especially since they pride themselves on their value of education. The same business owner claimed every Trini grows up hearing, "The future of Trinidad and Tobago is in your schoolbag," and stated that many Afro-Trinidadians are teachers and professors in New York. Other occupational niches include nursing, domestic work, technical fields, and small business.

How Can I Pray?

✳ Many Afro-Trinidadians arrive in New York with strong values, faith, and education but find their children choosing another path, which sometimes involves drugs, crime, and gangs. Pray that God would draw Afro-Trinidadian youth into fruitful and productive lives.

Trinidad and Tobago became independent from the United Kingdom in 1962, but its legal and education system are heavily influenced by the British system.

British

QUICK FACTS:

Place of Origin:
   United Kingdom (England, Scotland, Northern Ireland, Wales)

Location in Metro New York:
   Manhattan (West Village), or assimilated throughout Metro New York

Population in Metro New York:
   1,338,541 (ACS 2008 Total Ancestry); 82,804 (ACS 2008 Born in United Kingdom); 100,000 (Community Estimate)

Population in New York City:
   237,343 (ACS 2008 Total Ancestry); 32,321 (ACS 2008 Born in United Kingdom)

Primary Religion:
   Nonreligious

Secondary Religion:
   Christianity

Status of Christian Witness:
   Greater than or equal to 2% evangelical. Less than 5% evangelical.

Primary Language:
   English

Registry of Peoples Codes:
   102927, 108778, 110743, 110387

Significant Notes:
   ❋ The vast majority of the British in Metro New York come from England, followed by Scotland, Northern Ireland, and Wales.
   ❋ "There's probably no God, so stop worrying and enjoy your life." The British Humanist Association has put this slogan on public buses throughout the UK. Similar "bus campaigns" have been launched in Europe, Canada, and the US. See http://www.atheistbus.org.uk.
   ❋ Many evangelical organizations in the US have British roots, including the Salvation Army, which was founded in London in 1865.

"**W**hen we move here, we basically blend in. But we stand out, too—we're proud to be British!" explained Nicky, the owner of three very successful British businesses on Greenwich Avenue in Manhattan's West Village. Her shops are among the few places in Metro New York to find a proper English tea (the meal eaten in late afternoon, not the beverage) or a good fish and chips dinner. Despite the support of six thousand residents, Virgin Atlantic Airways, and New York-based British celebrities, a campaign to officially name the block "Little Britain" failed to convince a Manhattan Community Board in 2007. The reason cited by board members? "There's nothing specifically British about that block. There's no significant congregation of British people," they said.[1] While it is ironic that the British, who live in a city named after their own royalty, were denied a small street sign denoting their presence, it was hard to argue otherwise. Over 1.3 million people in Metro New York claim British ancestry,[2] but only a portion of these have a distinct British identity, and there is no stretch of land in Metro New York that can accurately be called "Little Britain." The British people hail from what is officially called the United Kingdom of Great Britain and Northern Ireland, composed of England, Scotland, Wales, and Northern Ireland. While all are British citizens, growing nationalism in recent years means that more people choose to identify themselves

as English, Scottish, Welsh, or Irish—a trend confirmed by responses to ancestry surveys in the US.[3] Community leaders suggest Metro New York is home to 100 thousand British.[4]

When Did They Come To New York?

With little resistance, the British navy took control of New Amsterdam from the Dutch in 1664, renaming it New York after the Duke of York, who later became King James II. British settlers arrived soon after. The British controlled New York City during the American Revolution, making it a refuge for colonists remaining loyal to the British Crown. Although a small number of British loyalists left after the war, the majority of the British stayed and transferred their allegiance to the new nation. Throughout the nineteenth century, a steady number of British immigrated but were greatly outpaced by other Europeans. From 1920-1969, the United Kingdom never filled its immigration quota, but many of those who did immigrate to the US were highly educated and skilled professionals. The most recent immigration wave began in the 1990s with many drawn by jobs in the fashion industry, the banking and financial sector, or with British multi-national corporations.

Where Do They Live?

The year 1783—before British loyalists and military had left—was likely the last time a large group of British citizens was concentrated anywhere in Metro New York! Today's British immigrants settle in communities reflective of their demographic identity rather than their ethnic identity. Artists and young professionals tend to live in urban neighborhoods such as the West Village. Those with families usually prefer the suburbs. Kearny, New Jersey, still bears the legacy of British ancestors who worked in a local thread mill in the early 1900s, including a store selling kilts and bagpipes, a fish and chips shop, and a strong tradition of producing top soccer players.

What Do They Believe?

"Perhaps ninety-seven percent are nonreligious," John, the director of St. George's Society, surmised. While Britain was once a leading Christian nation with a huge missionary force, the British no longer have a religious identity. Older people are the most likely to belong to a church, usually Episcopal (if English), Presbyterian (if Scottish), or Catholic. The trendy "New Atheism" promoted by British authors such as Richard Dawkins has capitalized on the corrosion of Britain's Christian heritage.

What Are Their Lives Like?

"It's 8 AM in New York. Beer and breakfast are on the table and football [soccer] or rugby is live on satellite TV!" That is how John described the scene in some New York sports bars frequented by the British. While the British are quite assimilated, sports draw them together. "Most are happy living in Metro New York," said John. "I've never met anyone who says it's horrible!"

How Can I Pray?

✳ Living in Metro New York, the British are exposed to a far more religious culture than at home. Pray that they would explore and experience biblical Christianity in this new context.

The British, like the Canadians, have many people living in Metro New York but are very "hidden" due to a lack of social organizations or an ethnic enclave.

Canadians

QUICK FACTS:

Place of Origin:
Canada

Significant Subgroups:
English Canadians (70%); French Canadians (30%)

Location in Metro New York:
Assimilated throughout entire New York Metro area, with a large concentration in Manhattan

Population in Metro New York:
100,000 (Community Estimate); 54,017 (ACS 2008 Born in Canada)

Population in New York City:
21,917 (ACS 2008 Born in Canada)

Primary Religion:
Christianity (mainline Protestant, Roman Catholic, evangelical)

Secondary Religion:
Nonreligious

Status of Christian Witness:
Greater than or equal to 5% evangelical. Less than 10% evangelical.

Primary Languages:
English, French

Registry of Peoples Codes:
101869, 103066

Significant Notes:

❋ Canadians affectionately refer to themselves as "Canucks" although it is possible some may take offense if an American uses the term.

❋ An estimated 70,000 to 99,000 undocumented Canadians are in the US.[4]

❋ Québec's most recent referendum to secede from Canada was defeated in 1995.

❋ Current Canadian Prime Minister Stephen Harper is an evangelical Christian who attends a Christian and Missionary Alliance church.

❋ The National Hockey League (NHL) consists of 24 American and 6 Canadian teams. In the 2008-09 season, 52% of NHL players were Canadian.[5]

"What gave away the fact that I'm Canadian?" asked the young man sitting across the table at a Tim Hortons doughnut shop in Times Square. Canadians have a special place in their hearts for Tim Hortons—their home-grown equivalent to Dunkin' Donuts—and they are more likely to be savoring a latte there than at Starbucks. Since detecting a Canadian by sight or speech can be a real challenge, frequenting Tim Hortons is one of the best ways to catch sight of a Canadian New Yorker! Canadians have been coming to the United States since colonial times, but in the last two decades the number of Canadians has grown, largely due to the passage of the North American Free Trade Agreement (NAFTA) in 1993. Although it is now easier for Canadians to work in the US, they must work at specific jobs for approved companies. Like the US, Canada was inhabited by native peoples, called First Nations, before it was settled by French and British colonists in the sixteenth and seventeenth centuries. Tensions have always run high between Canada's British and French cultures. Québec Province, the center of French-speaking Canada, has long desired independence. Historically, Metro New York's Canadian population has been roughly split between English and French Canadians although more of the recent arrivals have predominately been English-speaking. The Canadian Consulate estimates that 100 thousand Canadians live in Metro New York.

When Did They Come To New York?

Canadian immigration has fluctuated over the centuries. It peaked in the 1930s and reached its lowest point in the 1980s. Numbers picked up in the 1990s after NAFTA but have slipped since 2000. Because Canada has enjoyed long-term peace and prosperity, most

Canadians choose to come to Metro New York for better career opportunities or to experience life in the Big Apple.

Where Do They Live?

"You can't pick us out of a crowd," said the young Tim Hortons customer. "We don't look different, we speak the same language, we blend right in." Because they share so much in common with Americans, Canadians have never felt much need to live together and form a "Little Canada" in Metro New York. Canadians can be found throughout the area, from the city to the suburbs and beyond. Young professionals, who make up a significant portion of recent arrivals, tend to congregate in trendier neighborhoods of the city, while families settle in the suburbs. In Manhattan alone, Canadians make up the ninth-largest foreign-born population (ACS 2008).

What Do They Believe?

Canadians in Metro New York typically maintain the same religious faith they practiced in Canada. Seven out of ten Canadians identify themselves as either Roman Catholic or Protestant although recent surveys indicate that the religious landscape is changing. First, the number of Canadians who state they have "no religion" has increased to over sixteen percent.[1] Second, mainline Protestant denominations like the Anglican Church are losing members, particularly young people. Third, evangelical denominations are growing, with eight to twelve percent of Canadians claiming to be evangelical.[2] No focused ministry to Canadians is known in Metro New York.

What Are Their Lives Like?

Other than hanging out in one of Metro New York's Tim Hortons, going to Madison Square Garden when a Canadian hockey team is playing would be another likely way to encounter Canadians as they enjoy their national pastime. Most Canadians in Metro New York are well-educated, middle-to-upper-class professionals who work in banking, law, business, or the arts. Those who come to the US under NAFTA status must renew their work authorization annually. If an individual loses his job, he must secure another job offering NAFTA status, or go through the process of applying for US authorization and residency under other visa categories. Although their lifestyles are very similar to their American counterparts, Canadians are intensely proud of their heritage and dislike being mistaken for Americans.

How Can I Pray?

✷ Pray that the growing influence of evangelical Christianity in Canada will pique the interest of Canadians in Metro New York and draw them to explore Christianity on a deeper level.

✷ The largest concentration of French Canadians live in Québec, and the Québécois, as they prefer to be called, are around 0.5 percent evangelical Christian, making them one of North America's least reached ethnic groups.[3] Pray that their spiritual seeking would result in finding Christ.

While the Canadian Tim Hortons chain has taken over a few Dunkin' Donuts locations in New York, the largely Indian-owned Dunkin' Donuts franchises have more locations than any store in New York City.

Gujaratis

QUICK FACTS:

Place of Origin:
India (Gujarat State)

Location in Metro New York:
New Jersey (Edison, Iselin, Metuchen, Jersey City, Passaic, Cobbs Corner)

Population in Metro New York:
110,000 (Community Estimate)

Primary Religion:
Hinduism

Secondary Religions:
Islam, Christianity

Status of Christian Witness:
Greater than or equal to 2% evangelical.
Less than 5% evangelical.

Primary Language:
Gujarati

Secondary Languages:
English, Hindi

Registry of Peoples Code:
103544

Significant Notes:

✳ Indian Americans, predominately Gujarati, are the largest Asian-American ethnic group in New Jersey, representing 34% of the state's Asian population.[6]

✳ Mahatma Gandhi, leader of the Indian independence movement and Nobel Peace Prize winner, was born in Gujarat and is still revered by Gujaratis today.

✳ The 2009 India Day parade in Manhattan featured a few individuals dressed as Gandhi, carrying signs with messages decrying the influence of Christianity in India. One sign read, "Stop conversions under cloak of charity."

✳ There are a few ministries focused on evangelism and discipleship among Gujarati Hindus in New Jersey. Two churches have been planted from these efforts.

Mr. Patel proudly showed off the well-appointed rooms in his newest hotel in Brooklyn. Offering views of the Manhattan skyline and the Statue of Liberty, rooms cost as much as $350 per night. This luxury boutique hotel in upscale Park Slope is a far cry from the ubiquitous "Patel motels" that offer discount lodging for weary travelers along America's highways. Patels—"Patel" is the most common surname among Indians from the state of Gujarat—have come to dominate the US hospitality industry. Gujaratis now own forty-two percent of hotel properties in the US, worth a combined $40 billion.[1] An estimated twenty percent of Indians in Metro New York—around 110 thousand people—are Gujaratis, and the majority are Hindu.[2] Along with Punjabi Sikhs (p. 76) and Keralite Christians (p. 58), they make up the bulk of the Asian-Indian population, which is now the second-largest Asian ethnic group in Metro New York.[3] Coming to the US with high levels of education, a strong work ethic, and entrepreneurial spirit, Indians have made a significant impact. Physicians of Indian origin compose the largest immigrant group in the US medical community, accounting for one in every twenty practicing doctors.[4] Indian immigrants have become CEOs of corporations such as PepsiCo and Citigroup, while others have expanded small businesses into thriving enterprises like the Patel Brothers grocery chain, a Gujarati-owned business with forty-one stores across the US. However, the stereotype that all Indians are well-educated high achievers is inaccurate, as more recent arrivals come from diverse socioeconomic backgrounds, and many struggle to make a living.

When Did They Come To New York?

The first Gujaratis in Metro New York were students and professionals who came in the 1960s. The 1970s and '80s drew a large influx of professionals and business people who had the education, money, and connections to find jobs or set up businesses. Between family reunifications, business visas, and student visas, Indians have been one of the fastest-growing immigrant groups in Metro New York over the last few decades.

Where Do They Live?

"People in Gujarat Province may not know where Kennedy Airport is, but they know Oak Tree Road in Edison!" said a local pastor whose church hosts an ESL ministry for Gujaratis. Edison, New Jersey, has become the "Little India" of Metro New York and has the highest concentration of Gujaratis of any community in the country.[5] In fact, it is hard to find a non-Indian business on Oak Tree Road. While Queens was the first stop for Gujaratis, most wanted to own homes, so they moved to the suburbs as soon they had enough money. Seventy-fourth Street in Jackson Heights, Queens, continues to be a thriving Indian commercial center with many Gujarati-owned businesses.

What Do They Believe?

Haana, who works for a Gujarati newspaper in New Jersey, was adamant. "God is one god, and all religions worship him," she said, echoing a pluralistic theme commonly voiced by Hindus. Most Hindus claim to believe in one Supreme Being who

is worshipped by different names and incarnations, often represented by idols. Ninety percent of Gujaratis are Hindus. The most influential sect is the BAPS Swaminarayan Sanstha, founded in Gujarat in the nineteenth century.

Approximately twenty percent of Gujaratis in Metro New York belong to BAPS, which has become the leading institution for preserving Gujarati culture and language abroad. For this reason, many new immigrants are drawn to BAPS, even those who were not followers back home. A devout population of Muslim Gujaratis live in Metro New York and worship alongside other South Asian Muslims. Gujarati Christians are a small minority, and most come from Christian families in India.

What Are Their Lives Like?

"In some ways we are an endangered culture," explained Mr. Patel. "Our children are losing their grip on it, and Gujaratis in India are becoming westernized faster than we are here." Hoping to prevent extinction, Gujaratis work hard to stay connected and preserve their culture. Hindus, Muslims, and Christians each have numerous associations that host activities throughout the year to celebrate their cultures, strengthen their connections, and pass traditions on to their children.

How Can I Pray?

✳ The Gujaratis represent one of the most compelling church planting needs in Metro New York. Pray for God's power to break down spiritual barriers that keep Hindus and Muslims from accepting the truth of Christ's sacrificial love, which has redeemed humankind from eternal darkness.

Although Hinduism is often associated with India, its influence has spread throughout the world. Many Hindu deities are worshiped by Thai alongside Buddhism.

Thai

QUICK FACTS:

Place of Origin:
Thailand

Significant Subgroups:
Varies by region (e.g., Central Thai, Northern Thai, Southern Thai)

Location in Metro New York:
Queens (Woodside, Elmhurst, Jackson Heights)

Population in Metro New York:
30,000 (Community Estimate); 10,222 (ACS 2008 Thai who selected Asian alone as race); 9,667 (ACS 2008 Born in Thailand)

Population in New York City:
3,363 (ACS 2008 Thai who selected Asian alone as race); 3,352 (ACS 2008 Born in Thailand)

Primary Religion:
Buddhism

Secondary Religions:
Christianity (evangelical); Islam (Sunni)

Status of Christian Witness:
Less than 2% evangelical. Some evangelical resources available, but no active church planting within the past two years.

Primary Language:
Thai

Registry of Peoples Codes:
101940, 104960

Significant Notes:
❊ The Thai word *wat* refers to any place of worship except a mosque. A church is called a *wat krit*, and a Hindu temple is called a *wat khaek*.

❊ Since 2004, militant Muslims have claimed over 3,000 lives in the southern Thai province of Pattani, which was a small Islamic sultanate absorbed by Thailand in 1908.[6]

"The most important thing to know about us is that we accept everyone," said Ricky, a former tour guide from Thailand and regular worshipper at the Thai Buddhist temple (known as the Wat Thai) in Elmhurst, Queens. "We even have a special worship room upstairs just for people from other religions," he explained. One of the reasons behind this inclusiveness is the high rate of intermarriage between Thai and Americans. Instead of rejecting mixed-religion couples, Buddhist leaders typically encourage them to embrace both faiths and pass on to their children a "double heritage"—equal participation in the religious communities of both parents. This dual religious identity means that many Thai-American families are accustomed to attending Midnight Mass at a Catholic Church on Christmas Eve and performing merit ceremonies at the Wat Thai on Christmas Day.[1] One expert claims Thai Buddhist temples have become the most ethnically diverse Asian-American religious communities in the US.[2] Community leaders estimate Metro New York's Thai community numbers 30 thousand people.[3]

When Did They Come To New York?

Immigration from Thailand was nonexistent until the mid-1960s. During the Vietnam War, the Thai government allowed the US to use military bases and station thousands of American servicemen in Thailand. This led to a wave of marriages between US servicemen

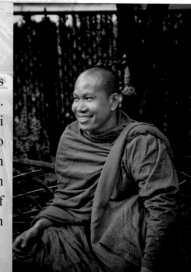

and Thai women in the 1960s and '70s. Once the door to the US was open, others came seeking educational and job opportunities. However, the ratio of women to men continued to be skewed. During the 1970s, three Thai women immigrated to the US for every Thai man. The 1980s saw the largest influx of Thai, with approximately 6,500 per year arriving in the US.[4] Today, Metro New York has the second-largest Thai population in the US after the Greater Los Angeles area (ACS 2008).

Where Do They Live?

"We are scattered around the New York area, but Woodside, Elmhurst, and Jackson Heights in Queens are home to many Thai," said Ricky. Several Thai restaurants and stores can be found along Broadway and Woodside Avenues in Elmhurst. Most neighborhoods boast at least one Thai restaurant, as the Thai have established a presence both in New York City and the suburbs of Metro New York. Thai Buddhist temples are also spread out across the Metro area, from Queens to the Bronx, and from Mahwah, New Jersey to Centereach, Long Island.

What Do They Believe?

Despite their inclusiveness, most Thai believe "to be Thai is to be Buddhist." Almost ninety percent of Thai, along with most Burmese (p. 164), are Theravada Buddhists. Theravada emphasizes the individual's responsibility to reach spiritual awakening by following the Eightfold Path of Buddha and rooting out "cravings" for sensual pleasures, which are the cause of human suffering. It is believed that once a person dies, his or her

soul does not persist into the next life, but a new personality is born, whose circumstances are determined by what was before. As a result, Theravada describes this continuity as rebirth, not reincarnation. The Thai tend to focus on the practical aspects of Theravada, such as *tam bun* or "earning merit," and *baap*, which means "avoiding demerit," in order to improve their present and future lives. In a survey of Thai Buddhists in America, ninety-two percent said *tam bun* was the primary reason for going to temple.[5] Metro New York also has a small Thai Muslim population, along with several hundred Christians—the spiritual descendents of missionaries who first came to Thailand in 1828. Although Metro New York has three Thai evangelical churches, located in Yonkers, Astoria, and Jackson Heights, they are small, and outreach to the community is limited.

What Are Their Lives Like?

"We come here for jobs—that's the only reason," Ricky explained. The Thai community in Metro New York primarily consists of first- and second-generation immigrants, and most come from the cities of Bangkok and Chiang Mai. While the Thai work in many different professions, significant numbers are involved in the restaurant business as owners or workers. Restaurants are often family enterprises, requiring all members, including children, to pitch in as needed.

How Can I Pray?

✳ Although the Thai often state, "All religions are equally good," they have been very resistant to Christianity. Pray they would see how Jesus has provided the "merit" they need for eternal life.

Most Thai Chinese trace their ancestry back to China's Guangdong Province, the origin of the Cantonese.

Mainland Cantonese

QUICK FACTS:

Place of Origin:
China (Guangdong, particularly Taishan and other Pearl River Delta areas)

Significant Subgroups:
Those from Taishan (represented by the Hoy Sun Ning Yeung Association) and those from outside Taishan (represented by the Lin Sing Association)

Location in Metro New York:
Manhattan (Chinatown); Brooklyn (Sunset Park, Bay Ridge, Benshonhurst); Queens (Flushing, Elmhurst)

Population in Metro New York:
Mainland Cantonese number unknown. Total Chinese Population: 650,482 (ACS 2008 Chinese, excluding Taiwanese, who selected Asian alone as race).

Population in New York City:
Mainland Cantonese number unknown. Total Chinese Population: 464,050 (ACS 2008 Chinese, excluding Taiwanese, who selected Asian alone as race).

Primary Religion:
Chinese Popular Religion

Secondary Religions:
Nonreligious, Buddhism, Taoism, Christianity

Status of Christian Witness:
Greater than or equal to 2% evangelical. Less than 5% evangelical.

Primary Language:
Cantonese (Yue Chinese)

Secondary Languages:
English, Mandarin

Registry of Peoples Code:
103701

Significant Notes:
❋ The term "Canton" came from a French pronunciation of Guangzhou, the capital city of the Guangdong Province in China.
❋ Standard Cantonese is spoken in Guangzhou, while Taishanese is a different Cantonese dialect in the same Yue language family. Taishanese was the dominant language among Chinese in New York City for a long period of time.

New York City is a place that unapologetically changes, evolves, and rebuilds. Historical buildings are torn down to make room for new developments, and ethnicities or races that have a sense of ownership over certain neighborhoods suddenly find themselves pushed out by economic or social factors. Since its inception in the late 1800s, Manhattan's Chinatown has "belonged" to the Cantonese, especially those from the Pearl River Delta in mainland China's Guangdong Province. As the size of Chinatown increased throughout the twentieth century, the City of New York primarily let Chinatown govern itself. An umbrella organization, the Chinese Consolidated Benevolent Association (CCBA), served in this capacity, with its president often referred to as the "Mayor of Chinatown." Furthermore, almost all Chinese joined associations, usually along family or provincial lines, that helped its members by providing jobs and social services. Those that did not have strong provincial or family ties formed associations called *tongs*, many of which date from the first Chinese immigrations in the late nineteenth century. Some of the *tongs* eventually became very powerful by gaining control of illicit businesses and enforcing their will through gangs, battling each other over territory and power and forcing almost all Chinese to pay for their "protective" services.[1] With an influx of new immigrants from other parts of China at the end of the twentieth century, the power of both the CCBA and *tongs* has subsided, and the city has started providing more social services and law enforcement in Chinatown. Many first-generation mainland Cantonese have passed away, and their descendants often choose to move away from the ethnic enclave. Although Cantonese is not the only Chinese language spoken in New York anymore, a large portion of the over 650 thousand

Chinese in Metro New York (ACS 2008) traces its roots back to Guangdong Province's Pearl River Delta.

When Did They Come To New York?

Retreating from civil war and responding to California's Gold Rush, thousands of Chinese from the Pearl River Delta, particularly Taishan, started leaving the coast of Guangdong Province and arriving in America in 1849. Taishanese people were contracted to mine for minerals and build railroads before industry changes and the Chinese Exclusion Act of 1882 largely confined them to the Chinatown ghettos of cities like San Francisco and New York. With the US allowing only a limited number of Chinese into the country until 1965, the Taishanese—and to a lesser extent other Cantonese—dominated Chinese life in Metro New York until 1965. At that point, new immigrants from Guangdong were allowed to reunite with their family members, but other Chinese also made their way to New York, including a large number of Cantonese from Hong Kong (p. 42). Over the last couple of decades, emigration from Guangdong has diminished, and second- and third-generation Cantonese often prefer an American or Chinese-American identity over their "rural" Taishan roots.

Where Do They Live?

While the second and third generations have scattered throughout Metro New York, first-generation mainland Cantonese, many of whom are elderly, still exist in Manhattan's Chinatown as well as its "extension" in Brooklyn's Sunset Park and the large Chinatown in Flushing, Queens.

What Do They Believe?

Although the Cantonese could be labeled nonreligious since they rarely attend places of worship, they are, in fact, pragmatically religious by seeking a balance in life through ritual. Like most Chinese in America, Cantonese religious life mainly involves ancestor veneration. Rituals done before Buddhist or ancestor shrines in homes, businesses, or temples are more an act of appeasement than worship. During interviews, Chinese pastors claimed that less than five percent of mainland Cantonese are evangelical Christian although the percentage is higher among the second and third generations.

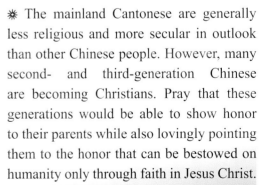

What Are Their Lives Like?

As the elder statesmen of the Chinese in Metro New York, the Cantonese have paved the way for others. By establishing job niches in laundries, restaurants, and garment work, the Cantonese created a path to success in America that required little English! Their ability to buy homes has led many away from the ethnic enclave although many return on weekends to visit and shop.

How Can I Pray?

✳ The mainland Cantonese are generally less religious and more secular in outlook than other Chinese people. However, many second- and third-generation Chinese are becoming Christians. Pray that these generations would be able to show honor to their parents while also lovingly pointing them to the honor that can be bestowed on humanity only through faith in Jesus Christ.

While Manhattan's Chinatown was primarily Cantonese for decades, the Fuzhounese are now the predominant Chinatown ethnic group.

Fuzhounese

QUICK FACTS:

Place of Origin:
Fujian Province in China (Changle, Mawei, Fuqing, Putian, Fuzhou City, Lianjian County)

Location in Metro New York:
Manhattan (Chinatown, Lower East Side); Brooklyn (Sunset Park Chinatown); Queens (Flushing Chinatown)

Population in Metro New York:
70,000 (Community Estimate)

Primary Religion:
Chinese Popular Religion

Status of Christian Witness:
Greater than or equal to 5% evangelical. Less than 10% evangelical.

Primary Language:
Fuzhounese (Min Dong Chinese)

Secondary Languages:
Mandarin, English, Cantonese

Registry of Peoples Code:
114085

Significant Notes:
❊ The Fuzhounese language, Mandarin, and Cantonese are mutually incomprehensible although many Fuzhounese speak some Mandarin.
❊ Other Chinese often look down upon Fuzhounese and consider them "country bumpkins."
❊ The Church of Grace to the Fujianese, with locations in Manhattan and Brooklyn, has grown to be one of the largest Chinese churches in Metro New York. Over one-fourth of their congregation was baptized in America, and thousands of Fuzhounese have been baptized through their church.[4]

The journey starts along the seafaring coastal towns of Fujian Province in China, less than one hundred miles away from Taiwan. Although Fuzhou City is the largest city in the area, the surrounding areas, such as Changle, Mawei, Fuqing, Putian, as well as Lianjiang County, have been the seedbeds of most illegal Chinese immigration to America over the past three decades. In these areas, snakeheads—the term used for those who smuggle Fuzhounese into America—openly market a covert venture into America as if they were selling a legitimate tourism package. With evidence of remittances all around and the astounding salaries the Fuzhounese are told they can make in America, the price of $30-60 thousand to set foot in New York City is too tempting for many Fuzhounese to pass up. Borrowing money up front from family or the snakeheads, who charge up to twenty-five percent interest annually, the migrants set out on their adventure along a variety of routes, most of which consist of long, crowded boat rides and an eventual crossing of the Mexican border. Upon arrival in New York City, the hub of the estimated 300 thousand Fuzhounese in America, they quickly find jobs through employment agencies, usually in a Chinese restaurant in the city or elsewhere in the US. It can take over five years for the smuggled Chinese immigrants to pay off the snakehead, and if they delay payment, they risk beatings or kidnappings of family members in China. Although Fuzhounese are very transient within the US, up to 70 thousand can be found in Metro New York at any given time.[1]

When Did They Come To New York?

Although some Fuzhounese were already in Metro New York, the mass migration from the surrounding areas of Fuzhou City started in the 1980s. These immigrants were largely illegal, but amnesties that occurred in 1986 and 1990 legalized many, allowing Fuzhounese to bring family over on reunification visas.[2] Many Fuzhounese are still smuggled through, however, and Fuzhou remains the largest source of recent Chinese immigration to America. When both Fuzhounese parents are in New York, their children are primarily sent back to China until they are of school age.

Where Do They Live?

In Manhattan's Chatham Square, a statue of Commissioner Lin Ze Xu—a Fuzhounese hero whose defiance of British importation of drugs led to the Opium War of 1839-1842—faces east towards East Broadway. The positioning of the statue is symbolic of a dramatic shift in New York's Chinese population, as the statue has its back turned to the old Chinatown center, dominated by the Cantonese, and looks out over East Broadway, the main Fuzhounese hub in the US. The Fuzhounese also make up a large portion of Brooklyn's Chinatown around 8th Avenue in Sunset Park.

What Do They Believe?

Traditionally, the seafaring Fuzhounese have prayed to the sea goddess Mazu for protection, and this practice has carried over to New York.[3] However, Fuzhounese religion is somewhat malleable, and although many do not attend places of worship, they mix Chinese traditional wisdom and Buddhist and Taoist rituals to bring balance to their lives. In the US, the Fuzhounese do not make their money by fishing, so protection from the sea takes a back seat to protection from immigration officials. As news has spread throughout the Fuzhounese community that religious asylum is a path to legalization, some Fuzhounese suddenly find themselves attracted to the Christian faith and seek to be baptized in a Christian church. Consequently, Chinese churches are strict about the baptismal process to ensure understanding, and many become genuine Christians. These baptisms take on increased significance for the Fuzhounese, whose journey to America has provided new life in all aspects. Over five percent of Fuzhounese are evangelical Christian.

What Are Their Lives Like?

Most Chinese restaurants in New York, and increasingly around the US, are run by Fuzhounese. They usually work six days a week and sometimes more, depending on whether the person is paying off debt. Mondays are big business days for Chinatown Fuzhounese, as Fuzhounese from all over the region come to buy restaurant supplies, phone cards, and other Fuzhounese essentials.

How Can I Pray?

✸ A movement is happening in Metro New York of Fuzhounese coming to Christ, but their transient nature and long work hours keep many from having genuine fellowship with other believers. Pray that these new Christians will mature in Christ and find a way to fellowship with others.

✸ The transient nature of the Fuzhounese could be an advantage. Pray that Fuzhounese Christians would hop from buffet restaurant to buffet restaurant sharing the gospel with others.

In the past couple of decades, Sunset Park in Brooklyn has become known as a Chinese and Mexican neighborhood.

Mexicans

QUICK FACTS:

Place of Origin:
Mexico (Puebla, Guerrero, Oaxaca, Mexico DF, Jalisco, Michoacán, Tlaxcala, Tabasco, Morelos); US (California)

Significant Subgroups:
Those from the Mixtecan region (65%); those from Mexico City and the surrounding areas (15%); those from other Mexican or US states (20%)

Location in Metro New York:
Brooklyn (Sunset Park, Bushwick, Williamsburg); Manhattan (Spanish Harlem, Clinton, Lower East Side); Bronx (South, Central); Queens (Corona, Astoria); Staten Island (New Brighton, Grymes Hill); New Jersey (Union City, West New York, Paterson)

Population in Metro New York:
579,377 (ACS 2008 Specific Origin Mexico); 340,193 (ACS 2008 Born in Mexico)

Population in New York City:
294,592 (ACS 2008 Specific Origin Mexico); 175,875 (ACS 2008 Born in Mexico)

Primary Religion:
Catholicism

Status of Christian Witness:
Greater than or equal to 2% evangelical. Less than 5% evangelical.

Primary Languages:
Indigenous languages, Spanish

Secondary Languages:
Spanish, English

Significant Notes:
✦ There are two Mexican men in New York City to every one Mexican woman.
✦ Many restaurants in New York City employ Mexicans as food preparers and dishwashers.
✦ Approximately 50% of Mexicans in Metro New York are from Puebla, 7% from Guerrero, and 8% from Oaxaca, even though these states are not included in the top four immigrant-sending states from Mexico into America as a whole.[4]

Chayito, a twenty-three-year-old immigrant from Mexico, stops off at a Spanish Harlem taco stand on his way home from a twelve-hour work day. His back aches, his mind and body are beyond fatigue, and he struggles incessantly to stop thinking about how much easier life was in his little town in the mountains of Puebla. Nevertheless, the smell of sizzling taco meat, the sound of Mexican music in the background, and the chattering of Spanish and Mexican indigenous languages around him incite a momentary sense of belonging and rest. Around 1980 it was hard to find a good taco in New York City. These days, Mexicans are in the passing lane to become the largest foreign-born group in the city over Dominicans. Nearly sixty-five percent of these Mexicans are from the Mixteca, a mountainous region of Mexico within the states of Puebla, Guerrero, and Oaxaca. Unlike other Mexican populations in the US, Mixtecans are just as comfortable speaking Zapoteco, Mixteco, or Nahuatl as they are Spanish. In the Mixteca region, these languages are, in reality, broader categories that describe a much more delineated range of languages and dialects sometimes understood only within a one-day walking distance of each town. For instance, ethnologue.com lists fifty-eight distinct languages under the parent family "Zapoteco" alone! Rounding off the Mexican population are approximately fifteen percent from Mexico City and its environs, and twenty percent from other states, some of whom have come from California and other places in the US.[1] There are an estimated 579,377 Mexicans in Metro New York, with 294,592 of these in New York City (ACS 2008).

When Did They Come To New York?

Growing up, Chayito heard all of the stories of how the Pueblan Don Pedro met a New Yorker in Mexico City in 1943 and consequently moved to the city, of

how hundreds of Pueblans followed in the 1960s and '70s to escape political persecution and low wages, and how the 1980s and '90s brought famine and what seemed like a massive exodus of every able-bodied male in the Mixteca to New York. He also heard how others throughout the Mexico City area and various Mexican states had recently followed the scent of money to "the capital of the world." With the wage differential between the US and Mexico being perhaps the largest in the world for any two countries side-by-side, how could the teenage Chayito resist a move?[2]

Where Do They Live?

While spread throughout the Metro area, Mexicans have mainly settled in traditional Latino neighborhoods in the city. They are most concentrated in Sunset Park (Brooklyn), Spanish Harlem (Manhattan), Corona (Queens), and throughout South and Central Bronx.

What Do They Believe?

Even though New York work schedules have made Catholic Mass attendance less frequent than in Mexico, Mexican New Yorkers still retain their vibrant Catholic faith, with the highlights of their year being celebrations of their various towns' patron saints and the Day of the Virgin of Guadalupe. Their intense devotion to saints plays a central part in their religious practice and has led some Mexicans to refer to themselves as Guadalupeños, a term that shows their identification with the Virgin of Guadalupe, the patron saint of Mexico. While other Hispanics in New York have converted on a large scale

to evangelical Christianity, Mixtecans largely retain their religious practices from home and keep traditions alive by sending children home to attend patron saint days.

What Are Their Lives Like?

When Chayito came to New York, he had dreams of quick money and elevated status. He never dreamed life could be so difficult. As he and his compatriots are the cheapest labor force in the city, they work tough jobs with little pay in the restaurant business, garment industry, and construction. Over one-half of the Mexicans in New York are under the age of twenty-five,[3] and many of these have become involved in gangs. While not all Mexicans plan to return to their hometowns to live, almost all retain strong ties to their homeland, sending money regularly and visiting on occasion.

How Can I Pray?

✳ New churches to reach out to the Mixteca are one of the biggest church planting needs in Metro New York. The Mexicans' rapid growth rate, language barrier, and devotion to patron saints pose a great challenge for the evangelical church to address. Pray for workers to start ministries and churches among this largely unreached people group.

Whereas Spanish Harlem is becoming largely Mexican, it used to be solely linked with Puerto Ricans.

Puerto Ricans

QUICK FACTS:

Place of Origin:
Puerto Rico (primarily San Juan)

Location in Metro New York:
Bronx (almost everywhere, including Mott Haven, Morrisania, West Farms, Unionport, Parkchester, Co-op City, Kingsbridge Heights); Manhattan (El Barrio, Lower East Side, Cathedral); New Jersey (Newark, Passaic, Paterson, Jersey City); Nassau (Brentwood, Pine Aire); Connecticut (Bridgeport)

Population in Metro New York:
1,378,221 (ACS 2008 Specific Origin Puerto Rico)

Population in New York City:
786,649 (ACS 2008 Specific Origin Puerto Rico)

Primary Religion:
Christianity (Roman Catholic, evangelical)

Status of Christian Witness:
Greater than or equal to 10% evangelical.

Primary Language:
Spanish

Secondary Language:
English

Registry of Peoples Codes:
108160, 210550

Significant Note:
❋ There are more Puerto Ricans in the five boroughs of New York City than in San Juan proper, making New York City the largest Puerto Rican city in the world. (The San Juan Metro area, however, has twice as many Puerto Ricans as the New York Metro area).

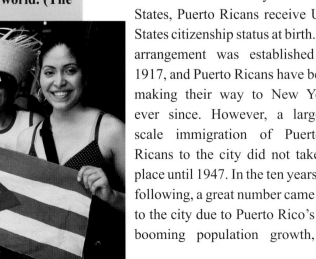

Numbering 786,649 in New York City and 1,378,221 in the Metro area (ACS 2008), Puerto Ricans have long been the largest Hispanic group in Metro New York. However, there are signs that their preponderance is waning. In 1990, Puerto Ricans made up 8.4 percent of the Metro New York population and 46.4 percent of Metro's Hispanic population. By 2008, these numbers had dwindled to 6.2 percent of the Metro New York population and only 30.4 percent of Metro's Hispanic population (ACS 2008). With the massive influx of South Americans, Central Americans, Mexicans, and Dominicans into the city, some researchers suggest that Puerto Ricans' majority influence over the Hispanic population in New York could come to an end in the next decade or two.[1] Nevertheless, as the ubiquitous Puerto Rican flag outside New York City apartment windows suggests, Puerto Rican pride is here to stay.

When Did They Come To New York?

As Puerto Rico is a territory of the United States, Puerto Ricans receive United States citizenship status at birth. This arrangement was established in 1917, and Puerto Ricans have been making their way to New York ever since. However, a large-scale immigration of Puerto Ricans to the city did not take place until 1947. In the ten years following, a great number came to the city due to Puerto Rico's booming population growth, lack of work opportunities, and poor standard of living. The abundant job availabilities in New York City's garment district and other service jobs served as a magnet for new Puerto Rican immigrants. While emigration from Puerto Rico slowed in the 1960s, a recession-induced wave of new Puerto Ricans came in the late 1970s, and the 1980s witnessed a steady stream of new immigrants due to increased violence, overcrowding, and unemployment on the island.[2] Many Puerto Ricans retire in Puerto Rico, while second- and third-generation Puerto Ricans steadily move out of the city into the surrounding counties, warmer climates such as Florida, or elsewhere in the Northeast, where living conditions are better and cheaper.

Where Do They Live?

East Harlem, commonly known as *el barrio*, or Spanish Harlem, received its name from the strong presence of Puerto Ricans in the neighborhood. The Puerto Rican flavor of East 116th Street and the surrounding area, however, is less pronounced these days, as Mexican taco stands and luxury condos in real estate-marketed "SpaHa" (Spanish Harlem) reflect competing entities for neighborhood identity. The Lower East Side has historically been an important Puerto Rican neighborhood, with such landmarks as the Nuyorican Poets Café, but their population

there is steadily declining. Almost all of the Bronx has a strong Puerto Rican contingent, and successful Puerto Ricans continue to move to New Jersey, Long Island, and Connecticut.

What Do They Believe?

Almost twenty percent lower than the total Hispanic count, around forty-nine percent of Puerto Ricans in America are Catholics, and around twenty-seven percent of Puerto Ricans are evangelical Christians, a number twelve percent more than Hispanics in general. The rest are mainline Protestants (nine percent), "other Christian" (four percent), or secular (nine percent).[3] In addition, some Puerto Rican Catholics and others practice varying levels of Santería, which is based on the traditional religious beliefs of the Yoruba from West Africa.

What Are Their Lives Like?

Puerto Ricans love to celebrate. At such events as the Three Kings Day and Puerto Rican Parade—one of the largest ethnic parades in New York City—their festive spirit is on full display. While Puerto Rican professionals abound, social problems such as crime, gangs, unemployment, and an alarmingly high divorce rate plague their urban community.

How Can I Pray?

✳ Pray that Puerto Rican Christians will actively make a difference in their community and that Christ would be victorious over the social ills that trouble many of their people.

✳ Pray that the vibrant evangelical churches led by Puerto Ricans throughout the city will effectively share the gospel with new immigrants from Central and South America.

It only takes one block for a neighborhood in New York to change character, as evidenced along Harlem's 116th Street where the historically Little Puerto Rico quickly becomes Little Senegal.

Senegalese

QUICK FACTS:

Place of Origin:
Senegal (Dakar)

Location in Metro New York:
Manhattan (Harlem); Brooklyn (Bedford-Stuyvesant); Bronx (Parkchester, University Heights, Highbridge)

Population in Metro New York:
30,000 (Community Estimate); 4,553 (ACS 2008 Single Ancestry)

Population in New York City:
25,000 (Community Estimate); 3,652 (ACS 2008 Single Ancestry)

Primary Religion:
Islam (Sufi Mouridism)

Secondary Religion:
Islam (Sufi Tijani)

Status of Christian Witness:
Less than 2% evangelical. Some evangelical resources available, but no active church planting within the past two years.

Primary Language:
Wolof

Secondary Languages:
Pulaar, French, English

Registry of Peoples Codes:
110856, 103074

Significant Notes:
❖ 116th Street in Harlem is the largest African commercial street in America, with businesses mainly owned by immigrants from Senegal, Guinea, Cote d'Ivoire, and Mali.

❖ At the annual Senegalese conference at the United Nations, a representative from Senegal explained that almost all phone calls into Senegal go into Touba although most of the family members of Senegalese immigrants live in Dakar. This phenomenon shows the extreme devotion and attachment Mourides in Metro New York have to their *marabout.*

On July 28th of every year, the Wolof gather at the northern tip of Central Park and march their way through Harlem up to bustling 125th Street—the men dressed in bright-colored *bubus* (outfits with shirts that extend past the knees and matching pants) and the women wearing white African dresses with matching head wraps. The few children actually raised in America lead the pack, followed by religious leaders from Senegal in a stretch limousine. A throng of religious devotees comes next. During their brief respite from grueling work schedules, they chant poetry by their religious sect's founder Amadou Bamba, catch up with their compatriots, or chat on their cell phones with family members in Senegal. Most Senegalese in Metro New York are Wolof, which is the most influential ethnic group in the country of Senegal, a country located on the west coast of Africa. Among the Wolof in Metro New York, most are Mourides, members of a Sufi Muslim religious movement founded by Amadou Bamba in the late 1800s, which emphasizes solidarity, hard work, and submission to one's *marabout,* an Islamic leader. The July 28th Amadou Bamba Day—complete with parade and evening conference at the United Nations Headquarters—has around two thousand participants annually, making it much larger than even Harlem's Pan-African Day Parade. There are an estimated 30 thousand Senegalese in Metro New York, seventy percent of whom are Wolof.[1] Rounding out the Senegalese population is a primarily Fulbe community, many of whom came to Senegal as refugees from Mauritania.

When Did They Come To New York?

Due to France's 1974 resolution to allow fewer immigrants from Senegal, and due to economic hardship in their country, many Senegalese started making their way to New York in the 1980s. Immediately, they carved an economic niche for themselves in the street-vending business. By 1984, many Senegalese came to study at local universities. Other educated Senegalese came for business purposes. The Senegalese influx into Metro New York continued rapidly until 2001 when stricter immigration policies and rising living expenses leveled off the Senegalese population in the city. Most of the Senegalese in Metro New York have emigrated from the capital city of Dakar.

Where Do They Live?

While the stretch of 116th Street in Harlem from Frederick Douglass Boulevard to Lenox Avenue has been dubbed "Little Africa," it is also more specifically nicknamed "Little Senegal" due to the disproportionate number of African businesses and restaurants owned by Senegalese. Many Wolof and other French-speaking West Africans are concentrated around this street, which hosts around ten African restaurants. The second-largest African commercial district in New York City is found along Brooklyn's Fulton Street, from Franklin Avenue to Bedford Avenue in Bedford-Stuyvesant. This area hosts a large concentration of Fulbe people from Senegal, Mauritania, and Guinea.

Even though Senegalese are very entrepreneurial and have a much larger presence in Harlem than Yemenis, many of the delis in the neighborhood are owned by Yemenis.

What Do They Believe?

Along 116th Street in Harlem, stores with names like "Touba Wholesale" and "Touba International Flavor" are adorned with Qur'anic verses, images of Amadou Bamba, and special charms from the store owner's *marabout* to ensure financial blessing. While the Mourides are devout Muslims, their practice of Islam is not considered orthodox by others, as they have an extreme devotion to their individual *marabouts* living in the holy city of Touba in Senegal. In Mouridism, Touba is revered as much as Mecca, and Amadou Bamba is revered as much as Mohammed. Non-Mouride Wolof and Fulbe mostly belong to the Tijani branch of Sufi Islam, and each group has its own mosques in the city.

What Are Their Lives Like?

Hard work defines Senegalese life in Metro New York. Many men leave their wife (or wives) and children in Africa while they work long hours in America to build a home and better life for their family in Senegal. Almost all Senegalese actively plan to return home one day.

How Can I Pray?

✳ Despite several decades of missionary work in Senegal, there are still only around one hundred evangelical Christians out of the 4.5 million Wolof in the world. Pray for a church planter to move to New York to minister among the Wolof in their own language or in French and that Wolof would start responding to the gospel.

Yemenis

QUICK FACTS:

Place of Origin:
Yemen

Significant Subgroups:
North Yemenis (80%); South Yemenis (20%)

Location in Metro New York:
Brooklyn (Bay Ridge, Atlantic Avenue); scattered in Queens, the Bronx, Harlem

Population in Metro New York:
20,000 (Community Estimate)

Primary Religion:
Islam (Sunni, Shi'ah)

Status of Christian Witness:
Less than 2% evangelical. Some evangelical resources available, but no active church planting within the past two years.

Primary Language:
Arabic (Sanaani, Hadrami)

Registry of Peoples Codes:
108627, 109729

Significant Notes:

❋ For the past five years, rebels loyal to slain Shi'ite cleric Hussein el-Houthi, a Zaydi Shi'ah leader, have been fighting Yemeni forces in northern Yemen. While Zaydi beliefs are very moderate in comparison to other Shi'ah, the Zaydi have become increasingly militant in the last few years. The conflict has escalated since late 2009, and rebels have made incursions into neighboring Saudi Arabia. Many fear it is becoming a proxy war between Saudi Arabia and Iran.[4]

❋ Metro New York is also home to a significant number of Yemeni Jews, who have at least one synagogue in Brooklyn.

❋ Yemen has one of the highest fertility rates in the world, and is also one of the poorest countries in the Arab world. Over 45% of Yemenis live below the poverty line, and unemployment is 35%.[5]

❋ A "Free South Yemen" protest was held in Washington DC in July 2009.

Standing on the corner of a Harlem intersection, Ali pointed to store after store nearby. "That one is Yemeni-owned," he said, pointing to a small corner deli. "So is that one," pointing to a hardware store. "And that one, and that one," motioning to the small grocery stores on the next corner. "We're all over!" Ali and his fellow Yemenis own an extraordinary number of New York City's independent delis and small grocery stores, also known as bodegas, which offer busy New Yorkers sandwiches, lottery tickets, and cigarettes twenty-four hours a day, seven days a week. Combining their business acumen and strong work ethic, Yemenis have acquired a significant portion of New York City's corner stores. Yemenis hail from Yemen, a country of 23 million and the only republic on the Arabian Peninsula. In 1990, North and South Yemen were united for the first time in centuries, but the unification process was a struggle, and civil war broke out in 1994. The South, which is rich in natural resources and had the support of the Saudi government, demanded independence. The conflict lasted only a few months until the South was defeated, but over seven thousand casualties were claimed.[1] Yemen still faces a strong Southern independence movement and is also troubled by violent Shi'ah rebels in the northern part of the country and an increasing Al-Qaeda presence. Metro New York's Yemeni

population of approximately 20 thousand consists of both North and South Yemenis, and while they disagree on Yemeni politics, most are on friendly terms with one another.[2]

When Did They Come To New York?

The first Yemenis came in small numbers in the late 1800s, settling alongside early Syrio-Lebanese and Palestinian immigrants. Most Yemenis, though, arrived after 1965, following a "chain migration" pattern by which those already settled would host new arrivals, helping them find housing and work. The 1990s saw a big surge, as many Yemenis lost jobs as a result of the first Gulf War. It is rare to find an entire Yemeni family in Metro New York, as ninety percent of Yemeni immigrants are men who work to support their families back home.[3]

Where Do They Live?

"We're everywhere," said Nabil, a young Yemeni man who works in his father's bodega in Brooklyn. "There's really not one spot where we all live, except for Bay Ridge." Bay Ridge, Brooklyn, has the largest Arab-American community in New York City, and Yemenis are part of the mix. Yemenis live and own stores all around the city, mainly in developing neighborhoods within Brooklyn, Queens, and the Bronx, as well as Harlem, where rents are more affordable.

What Do They Believe?

In Yemen, over half of the population is Sunni Muslim. The large Shi'ite minority, dominated by the Zaydi Shi'ah sect, is concentrated in North Yemen. Metro New York's Yemeni community consists of both Sunni and Shi'ah, and differing levels of devotion to

Islam are often apparent. A walk through a Yemeni bodega speaks volumes about the religious outlook of the owner. Some strictly follow halal regulations, while others sell pork and alcohol products forbidden by Islam. Some Yemenis use their stores as proselytizing venues, posting Muslim prayers and tracts for shoppers to read. Many even have a prayer mat pointed towards Mecca on the floor, so both owners and customers can pray at the appointed times during the day. There are two Yemeni mosques in Brooklyn: one on Atlantic Avenue and the other on 3rd Avenue in Bay Ridge. Currently, there is no known evangelical ministry focused on Yemenis in Metro New York.

What Are Their Lives Like?

"A Yemeni man might have an extra five hundred dollars a month, which won't go far to support a family in New York," explained Ali, "but the money is worth a lot in Yemen. The family can live much better." For generations, Yemeni men have been leaving their families and heading to other parts of the world in order to provide for their families. Many look forward to monthly DVDs of family celebrations to keep them connected. While in Metro New York, Yemeni men work hard, typically logging twelve to fifteen hours a day, seven days a week. Many will work for nine to ten months straight and spend the remainder of the year back home in Yemen. Very few plan to stay in the US long term, as most are using their money to build homes and invest in businesses in Yemen.

How Can I Pray?

✳ Yemen is one of the least-evangelized countries in the world, yet Yemenis in Metro New York are very accessible and easy to befriend because their businesses put them in the public eye. Pray that Christians will capitalize on these open doors to reach Yemenis with the gospel.

Besides Yemenis, the other large presence in the deli business is Dominicans. With their Hispanic influence, "bodega" (a Spanish word for "grocery store") has become common New York vocabulary.

Dominicans

QUICK FACTS:

Place of Origin:
Dominican Republic (primarily Santo Domingo)

Location in Metro New York:
Manhattan (Washington Heights, Inwood, Hamilton Heights, Cathedral); Bronx (Kingsbridge Heights, Highbridge, University Heights, Morris Heights, Tremont, Fordham); Queens (Corona); New Jersey (Passaic, Paterson, Perth Amboy); Brooklyn (Williamsburg); Rockland (Haverstraw); Westchester (Sleepy Hollow); Nassau (Freeport)

Population in Metro New York:
842,907 (ACS 2008 Specific Origin Dominican Republic); 490,934 (ACS 2008 Born in Dominican Republic)

Population in New York City:
580,007 (ACS 2008 Specific Origin Dominican Republic); 348,741 (ACS 2008 Born in Dominican Republic)

Primary Religion:
Christianity (Roman Catholic, evangelical)

Status of Christian Witness:
Greater than or equal to 10% evangelical.

Primary Language:
Spanish

Secondary Language:
English

Registry of Peoples Code:
109534

Significant Notes:
❊ According to the 2008 American Community Survey, 62% of Dominicans in the United States live in Metro New York.

❊ Dominicans are the largest immigrant group in Metro New York, and they make up around 7% of New York City's population (Puerto Ricans have a larger population, but are technically not immigrants since they receive US citizenship at birth).

Known for their baseball prowess and the merengue, Dominicans have been further introduced to a wider American audience through the Tony-award winning musical In the Heights, a rap-infused Broadway show set in Upper Manhattan's Washington Heights, the social center of Dominican life in the United States. In the musical, the main character struggles with a longing to return to the Dominican Republic but, like many of the nearly one million Dominicans in Metro New York, realizes that the city has become home. Dominicans are the largest immigrant group in the city and make up about seven percent of New York City's population (ACS 2008). Among children in public schools, this number is even higher. Now that they have a large, established, and recognized community, Dominican New Yorkers play an increasing role in both city and Dominican Republic politics. Leonel Fernández, who is now serving his third term as the President of the Dominican Republic, actually grew up in Washington Heights, and the political clout of Dominican New Yorkers influenced legislation in 1994 that allowed Dominican Americans to become citizens of both countries.[1] In 1991, the Dominican presence influenced a redistricting of the New York City Council, creating a new seat in northern Manhattan that has been held by a Dominican ever since.[2] With Metro New York's diminishing Puerto Rican population, and with the continued increase of Dominicans, a shift in local Latino power could be taking place.

When Did They Come To New York?

Following the 1961 assassination of dictator Rafael Trujillo and the 1965 civil war between supporters of differing political factions—a struggle that ultimately ended in a Lyndon B. Johnson-ordered invasion of US troops to restore peace—Dominicans migrated en masse to New York City. For a couple of decades, these migrants were largely those who were on the losing side of the political struggle or were otherwise politically repressed. Starting in the 1980s, though, the deteriorating Dominican economy provided extra motivation for people from every class of society to find a place in the already-famous Dominican *barrio* in Washington Heights. In 1991, the minimum monthly salary for full-

time work was thirteen times higher in New York than in the Dominican Republic.[3] While the Dominican Republic's economy and political situation have become much more stable in the twenty-first century, Dominicans still account for a large percentage of immigration to the city.

Where Do They Live?

Towards the end of In the Heights, the local beauty salon closes down in Washington Heights in order to reopen in West Bronx. This event accurately reflects what is happening in the Dominican community. In 2000, there were 125,063 Dominican-born in Manhattan and 124,032 in the Bronx. By 2008, the Bronx had a larger Dominican population, with 140,856 Dominican-born compared to Manhattan's 100,312. Dominicans have also dispersed throughout the Metro area, with Corona, Queens, and Passaic, New Jersey, among other places, having large concentrations.

What Do They Believe?

Religion is an important part of Dominican life, and while almost everyone in the Dominican Republic is Catholic, many Dominicans are becoming evangelical Christians in Metro New York. A recent study shows that forty-six percent of New York Dominicans consider themselves born-again or evangelical.[4]

What Are Their Lives Like?

Two of baseball's biggest stars, Alex Rodriguez and Manny Ramirez, spent some of their childhood in Washington Heights, and many young Dominican men put their hope in baseball for a better future. Dominicans are also known for running bodegas (small, corner grocery stores), driving "gypsy" taxicabs, and working in the garment, hotel, and restaurant industries.

How Can I Pray?

✳ Many Dominicans are becoming faithful followers of Christ, either as evangelical Protestants or as Catholics who believe it is necessary to be a "born-again" believer. Pray that Dominicans will have a spiritual, and not just a political, impact on Metro New York.

While Dominicans have the largest foreign-born population in Metro New York, the Chinese have the second-largest.

Hong Kongese

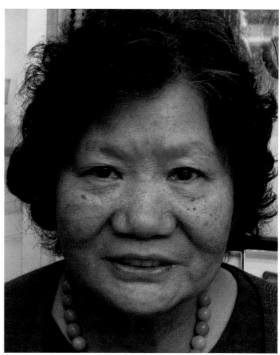

QUICK FACTS:

Place of Origin:
Hong Kong

Location in Metro New York:
Manhattan (Chinatown); Queens (Flushing, Jackson Heights, Elmhurst); Brooklyn (Sheepshead Bay, Sunset Park)

Population in Metro New York:
48,664 (ACS 2008 Born in Hong Kong)

Population in New York City:
33,891 (ACS 2008 Born in Hong Kong)

Primary Religion:
Chinese Popular Religion

Secondary Religions:
Nonreligious, Buddhism, Taoism, Christianity

Status of Christian Witness:
Greater than or equal to 2% evangelical. Less than 5% evangelical.

Primary Language:
Hong Kong Cantonese

Secondary Languages:
English, Mandarin

Registry of Peoples Code:
103701

Significant Notes:
✺ Hong Kongese refer to themselves as "Cantonese" and are also known as "Hong Kongers."

✺ In the Sino-British Joint Declaration of 1984, the two agreed that Britain would transfer sovereignty over Hong Kong to the People's Republic of China in 1997 and that the socialist system would not be practiced in Hong Kong, nor would Hong Kong's capitalist system or way of life be changed, for a period of 50 years.

✺ Most of the Hong Kongese in Metro New York are in the US legally.

✺ Several Hong Kongese have had success in Hollywood, including Bruce Lee, Jackie Chan, John Woo, and Chow Yun-Fat.

Chinatowns throughout Metro New York received a makeover when the Hong Kongese started investing in the city in the last several decades. Coming from a city that sits at the top of the financial world alongside London and New York City, Hong Kongese have created larger, glossier, and more sophisticated Chinese businesses throughout the city. Many Hong Kongese trace their ancestry back to Guangdong Province, and they are proud of their use of Cantonese as their standard language although many also learn English and Mandarin. They are capitalists, cosmopolitan, educated, organized, and largely influenced by the West due to Britain's colonization of Hong Kong until sovereignty was transferred to the People's Republic of China (PRC) in 1997. As mainland Cantonese immigration has dwindled over the last few decades, many of the first-generation "Cantonese" in Metro New York are Hong Kongese.

When Did They Come To New York?

Hong Kongese immigrated with other Cantonese in the late 1840s, but it was not until the Hart-Celler Act of 1965 that a large number of Hong Kongese made their way directly to Metro New York. Although some of these immigrants were refugees from mainland China who escaped to Hong Kong and spoke Mandarin, most were Cantonese speakers who helped maintain Cantonese as the de facto language of Chinese New York. When an announcement was made in 1984 that Britain's sovereignty over Hong Kong would be transferred to Communist China in 1997, cosmopolitan and capitalistic Hong Kongese became very anxious about what would take place. A mass emigration ensued. One Hong Kongese woman who came to New York during this time insisted, "We don't have anything against Chinese government—we just want Hong Kong

to be free. We just want our freedom." The Tiananmen Square incident in 1989, in which hundreds of public protestors were killed by the PRC military, only increased Hong Kongese anxiety. Hundreds of thousands of Hong Kongese left the city, some of whom never returned, and some of whom returned with foreign passports that served as their "insurance policies" in case things did not work out under PRC rule. A disproportionate number of these emigrants were wealthy professionals who felt that Hong Kong's political situation was not good for investment. As a result, New York became a choice destination due to its sizeable Cantonese community, financial opportunities, and the same posh brands they had become accustomed to in Hong Kong. Hong Kong's transition out of manufacturing into financial services left many working-class people jobless in the 1980s and 1990s as well, prompting many of them to move to New York. With a "one country, two systems" policy that has been honored by the PRC since 1997, Hong Kong's economy is doing well. Consequently, emigration from Hong Kong has lessened, and some professionals in New York are moving back to Hong Kong.

Where Do They Live?

Hong Kongese are still largely concentrated in Metro New York's Chinatowns. The largest concentrations are in the Chinatowns of Manhattan and Flushing, Queens, although

What Do They Believe?

Along with other Chinese, over half of Hong Kongese never attend places of worship, which makes them the least religious immigrant group from East Asia.[1] However, unlike mainland Chinese who have been influenced by communism, Hong Kongese are nonreligious due to—among other factors—their materialism. A Hong Kongese pastor in Queens claimed that less than five percent of Hong Kongese in New York are evangelical Christian, which he estimated was lower than the percentage in Hong Kong. A Hong Kongese member from his church claimed, "When I became a Christian, my family thought it was ridiculous. They were so interested in making money, when I gave money to the church they thought it was stupid, like throwing money to the wind."

What Are Their Lives Like?

Compared to other Chinese, Hong Kongese are disproportionately involved in owning real estate and garment businesses. Even though many Hong Kongese professionals are present, the working-class Hong Kongese outnumber them in Metro New York.

How Can I Pray?

✳ Many Hong Kongese were exposed to the gospel back home but have chosen to live for their material success. Pray that they would invest in the "eternal" instead of the "temporal."

Around one-half of the Indonesians in Metro New York are Chinese-Indonesians.

Indesians

QUICK FACTS:

Place of Origin:
Indonesia

Significant subgroups:
Chinese-Indonesian (50%); Minahasa/ Manado (35%); Acehnese, Ambonese, Balinese, Batak, Bugis, Javanese, Minangkabau, Poso, Sundanese, West Timorese (15%)

Location in Metro New York:
Queens (Elmhurst, Corona, Woodside, Forest Hills); New Jersey (Edison); Long Island (Nassau)

Population in Metro New York:
8,000-15,000 (Community Estimate); 6,677 (ACS 2008 Born in Indonesia)

Population in New York City:
4,485 (ACS 2008 Born in Indonesia)

Primary Religion:
Christianity

Secondary Religions:
Sunni Islam, Buddhism, Animism, Bali Hinduism

Status of Christian Witness:
Greater than or equal to 10% evangelical.

Primary Language:
Bahasa Indonesian

Secondary Languages:
Multiple ethnic-specific languages, English, Dutch

Significant Notes:
☀ In general, the Indonesian population in Metro New York is around 60% Christian, 20% Muslim, and 20% Buddhist.[4] There are 21 Indonesian churches in Metro New York.
☀ Perhaps the most influential imam in Metro New York is Shamsi Ali, an Indonesian who leads prayers in a couple of mosques, including the largest mosque in New York City.
☀ The largest religious festival of the year at Masjid al-Hikmah, the Indonesian mosque in Long Island City, Queens, attracts an estimated 2,000 people.[5]
☀ Indonesians in Metro New York are more organized within their ethnic associations than they are as a whole.

During the beginning stages of a new church start in Woodside, Queens, Pastor Lasut* brought in an unusual speaker to lure Indonesians to a worship service. The guest speaker, named Victor,* was flown in from Indonesia for the occasion. He had been a Bible student in Jakarta in 1999 when a horde of Islamic radicals swept into his Bible school, burning down campus buildings and violently attacking several students. Victor himself was captured, tied up, and beaten before being knocked unconscious by the blow of a sickle. When he woke up, his head was partially severed. After he was rushed to a hospital, a doctor merely sewed up the outside of his neck, claiming that the damage was so bad internally that nothing could be done to save him and that he would die within a few days. At that point, Victor claimed that his spirit left his body and that Jesus spoke to him, indicating that it was not time to die yet. When his spirit returned to his body, a cracking sound was heard inside of Victor's neck and he was completely healed. Today, Victor travels full-time, telling the story of what God has done for him. Although group violence certainly existed during the "New Order" reign of President Suharto from 1967-1998, the majority of Indonesia's fatal violence in the 1980s and early 1990s was state-perpetrated against the peoples of independence-minded regions,

such as East Timor and Aceh. At the end of Suharto's reign and into the teething years of Indonesia's democracy from 1997-2001, a diversified series of inter-religious and inter-ethnic violence swept across Indonesia and resulted in thousands of fatalities. The majority of these conflicts were clashes between Muslims and Christians, but anti-Chinese sentiment also led to violent outbursts.[1] Fleeing the persecution in their homeland, Indonesian Christian and ethnic Chinese immigrants quickly made up the majority of the Indonesian population in Metro New York. Out of the over eight thousand Indonesians in Metro New York, approximately one-half are ethnically Chinese, and sixty percent are Christians.[2] The Minahasa, also called Manado, are the other major ethnic group represented in the Indonesian community although several ethnic groups have a significant presence.[3]

When Did They Come To New York?

With widespread inter-religious and inter-ethnic conflicts plaguing Indonesia in the late 1990s and into the twenty-first century, a corresponding uneasiness over the country's economic stability brought a fresh wave of Indonesians into Metro New York. Before this time, the Indonesian population in Metro New York was largely hidden. The exodus from Indonesia included both Christians and Muslims, almost all of whom attribute dissatisfaction with their country's outbreak of violence as a reason for leaving.

New York, even though Indonesians are spread throughout Elmhurst, Corona, Woodside, and Forest Hills in Queens. Many successful Indonesians move out of the city to buy homes in New Jersey and Long Island.

What Do They Believe?

Although Indonesia is the largest Muslim country in the world, most Indonesians in Metro New York are Christian. Sometimes this Christian identity comes from having an ethnic Christian heritage, such as that found among the Minahasa and Batak, but sometimes it is as a result of recent conversion, as evidenced among many ethnic Chinese as well as Muslims who have become disenchanted with their religion due to Muslim-perpetrated violence in their home country.

What Are Their Lives Like?

With much of the population undocumented, Indonesians are mainly relegated to service jobs in restaurants, construction, and other low-paying occupations. Most Indonesians socialize with one another along ethnic and religious lines in their places of worship.

How Can I Pray?

✳ Indonesian Muslims in Metro New York are very open to dialogue about faith due to the atrocities back home. Pray that Christians will forgive Muslims and lovingly share about Christ.

Where Do They Live?

With two Indonesian restaurants side-by-side on Whitney Avenue in Elmhurst, Queens, this street qualifies as an Indonesian enclave more than any other in Metro

Many Indonesians, as well as Jews from Eastern Europe, moved to Metro New York due to religious persecution.

Satmar Jews

QUICK FACTS:

Place of Origin:
Satu-Mare, Hungary (now part of Romania)

Significant Subgroups:
None along ethnic lines. Division exists between Satmars who support two different rebbes, and not a small amount of confusion, as both sides claim allegiance of over half the Satmar community.

Location in Metro New York:
Brooklyn (Williamsburg); Orange (Kiryas Joel)

Population in Metro New York:
65,000 (Community Estimate)

Primary Religion:
Judaism (Satmar Hasidism)

Status of Christian Witness:
Less than 2% evangelical. Some evangelical resources available, but no active church planting within the past two years.

Primary Language:
Yiddish

Secondary Language:
English

Significant Notes:
❋ The vision for Kiryas Joel came from Satmar Rebbe Joel Teitelbaum's desire to create a community governed by ultra-Orthodox tenets, where the Satmar would be shielded from any outside influences. The community has its own website: http://www.kjvoice.com.

❋ Kiryas Joel grew faster than any other community in New York State between 2000 and 2006. The population increased from approximately 13,000 to 20,000.[6]

❋ The Satmar educational system is focused strictly on religious studies. College or professional studies are not options for the Satmar, which means they have very few avenues of employment outside their own community.

"**Y**ou spoke Hebrew, you Zionist! Skip three turns and pay $500."[1] So reads one of the "repentance" cards in Handl Erhlikh (Be Virtuous), a Monopoly-like board game designed to teach young Satmar girls how to live a pure Jewish life. The Satmar are the largest Hasidic group in Metro New York, with an estimated 65 thousand followers.[2] Their extreme anti-Zionist position has put them at odds with most of the Jewish world, which supports the nation of Israel. However, such contradictions and conflict pervade the Satmar story. In 1944, as the Nazis moved into Hungary, the Satmar rebbe, Joel Teitelbaum, was one of 1,700 Jews rescued by the Zionist leader Rudolph Kastner. Despite this, Teitelbaum was an unyielding opponent of the Zionist movement, indoctrinating the Satmar with the idea that modern Israel is an ally of Satan.[3] The Satmar's resistance to the modern world is another study in contradiction. While forbidden to watch television themselves, they sell them to others, operating thriving consumer electronics businesses, such as B&H Photo Video in New York City. The Satmar are also no strangers to conflict. They have feuded for years with the Lubavitcher, the other Hasidic "superpower," over support for Israel and the Lubavitcher's outreach to non-Orthodox Jews. Recent internal conflict has devastated the Satmars as well. Since the death of Rebbe Moishe Teitelbaum in 2006, two of his sons have been fighting to succeed him. The Satmar are now split into two warring camps and have taken their fight to the New York State Supreme Court.

When Did They Come to New York?

After his rescue, Rebbe Joel Teitelbaum came to New York in 1947. Other survivors followed, and the Satmar (whose name comes from their hometown of Satu-Mare) settled in Williamsburg, Brooklyn. By the early 1970s, the Satmars needed more space. They purchased land in Orange County, New York, an hour's drive from the city. The new community was named Kiryas Joel—Joel's Village—after their beloved rebbe.

Where Do They Live?

Although the two Satmar worlds—urban Williamsburg and semi-rural Kiryas Joel—look very different, they are much the same. While Williamsburg's gritty streets are packed with crowded apartment buildings and shops, the winding roads of Kiryas Joel are lined with single-family homes, townhouses, and a couple of shopping centers. However, each community is centered on the *besmedresh*, or the house of study, and the synagogue. The most common feature in both areas? The enormous number of children! Williamsburg's playgrounds are dominated by young Satmars, while dozens of children play in the front yards of Kiryas Joel. Baby strollers and tricycles are everywhere, chained to fences in Kiryas Joel and parked in Williamsburg apartment lobbies.

What Do They Believe?

"O daughters of Jerusalem [...] do not awaken love before it pleases." Satmar Rebbe Joel Teitelbaum used this verse from Song of Solomon as his basis for believing that the founding of Israel was an act of impatience and a failure

to wait for the Messiah to establish the promised kingdom in Jerusalem. Teitelbaum also taught that the Holocaust and the continual bloodshed in the Holy Land were direct punishment to Jews for usurping the role of the Messiah. Thus, the Satmar are not allowed to show any support for Israel or even speak modern Hebrew.

What Are Their Lives Like?

"We do believe in family planning—we plan to have families of sixteen to eighteen children!" This half-joking response was attributed to a Kiryas Joel resident defending the Satmar's prohibition of birth control. The birthrate among the Satmar—now at ten children on average per woman—is possibly the highest among any group in the US.[4] With large families and very limited job opportunities, poverty is rampant among the Satmar. Kiryas Joel is now the poorest community in the US, with two-thirds of the residents living below the poverty line and forty percent receiving food stamps.[5]

How Can I Pray?

✳ The Satmar communities in Williamsburg and Kiryas Joel are very insular. With no known Christians from a Satmar-Jewish background and with limited access into the Satmar community by outsiders, pray that God reveals that Jesus is the Messiah in creative and powerful ways.

Whereas Jews are inextricably linked with the nation of Israel, some Jews such as the Satmar are anti-Zionist.

47

Israelis

QUICK FACTS:

Place of Origin:
Israel (Tel Aviv, Jerusalem)

Significant Subgroups:
Multiple, many of which have a loose identity with Israel, instead associating with a Jewish sect or ethnic identity from their previous location. Younger US immigrants born in Israel have the strongest Israeli identity and are often called "Sabras."

Location in Metro New York:
New Jersey (Fair Lawn); Queens (Kew Gardens Hills, Forest Hills, Woodmere, Meadowmere Park, Cedarhurst, Ocean Point, Rego Park); Brooklyn (Borough Park, Georgetown, Midwood, Gravesend, Williamsburg); New Jersey (Fair Lawn); Staten Island (New Springville); Manhattan (Lenox Hill, East Village); Rockland (Monsey, Kaser); Orange (Kyrias Joel); Long Island (Great Neck)

Population in Metro New York:
200,000 (Community Estimate); 46,656 (ACS 2008 Born in Israel)

Population in New York City:
25,135 (ACS 2008 Born in Israel)

Primary Religion:
Judaism

Status of Christian Witness:
Less than 2% evangelical. Some evangelical resources available, but no active church planting within the past two years.

Primary Language:
Hebrew

Other Languages:
English, Yiddish, Ladino

Registry of Peoples Code:
104088

Significant Notes:
✣ Around 50% of Israelis in the United States live in either New York City or Los Angeles.
✣ There is no primarily Israeli church or messianic synagogue known to exist in Metro New York.

They are the paradoxical exiles. For all the politics. All the fighting. All the migration. All the pride. All the money spent to form, establish, and solidify Israel. For all the effort it took to bring the exiles back into "the promised land," the people were not supposed to leave so willingly. Yet, despite the chagrin of their compatriots, Israelis have flooded into the New York Metro area for decades. Among the Zionists they are labeled *yordim*, meaning they have descended or gone down, as opposed to the *olim*, who have ascended or gone up by immigrating to Israel.[1] Despite the stigma, around 200 thousand Israeli immigrants as diverse as Israel itself now call Metro New York their temporary home.[2] They are religious and secular, young and old, Jewish and Arab, Ashkenazi and Sephardic, and even Zionist and anti-Zionist. Despite their differences, many Israelis plan on one day returning to the land they call home.

When Did They Come to New York?

Israelis have been making their way to New York City, the neo-promised land for Jews, from the moment the nation of Israel began. The 1950s and early '60s witnessed a steady wave of Israelis drawn to the economic and educational opportunities America had to offer, not to mention the much more stable political environment. The pull of safety in New York spiked immigration in the 1970s due to the uncertainty and fear that swept over

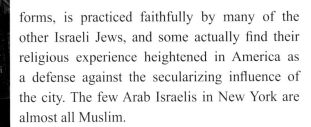

many Israelis in the aftermath of the 1973 Yom Kippur War. From the 1980s into the twenty-first century, a large contingent of educated young people found skilled employment in Israel lacking, and packed their bags for the opportunities and adventure of New York.[3] The stream of young Israelis into New York, many right out of the army, continues to this day.

Where Do They Live?

For Israelis, New York is a tale of two cities. Slip into Borough Park, Brooklyn, for a meander down 13th Avenue, and one can peek into the world of Orthodox Jews (many from Israel), whose lives are governed by a strict observance of the Judaic laws. On the other hand, head down to the clubs in Manhattan's Meatpacking District late one Friday, and it would not be unusual to find a staggering tribe of young Israelis. Of course, everything in between exists as well.

What Do They Believe?

A slight majority of Israeli Jews in New York claim that their Jewish identity is more cultural and ethnic than religious. However, it is not uncommon for them to participate in religious festivities from time to time, even though this is also interpreted as identifying culturally with their people. Judaism, in all its various forms, is practiced faithfully by many of the other Israeli Jews, and some actually find their religious experience heightened in America as a defense against the secularizing influence of the city. The few Arab Israelis in New York are almost all Muslim.

What Are Their Lives Like?

The diversity of Israelis becomes very evident when looking at their assortment of settlements in the Metro area. Those with a more Orthodox bent often settle among other Orthodox Jews in Borough Park or Williamsburg in Brooklyn, or even the Hasidic enclave of Monsey in Rockland County. The seaside communities of Georgetown in Brooklyn and Woodmere in Queens have a concentrated Israeli population, as do the suburban areas of New Springville, Staten Island, and Fair Lawn, New Jersey. Nevertheless, the most noticeable "Little Israels" in New York today are along Main Street in Kew Gardens Hills, Queens, and St. Marks Place in Manhattan's East Village, which has developed into a haven for the younger Israelis flocking into the city.

How Can I Pray?

✳ There are no known church planters specifically focused on reaching the Israelis, and there is no primarily Israeli church known to exist in New York City either. Pray for laborers.

✳ Many young Israelis have come to New York City on a search, be it for money, education, or adventure. Pray that their search would end and then begin anew—in Jesus the Messiah.

Although Zionists find much support in the very Jewish city of New York, Palestinians also have a large presence and are not afraid to demonstrate for their political causes.

Palestinians

QUICK FACTS:

Place of Origin:
West Bank area (Ramallah, Bethlehem, Jerusalem, surrounding villages), as well as Gaza, Lebanon, Syria, Jordan

Significant Subgroups:
Mainly religious

Location in Metro New York:
Brooklyn (Bay Ridge); New Jersey (Paterson, Lake View, Clifton, Haledon, Prospect Park, Passaic, North Bergen); Staten Island (New Brighton)

Population in Metro New York:
30,000 (Community Estimate); 10,805 (ACS 2008 Total Ancestry Reported)

Population in New York City:
4,317 (ACS 2008 Total Ancestry Reported)

Primary Religion:
Muslim (Sunni)

Secondary Religion:
Christianity (Orthodox)

Status of Christian Witness:
Less than 2% evangelical. Some evangelical resources available, but no active church planting within the past two years.

Primary Language:
Arabic

Registry of Peoples Code:
107785

Significant Notes:
❊ Of the Palestinians living in the United States, 11% are in Metro New York (ACS 2008).
❊ Main Street in Paterson is called "Little Ramallah" since 65 out of the 83 villages surrounding Ramallah are represented there.[2]
❊ Palestinian Christians in the Americas primarily settle in Chile, Chicago, and California.

"After September eleventh, my neighbor told me he wouldn't be coming to my carwash anymore," shared Sam, a Palestinian man who has lived in Paterson, New Jersey, for twenty-five years. "He said he didn't want to funnel money to terrorists." Living under suspicion compounds the Palestinians' anguish about losing their homeland in 1948 and being forced to live in militarized zones where their freedoms are restricted and violence is a part of life. Because Palestinians in the US watch events in the West Bank and Gaza in real-time on satellite TV and talk with relatives there regularly, they identify with the oppression and violence. They want justice—to be autonomous people with their own land. Community leaders estimate there are 30 thousand Palestinians in the New York Metro area. Here they face intrinsic tensions: They came to the US for a better life, yet the US has historically supported Israel (their enemy). New York City is where their "oppressors" have achieved power, wealth, and success. Nevertheless, Palestinians have a voice here. They are not afraid to demand justice for their people, as evidenced by the January 2009 Times Square march protesting Israel's attacks on Gaza.

When Did They Come To New York?

Palestinian Christians first came to New York City in the 1880s, with small numbers of refugees arriving after the 1948 war. The majority of Palestinian immigrants in the New York Metro area—predominantly Muslims—came after 1967, peaking in the 1990s. Most came

to make a better life for their families and to escape the violence and lack of opportunities in the West Bank. The tightened immigration policy following the 9/11 attacks has greatly reduced Palestinian entry into the United States.

Where Do They Live?

A significant Palestinian community lives in the Paterson, New Jersey area with businesses concentrated downtown along the intersection of Main and George Streets. The Bay Ridge area of Brooklyn between 4th and 8th Avenues and 60th and 80th Streets also hosts a large community, with their businesses located along 5th Avenue and Ovington. While the younger population prefers the excitement of Brooklyn, families are beginning to move to the northeast New Brighton area of Staten Island where they have established businesses around northern Bay Street.

What Do They Believe?

An estimated ninety-five percent of the Palestinian population in Metro New York is Sunni Muslim, and the remaining five percent, Christian. Their first allegiance, however, is typically to their Palestinian identity. Palestinians worship alongside other Muslims; they do not have their own worship centers. Palestinian Muslims claim to be very accepting of all faith communities, as they just want to "live in peace with everyone." Most Palestinian Christians are Orthodox and worship at Arabic-speaking churches, such as Saint Nicholas Antiochian Orthodox Cathedral of Brooklyn.

What Are Their Lives Like?

Standing outside of his bagel shop in Staten Island, Freddy, an immigrant from Gaza exclaimed, "It is sad that kids have to come in here asking to know the truth. They should be able to get this through American media, but they don't." During and after the Israeli-Gaza conflict in 2009, Palestinians longed for their voice to be heard, and the plight of their people constantly occupies their thoughts and activities. Many still send financial support to relatives in the Middle East and visit as often as possible. With Palestinians holding conservative and traditional family values, young adults typically seek Palestinian spouses approved by their parents, and their weddings function as significant community events.[1] Palestinians are very hospitable and are especially open to talking to outsiders when they can express their political views to—in their own words—"spread the truth." As one Palestinian man in New Jersey claimed, "Al-Jazeera is far better than other television networks because they put everything live—no fake news."

How Can I Pray?

✳ Palestinians feel oppressed and ignored by the world; they see political justice as their only hope for a better life. Pray that their minds and hearts would be opened to the true God of Abraham, who grants genuine hope and lasting peace through Christ.

✳ Palestinians long to be heard. Pray that Christians would listen to and befriend them.

The largest Metro New York Palestinian and Turkish enclaves are both in Paterson, New Jersey.

Turks

QUICK FACTS:

Place of Origin:
Turkey

Significant Subgroups:
Turks, Circassians, Karachay, Crimean Tatar, Azeri, Meskhetian, Kurds, Laz

Location in Metro New York:
Queens (Sunnyside); New Jersey (Paterson, South Paterson, Lakeview); Connecticut (West Haven)

Population in Metro New York:
70,000 (Community Estimate); 48,977 (ACS 2008 Total Ancestry Reported); 32,110 (ACS 2008 Born in Turkey)

Population in New York City:
18,183 (ACS 2008 Total Ancestry Reported); 12,178 (ACS 2008 Born in Turkey)

Primary Religion:
Islam (Sunni, Alevi)

Status of Christian Witness:
Less than 2% evangelical. Initial (localized) church planting within the past two years.

Primary Language:
Turkish

Secondary Languages:
English, Kabardian, Adyghe, Karachay-Balkar

Registry of Peoples Codes:
113818, 102312, 102815, 100079

Significant Notes:
✻ Approximately 40 Turkish Christian believers are known to exist in Metro New York.
✻ Some Turkish mosques and cultural centers in Metro New York include Queens (Turkish Islamic Cultural Center, Sunnyside); Brooklyn (Fatih Camii Mosque, Sunset Park; Crimean Turks Mosque, Borough Park); New Jersey (Karachay Turks Mosque and Cultural Association, North Haledon; Circassian Education Association, Wayne; Muslim Mosque, Inc., and the United Islamic Center, Paterson); and Chestnut Ridge (Halveti-Jerrahi Tariqa).

"**A**mericans find us confusing. They ask, are you European or Middle Eastern? Western or Eastern?" Mehmet,* a Turkish language teacher, smiled as he explained, "I say we are a little of everything!" The nation of Turkey, descended from the mighty Ottoman Turkish Empire, literally sits as the bridge between the East and West—half on the continent of Europe and half in Asia. The Ottoman Turks once held vast power in the Middle East and Central Asia but began to decline in the sixteenth century and gradually lost most of their territory. Following Turkey's defeat in World War I and a bitter war with Greece, the Republic of Turkey was established in 1923 by Mustafa Kemal, known as Ataturk, or "Father of the Turks." Ataturk desperately wanted Turkey to be a modern nation, so he instituted aggressive reforms to subjugate Islam to the government and eliminate all ethnic and linguistic differences among the people. His efforts made Turkey into a thoroughly secular state, despite being ninety-eight percent Muslim, with a diverse population fused into one Turkish identity. As Mehmet explained, "My grandmother is technically a Georgian, but she has lived in Turkey all her life. She would be offended if someone said she wasn't Turkish." Metro New York's Turkish population is estimated to number 70 thousand.[1] While most simply identify themselves as Turk, others come from Turkish minority groups such as the Karachay, Circassians, Crimean Tatars, Azeri, and Meskhetians. Small numbers of Kurds (an Indo-Persian people) and Laz (who are descended from Greeks) are also present.

When Did They Come To New York?

The Karachay and Circassians were the first groups of Turks to arrive in Metro New York just following World War II. Both established communities in Paterson, New Jersey, that continued to grow steadily. Most Turkish immigrants in Metro New York, however, are far more recent arrivals who fled Turkey's financial crisis in 2001, seeking jobs and economic stability. Many young Turks come to get a US college degree, hoping to secure a job that will provide them with a business visa. Turkish citizens are one of the fastest growing groups of foreign students in the US.[2]

Where Do They Live?

Turks have formed several distinct communities in Metro New York. The oldest and largest Turkish community in the US is in Paterson, New Jersey, which is also home to thousands of Palestinians. Turkish shops and restaurants stand next to their Arabic counterparts on Main Street. In West Haven, Connecticut's Turkish capital, one can find Turkish food on Campbell Street and a mosque with a view of the water. Sunnyside, Queens, has a large and growing Turkish community, and many wealthier, professional Turks have moved to suburban Long Island.

What Do They Believe?

"If you have eight Turks in a room, there might be four levels of loyalty to Islam," explained Sue,* a missionary to Turks in New Jersey. Because of Turkey's secular status, Turks have been free

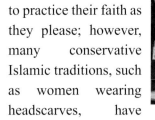

to practice their faith as they please; however, many conservative Islamic traditions, such as women wearing headscarves, have been prohibited at times. While most Turks continue to be secular Muslims when they come to Metro New York, many others find that living in the US allows them to practice a more conservative version of Islam than they could in Turkey. The vast majority of Turks in Metro New York are Sunni Muslims although there is a Turkish Sufi order in Rockland County. The one Turkish church in New Jersey, a spiritual home for several believers, was just started in the last few years with several new converts to Christianity.

What Are Their Lives Like?

"Many Turks heard bad things about Americans back in Turkey," Sue noted. "When they come here, they see those things aren't true. Still, many remain in their own enclaves, just to be safe." Turks deeply value family and friendships although it takes time to build relationships with them. Because ethnicity was downplayed in Turkey, Turkish groups here really enjoy celebrating their culture. The Karachay and Circassians, for example, have active cultural associations in New Jersey.

How Can I Pray?

❊ Pray for the small group of Turkish believers in New Jersey, many of whom are the only Christians in their families. Pray for growth in their love and knowledge of the Lord.

❊ Several missionaries are known to be living among Turkish communities in Metro New York. Pray that they will be able to build strong relationships in the community and have opportunities to share the gospel in multiple venues.

The Syrio-Lebanese Christian community that started migrating to New York in the 1870s came with Turkish passports, due to the reach of the Ottoman Empire.

Syrio-Lebanese Christians

QUICK FACTS:

Place of Origin:
Lebanon, Syria

Significant Subgroups:
Lebanese (55%); Syrian (45%)

Location in Metro New York:
Brooklyn (Bay Ridge); Westchester (Yonkers);
New Jersey; Connecticut

Population in Metro New York:
42,000 (Community Estimate); 63,439 (ACS
2008 Total Ancestry Reported from Lebanon
and Syria, including all religions)

Population in New York City:
25,052 (ACS 2008 Total Ancestry Reported from
Lebanon and Syria, including all religions)

Primary Religion:
Christianity (Eastern Rite Catholic, Orthodox)

Status of Christian Witness:
Less than 2% evangelical. Some evangelical
resources available, but no active church
planting within the past two years.

Primary Languages:
Arabic, English

Registry of Peoples Codes:
210540, 109662, 105688

Significant Notes:
❈ Immigrants from Greater Syria account for
two-thirds of the estimated 2.5 million Arab-
Americans in the US.[4]
❈ Although Lebanon is now two-thirds
Muslim, the government distributes power
among Christians and Muslims. Half the seats
in Parliament are held by Muslims and half
by Christians. The President is a Maronite
Christian, the Prime Minister is a Sunni Muslim,
and the Speaker of Parliament is a Shi'ite
Muslim. This is called the
"confessional system."[5]
❈ Metro New York is home to at least 6
Maronite churches, 6 Melkite churches, 12
Antiochian and 6 Syrian Orthodox churches.

"Our church has new immigrants worshipping alongside fourth- and fifth-generation members," said Father Root, whose Maronite Church in Brooklyn serves the Syrio-Lebanese Christian community. In the late 1800s, the first Arab immigrants began arriving in Metro New York. Most of these Arabs were Syrio-Lebanese Christians who hailed from what was called Greater Syria, part of the Ottoman Empire. After World War I, the region came under French control. Lebanon subsequently gained independence in 1943 and Syria in 1961. Desperately poor with few skills, many Syrio-Lebanese Christians became itinerant peddlers in the US, going door-to-door to sell items such as

sewing supplies, small tools, and dry goods from a backpack or two-wheeled cart. The "Syrian Peddler" was a fixture in the early twentieth century, as he made his rounds through small towns across America. Eventually, many were able to set up their own shops and move up the economic ladder. Today, Metro New York's Syrio-Lebanese Christian population is estimated to number around 42 thousand.[1]

54

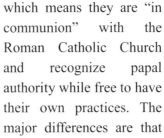

When Did They Come To New York?

There was little emigration from Greater Syria until the Great Migration of 1880-1920, when approximately 90 thousand Syrio-Lebanese settled in the US.[2] Most of these early immigrants were from the area around Mount Lebanon. While many sought religious freedom or to avoid conscription in the Ottoman army, most came to Metro New York for the opportunities it offered. After the Great Migration, US restrictions kept emigration from the Middle East at low levels until 1965, by which time Syria and Lebanon were independent countries. A major wave of Lebanese arrived between 1975 and 1991, fleeing a long and destructive civil war. Syrian immigrants also came steadily from the mid-1960s through the 1990s. With these and other Arab immigrants, New York City's Arab population doubled between 1965 and 1990.[3]

Where Do They Live?

After first settling in Lower Manhattan, early Syrio-Lebanese Christians migrated to Brooklyn, establishing a thriving commercial district along Atlantic Avenue in the South Ferry area. They began moving to Bay Ridge, Brooklyn, in the 1950s, which now has the largest Arab concentration in New York City. Subsequent generations continue to live and operate businesses there although many have spread out into areas of Westchester County, Connecticut, and New Jersey.

What Do They Believe?

"The disciples were called Christians first at Antioch." Referring back to Acts 11:26, Syrio-Lebanese Christians trace their roots to believers who sat under the teaching of the Apostle Paul and Barnabas in the ancient Syrian city of Antioch (in modern-day Turkey). They eventually split into three churches: Maronite, Melkite, and Orthodox. The Maronite and Melkite are Eastern Catholic Churches, which means they are "in communion" with the Roman Catholic Church and recognize papal authority while free to have their own practices. The major differences are that the Maronites, who lived in the mountains of Lebanon, preserved the original Antiochian liturgy and have a strong Lebanese identity. The Melkites, on the other hand, lived in the cities and were influenced by the Greeks. They adopted the Byzantine liturgy and are considered a pan-Arabic church. The Antiochian Orthodox and Syrian Orthodox, however, are Eastern Orthodox Churches that came out of the East-West Schism in 1054—each with its own patriarch. While most Syrio-Lebanese Christians belong to one of the traditional churches, some have left to join evangelical churches.

What Are Their Lives Like?

Strong families are the core of the Syrio-Lebanese Christian community, and women hold the place of honor as the center of each family unit. The hard work and sacrifice of the early immigrants has paid off, as many of their descendents have achieved the "American Dream" in Metro New York. Both men and women are typically well educated and represented in many professions. While the days of the "Syrian peddlers" are long gone, a high percentage of their descendents continue to be engaged in commerce and retail operations as business owners and salespersons.

How Can I Pray?

✳ The first Christians in Antioch were a powerful missionary force, sending Paul and Barnabas on their first missionary journey. Pray for Syrio-Lebanese Christians to use their common nationality and Arabic skills to reach Muslims, one of the largest mission fields in Metro New York.

While the Syrio-Lebanese Christian community was the first large Arab community in New York, the most noticeable Arab community today is Egyptian.

Egyptians

QUICK FACTS:

Place of Origin:
Egypt (Cairo, Alexandria)

Significant Subgroups:
Copt (50%); Arab (50%)

Location in Metro New York:
New Jersey (Jersey City, Bergen, Bayonne, Hazelton, Avenel); Queens (Astoria); Brooklyn (Fort Hamilton, Bay Ridge)

Population in Metro New York:
110,000 (Community Estimate); 47,728 (ACS 2008 Total Ancestry); 35,344 (ACS 2008 Born in Egypt)[2]

Population in New York City:
17,117 (ACS 2008 Total Ancestry); 12,906 (ACS 2008 Born in Egypt)

Primary Religions:
Christianity (Coptic); Islam (Sunni)

Status of Christian Witness:
Greater than or equal to 2% evangelical. Less than 5% evangelical.

Primary Language:
Arabic

Secondary Language:
English

Registry of Peoples Codes:
102879, 102880

Significant Notes:
❀ Although the Coptic Christians only make up around 9% of Egypt's population, they might outnumber Egyptian Muslims in Metro New York.
❀ Jersey City has the largest Egyptian Copt community in the United States.
❀ There are 22 Coptic churches in Metro New York.

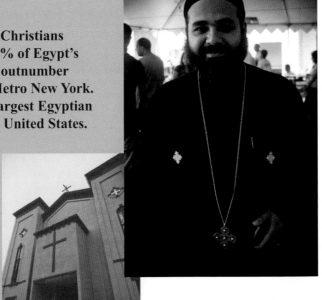

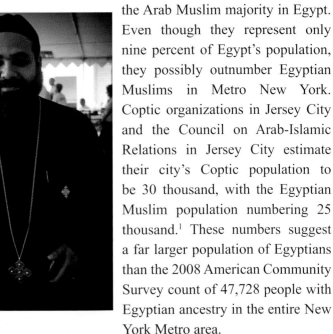

When centuries-rooted animosity underlies interethnic relations, common nationality and immigrant status may enable newfound affinity. But even one tragic event can ignite a fire of hatred and racial tension. Such was the case in January 2005, when the center of Metro New York's Egyptian population was shaken up by the murder of four Egyptian Coptic Christians in Jersey City. Although the case was dismissed as having a robbery motive, many Egyptian Copts felt that the investigation left many questions unanswered and were convinced that the murder was religiously motivated and instigated by Egyptian Muslims. The Coptic Christians—who claim to be the true descendents of the ancient Egyptians and date their Christian heritage to the first century when St. Mark visited Alexandria—have long been persecuted by the Arab Muslim majority in Egypt. Even though they represent only nine percent of Egypt's population, they possibly outnumber Egyptian Muslims in Metro New York. Coptic organizations in Jersey City and the Council on Arab-Islamic Relations in Jersey City estimate their city's Coptic population to be 30 thousand, with the Egyptian Muslim population numbering 25 thousand.[1] These numbers suggest a far larger population of Egyptians than the 2008 American Community Survey count of 47,728 people with Egyptian ancestry in the entire New York Metro area.

When Did They Come To New York?

Both Egyptian Copts and Arabs have been steadily moving into New Jersey and New York City since the advent of the Immigration and Nationality Act in 1965. Favoring professionals, this policy change enabled many educated Egyptians to reside in America legally, many of whom were eager to leave the politically unstable situation in their country. While the availability of these professional jobs has waned over the last couple of decades, the steady flow of Egyptians into Metro New York still often has a university education.

Where Do They Live?

As the Coptic murder case attests, religious and ethnic tensions abound within the Egyptian community. However, as is common in the New York Metro area, people from the same nation live alongside each other to create their own space of familiar culture, language, food, and services. While the main Egyptian enclave in America is along JFK Boulevard in Jersey City, a new "Little Egypt" has developed on Steinway Street between 28th Avenue and Astoria Boulevard in Astoria, Queens. A general Arab enclave, including a large number of Egyptians, is continuing to develop in Bay Ridge, Brooklyn, as well.

What Do They Believe?

With a Christian history that dates back to the first century for the Copts, and a Muslim history that dates back to the seventh century for the Arabs, both groups have a faith that is firmly entrenched in history, culture, customs, and honor. When one group becomes involved in either oppression or

proselytization of the other, feuds normally result. The Copts suggested this was the case in the murder story above, as one of the slain was actively involved in attempts to convert Muslims to Christianity over the Internet. A small percentage of Egyptian Copts and Arabs are evangelical Christian.

What Are Their Lives Like?

Although zealots exist in both the Egyptian Coptic and Arab Muslim camps, Egyptians are often secular in mindset and behavior. The sharing of *shisha*, a fruit-flavored tobacco smoked though water pipes called hookahs, is actually more common between the two groups than the feuds that make the headlines. Nevertheless, it is still most common for a Copt to marry and socialize with a Copt, and a Muslim to marry and socialize with a Muslim. Whereas some Copts are active politically to ensure safety and rights for their people back home, most Egyptians are content to leisurely enjoy each other's company at the hands of their financial success in America.

How Can I Pray?

✳ Muslims have recently been coming to Christ in Egypt more than in many Muslim countries in the world. Pray that Egyptians in Metro New York would find salvation through Christ as well.

Both Egyptian Copts and Indian Keralites trace their Christian roots back to one of the original disciples of Jesus.

Keralites

QUICK FACTS:

Place of Origin:
India (Kerala Province)

Significant Subgroups:
Mainly along religious lines

Location in Metro New York:
Queens (Glen Oaks, Floral Park, Bellerose)

Population in Metro New York:
100,000 (Community Estimate)

Primary Religion:
Christianity

Secondary Religions:
Hinduism, Islam

Status of Christian Witness:
Greater than or equal to 10% evangelical.

Primary Language:
Malayalam

Secondary Languages:
English, Hindi

Registry of Peoples Codes:
113714, 112914

Significant Notes:

☀ Keralites typically call themselves "Malayali," a name derived from their language, which is Malayalam.

☀ In Kerala, only 22% of the population is Christian.[4] Christians, however, have dominated the nursing profession, which is why the vast majority of Keralites in Metro New York are Christian.

☀ Approximately 85% of Keralites in Metro New York identify themselves as Christian and 20% as evangelical Christian. There are close to 100 evangelical churches serving the Malayali community.

☀ The main Keralite Christian groups are Malankara Orthodox, Syrian Orthodox, Kananaya Orthodox, Syro-Malabar Catholics, Syro-Malankara Catholics, Kananaya Catholics, Marthoma (Anglican), and Church of South India evangelical churches.

"While most Keralites in Metro New York call themselves Christians, they believe their faith is inherited. That makes them very hard to reach," said Pastor Raju, who has been ministering among Keralites (most often called Malayali, in reference to their ethnolinguistic group) since 1991. Malayali Christians claim to trace their history back to Apostolic times. According to tradition, the Apostle Thomas arrived in Kerala, a tiny state on the southwest coast of India, in 52 AD. After converting several upper-caste Hindus and founding many churches, he was martyred in Kerala in 72 AD. Although the "St. Thomas tradition" has its detractors, most Keralite Christians hold proudly to the belief that they are the spiritual descendents of the doubting Apostle. Christianity's influence in Kerala is indisputable. It has the highest educational attainment and literacy rate of any Indian state, which is the legacy of British missionaries who introduced universal education. The missionaries also established training programs for women, most notably nursing schools. Because nursing was considered "low-status" by other religions, it became a niche profession for Malayali Christian women. In the late 1960s, nurses were desperately needed in Metro New York to care for the large population of wounded Vietnam veterans. Thousands of Malayali Christian nurses were recruited, paving the way for their families and future immigrants to start a new life in the US. An estimated 100 thousand Keralites live in Metro New York today.[1]

When Did They Come To New York?

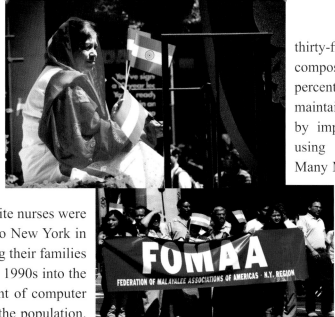

With aquamarine lagoons, sandy beaches, and palm forests, Kerala is a tourist paradise with limited job opportunities, so its people have a long history of emigrating to find work. Keralite nurses were first recruited to work in Metro New York in the 1960s. They began bringing their families in the '70s. Later waves in the 1990s into the early 2000s added a contingent of computer and business professionals to the population. Many of these later immigrants were Hindus with a small number of Muslims.

Where Do They Live?

"New York City was the initial destination for Malayali nurses because there were a lot of jobs, cheap housing, and public transportation," explained Pastor Raju. Once family members arrived and enough money was saved, families began to buy homes in the suburbs of Long Island, New Jersey, as well as Westchester and Rockland Counties in upstate New York. Later immigrants settled alongside them. A substantial number of Malayali live in the neighborhoods of Glen Oaks, Floral Park, and Bellerose in eastern Queens, where a few Indian shops and restaurants line Hillside Avenue.

What Do They Believe?

It is hard to fathom that the one ancient Apostolic church in Kerala has evolved into more than twenty Christian sects. Centuries of colonial influences fragmented the Christians among various Orthodox, Catholic, and Protestant churches—all represented among Metro New York's Keralite population, which is approximately eighty-five percent Christian. Among Christians, Catholics are the largest group with forty-one percent, Orthodox account for

thirty-five percent, and Protestants compose the remaining twenty-four percent.[2] Orthodox and Catholics maintain the strongest cultural connection by importing priests from Kerala and using Malayalam-language liturgies. Many Malayali evangelical churches are transitioning leadership to the second generation, becoming more Americanized, holding English services, and seeking members outside the Malayali community. About fourteen percent of Keralites in Metro New York are Hindu and one to two percent are Muslim.[3]

What Are Their Lives Like?

"The average Keralite family has at least one person working in the health care field," said Kurien, the leader of a Kerala association in Metro New York. For most Keralites, life revolves around work (usually at a hospital) and church. Their unique immigration story—with women arriving first—has created interesting family dynamics. While women often dominate in the work world, men definitely wield the power in the church. As a result, young women often leave Malayali churches for American churches because they desire a more significant role.

How Can I Pray?

✳ Having a long history of Christianity in a country that is largely Hindu, Malayali Christians are susceptible to considering "Christian" an ethnic identity marker rather than a mark of their relationship with Christ. Pray for their identity to be found in Christ and not merely Christian heritage.

Both the Keralite and Filipino migrations to New York were led by women nurses taking advantage of nurse shortages in New York hospitals.

Filipinos

QUICK FACTS:

Place of Origin:
Philippines

Location in Metro New York:
New Jersey (Greenville, Jersey City, Bergenfield, West Bergen, Edison); Queens (Woodside, Elmhurst)

Population in Metro New York:
300,000 (Community Estimate); 208,540 (ACS 2008 Filipinos who selected Asian Alone as race); 161,482 (ACS 2008 Born in Philippines)

Population in New York City:
70,448 (ACS 2008 Filipinos who selected Asian Alone as race); 54,608 (ACS 2008 Born in Philippines)

Primary Religion:
Christianity (Roman Catholic)

Secondary Religions:
Christianity (evangelical); Iglesia Ni Cristo

Status of Christian Witness:
Greater than or equal to 5% evangelical. Less than 10% evangelical.

Primary Languages:
Tagalog, English

Registry of Peoples Code:
109692

Significant Notes:
❋ Filipinos are now the 3rd-largest Asian group in Metro New York, behind Chinese and Indians but ahead of Koreans.
❋ According to the 2000 Census, Filipino households in New York City earn far more money than any other large immigrant group.

As far as Metro New York immigrant groups go, the Filipinos are the quintessential chameleons. With the history of the Philippines littered with influence from diverse nations and peoples, its people have been uniquely prepared to adapt, blend, and integrate. Filipino genetics, names, features, culture, and language draw influence from peoples as diverse as Taiwanese aborigines, Indonesians, Malays, Chinese, Indians, Japanese, Spaniards, and Americans. As a result, a Filipina New Yorker is just as comfortable marrying a man from Puerto Rico as she is a man from China. The Filipino ability and willingness to adapt has led to the Philippines' sending its greatest export commodity—its people—all over the world. In 2007, the Philippines was the fourth-largest remittance-receiving country in the world, right behind India, China, and Mexico.[1] At any given time, an equivalent to almost one-fourth of the Philippines' domestic work force is working abroad, which gives the country the honor of having the highest rate of outmigration per population of any country in East or Southeast Asia.[2] With large expatriate communities in places as varied as America, Saudi Arabia, Dubai, Taiwan, Japan, Italy, and Malaysia, Filipinos have had little difficulty adjusting to the fast-paced culture of Metro New York. A now-defunct Filipino radio station estimated their community to number over 300 thousand in Metro New York, while the 2008 American Community Survey estimated 208,540 Filipinos in the Metro area.

When Did They Come to New York?

The Philippines was a territory or commonwealth of America from 1898 to 1946. From that time on, Filipinos have migrated to America in various waves. While the sugar fields of Hawaii and the fish canneries of Alaska lured many Filipino immigrants at the beginning of the twentieth century, Metro New York did not receive a large number of Filipino immigrants until 1965 immigration policy changes welcomed skilled workers from a variety of countries. Faced with a nursing shortage, New York hospitals actively recruited Filipinos in the 1970s, '80s, and '90s due to their English ability and education in American-style institutions. In the 1990s, seventy-two percent of Filipinas who came to New York were registered nurses, and Filipinos represented around ten percent of the city's nurses.[3] Once established, these nurses were able to bring their families over on reunification visas. The migration of nurses and their families was augmented by other Filipino professionals, such as physical therapists and computer programmers, making the ever-growing Filipino community the third-largest Asian group in Metro New York today.

Where Do They Live?

Like many immigrant groups in the Metro area that are predominantly professionals, Filipinos live in a variety of places. They often choose housing based on proximity to their work, so it is no surprise that Filipino clusters are often located near major hospitals. The largest Filipino enclave in the Metro area is in Jersey City around Newark Avenue from JFK Boulevard to Palisade Avenue. The neighboring cluster around Manila Avenue was the original enclave. In Queens, a smaller portal to all things Filipino can be found around 69th Street and Roosevelt Avenue in Woodside.

What Do They Believe?

For Filipinos, the Christian church is not simply a spiritual home but a place to ward off loneliness and insecurity and to gain Filipino friends, news, and cultural connection. As a result, religious devotion actually increases in Metro New York among most first-generation Filipinos compared to their homeland. At least eighty percent of Filipinos identify themselves as Catholic, close to ten percent as evangelical Christian, and the rest as Iglesia Ni Cristo (a sect originated in the Philippines), Jehovah's Witness, or other.

What Are Their Lives Like?

In the 2000 Census, out of the largest immigrant groups, Filipinos in New York City were by far the wealthiest in terms of household income. They made a whopping $20,500 more a year than the second group (Indians) and made eighty-seven percent more than the city median. Filipino professionals work long hours to make this money but also find time for leisure activities, which include ballroom dancing, gambling, and golf.

How Can I Pray?

✴ Pray that the Filipino church will use their cross-cultural skills in missional endeavors.
✴ Pray that Filipino wealth will fuel Kingdom efforts instead of materialism.

While Filipinos have a mixed ancestry, Malays are one of the most dominant influences.

Malaysians

QUICK FACTS:

Place of Origin:
Malaysia

Significant Subgroups:
Chinese (85-90%); Malay (10-15%)

Location in Metro New York:
Queens (Flushing, Elmhurst); Manhattan (Chinatown)

Population in Metro New York:
40,000 (Community Estimate); 10,197 (Census 2000 Born in Malaysia)

Population in New York City:
7,752 (Census 2000 Born in Malaysia)

Primary Religion:
Buddhism

Secondary Religions:
Christianity (evangelical); Islam (Sunni)

Status of Christian Witness:
Greater than or equal to 10% evangelical.

Primary Languages:
Malaysian, Cantonese

Secondary Languages:
Mandarin, Hokkienese, English

Registry of Peoples Codes:
103701, 102140, 106144

Significant Notes:

❉ Article 160 of Malaysia's Constitution defines an ethnic Malay as someone who professes the Muslim faith. Those who leave Islam are no longer considered Malay and forfeit *bumiputra* rights.[4]

❉ About 9% of Malaysia's population is Christian, most of whom are indigenous people in East Malaysia. Like other Christians in the Muslim world, they use the word "Allah" for God. The Malaysian government forbade them to use "Allah" but revoked their decision in December 2009.[5] Arson attacks on churches took place in retaliation.

"Open to *bumiputra* entrepreneurs only," states the eligibility requirements for a business loan through a Malaysian bank.[1] Ask a Malaysian in Metro New York what this means, and one is likely to get an earful. After gaining independence in 1957, the government of Malaysia established a race-based affirmative action system in order to increase the economic power of ethnic Muslim Malays, the *bumiputra*, or "sons of the earth." Despite their status as the majority ethnic group, the Malays were more likely to be poor and uneducated in comparison to minority groups such as the Chinese and Indians, who came to Malaysia during the British colonial period as laborers in the tin mines and plantations. Highly motivated and hardworking, the Chinese in particular came to dominate Malaysia's business and professional sector, growing far wealthier than the ethnic Malays. Hoping to level the playing field, Malaysia enacted a quota system in the 1970s to favor *bumiputra* in higher education and civil service. They also receive discounts to purchase new homes. Although 2009 reforms have lifted the restriction in many economic sectors, businesses desiring to be listed on Malaysia's stock exchange have long been required to have thirty percent *bumiputra* ownership. Faced with such discrimination, ethnic Chinese Malaysians have been far more likely to leave Malaysia than ethnic Malays. While Chinese make up twenty-four percent of Malaysia's population, they account for close to ninety percent of Metro New York's 40 thousand-strong Malaysian community.[2] As Helen, the owner of a Chinese Malaysian restaurant in Flushing, explained, "I have been here for twenty-four years, and I've only met a handful of Malays."

When Did They Come To New York?

In the early years of *bumiputra* policy, the Malaysian economy expanded, making it easier for the Chinese to accept the preferential treatment of Malays. However, when the Malaysian economy took a downturn in the mid-1980s, Chinese began to leave in large numbers. Most were wealthy enough to come on tourist visas and stay, like Helen, who worked as a nanny, eventually obtaining a green card before opening her restaurant. Although some returned home when Malaysia's economy picked up again in the 1990s, census data shows the Malaysian population in New York City alone grew by 170 percent between 1990 and 2000.[3] A steady stream of Malaysians has continued to arrive since 2000.

Where Do They Live?

"We are very different from mainland Chinese!" Helen said adamantly. Since Chinese Malaysians are fluent in Cantonese, and some speak Mandarin or Hokkienese, it is easy for them to live and work in Metro New York's large Chinese communities, such as Flushing and Elmhurst in Queens or Manhattan's Chinatown. However, it is clear they maintain their own identity. Ethnic Malays seem to blend in around Metro New York—they are not known to congregate in specific areas.

What Do They Believe?

"Because they held onto Buddhism and ancestor worship, Chinese Malaysians are harder to reach with Christianity than mainland Chinese, who have been atheists for sixty years," explained Pastor Yee, a Chinese pastor in Flushing. Although eighty percent claim to be Buddhist, materialism and financial success seem to be the real gods for most Chinese Malaysians. This leads them to take a consumer approach to religion—they will worship whatever or whoever blesses them with success and happiness. Often, they will have a Buddha statue at their business and a shrine for ancestor worship at home. Close to twenty percent of Chinese Malaysians in Metro New York are evangelical Christians. While no exclusively Chinese Malaysian churches exist, several Chinese churches have a strong Chinese-Malaysian presence. Like Indonesian and Singaporean Muslims, ethnic Malays align with the Shaf'i school, the second-largest school in Sunni Islam.

What Are Their Lives Like?

When Chinese Malaysians get together, it is usually on special occasions at one another's homes. Pastor Yee explained, "There's little sense of community among Chinese Malaysians. Their lives revolve around work and family, typically putting in long hours to earn as much as possible." Helen added, "We don't really interact with mainland Chinese or Malays at all."

How Can I Pray?

✳ Many Chinese Malaysians reject Christianity because they find the emphasis on humility and suffering offensive. Pray they would grasp God's holiness and seek His mercy and saving grace.

Even though ethnic Chinese make up only one-fourth of the Malaysian population, almost all Malaysians in Metro New York are ethnic Chinese.

Mainland Han

QUICK FACTS:

Place of Origin:
Northern and Eastern Provinces of Mainland China (primarily Beijing and Shanghai)

Significant Subgroups:
Multiple subgroups based on town or province of origin (e.g., Shanghai or Beijing), preferred language (e.g., Mandarin or Wu), and uptown or downtown identity

Location in Metro New York:
Queens (Flushing, Elmhurst); also scattered in Long Island, New Jersey, Connecticut, Westchester

Population in Metro New York:
Mainland Han number unknown. Total Chinese Population: 650,482 (ACS 2008 Chinese, excluding Taiwanese, who selected Asian alone as race)

Population in New York City:
Mainland Han number unknown. Total Chinese Population: 464,050 (ACS 2008 Chinese, excluding Taiwanese, who selected Asian alone as race)

Primary Religion:
Nonreligious

Secondary Religion:
Chinese Popular Religion, Buddhism, Taoism, Christianity

Status of Christian Witness:
Greater than or equal to 2% evangelical. Less than 5% evangelical.

Primary Languages:
Mandarin, Wu

Secondary Languages:
Mandarin, English

Registry of Peoples Codes:
102143, 103686

Significant Note:
✳ Although Cantonese and Mandarin speakers share a common written Chinese language, their spoken languages are mutually unintelligible.

Mandarin is the most commonly spoken language in the world, but it has historically been a minority language among Chinese New Yorkers due to Cantonese predominance. Now, it is quickly becoming the lingua franca of Chinese New York, even though only an estimated ten percent of Chinese in Metro New York speak it as their first language.[1] With the growth of the Chinese economy and the importance of Mandarin for business, many Cantonese families are even sending their children to schools to learn Mandarin. Symbolic of the change, the Chinese Consolidated Benevolent Association—the traditionally Cantonese umbrella organization founded in 1883—elected for the first time in 2008 a president whose mother tongue was Mandarin.[2] In the Metro area, aside from originally mainlanders from Taiwan (p. 70) and Southeast Asia, the main Mandarin speakers are Han Chinese from the northern and eastern provinces of China, particularly from big cities like Beijing and Shanghai. The Fuzhounese (p. 30), Wenzhounese (p. 108), and mainland Cantonese (p. 28) are also mainland Han but are treated in their own profiles. Shanghainese speak their own language, called Wu, but most speak Mandarin well, especially since "please speak Mandarin" signs dominate the school walls in China. Besides ethnicity, one of the sharp identity markers of Metro New York Chinese is whether or not they are "downtown" or "uptown." The

"uptown Chinese" are wealthy professionals who have high levels of education. Most of these are American-born Chinese or from the main Chinese financial or educational centers, such as Shanghai, Hong Kong, or Beijing. The "downtown Chinese" have little education and few English skills and work in restaurants, garment shops, and other service jobs.[3]

When Did They Come To New York?

After losing control of mainland China to the Communist Party, the government of the Republic of China retreated to Taiwan in 1949. For thirty years, the United States formally acknowledged the Republic of China as the sole legitimate government over all of China, which restricted migration from the mainland. However, many Shanghainese managed to find their way to New York in the 1970s through Hong Kong and Taiwan. When diplomatic policies changed in 1979 and the US recognized the legitimacy of the Communist People's Republic of China, migration doors opened once again from the mainland. Both "uptown" and "downtown" Chinese immigrated to New York throughout the 1980s and '90s. Since that time, most immigration has consisted of Mandarin-speaking graduate students from Beijing and Shanghai, some of whom have stayed to work in the New York Metro area.

Where Do They Live?

Since the 1980s, the Chinatown in Flushing, Queens, has largely hosted Mandarin-speaking immigrants from Taiwan, Shanghai, and northern China. Many of the "uptown Chinese" reside in the suburbs of Long Island, Connecticut, Westchester, and New Jersey.

What Do They Believe?

At the corner of Canal and Bowery Streets in Manhattan lies the Mahayana Buddhist Temple, the largest Buddhist temple in New York City. Its presence represents the influence Mahayana Buddhism has had on mainland Han Chinese. However, most mainland Han in New York are nonreligious, especially those who are recent immigrants and were raised entirely under communist rule. Whatever Buddhist identity remains upon arrival in New York is often shed by "uptown Chinese," who have trouble connecting what they perceive to be superstitious practices in Buddhism to their backgrounds in reasoning and logic. For the religiously inclined, many "uptown Chinese" find Christianity to be a great alternative and either establish "intellectual" Chinese churches or attend churches where sermons appeal to the intellect as well as the heart.

What Are Their Lives Like?

Sharon, a leader of a Mandarin language school in New Jersey claimed, "Most Chinese move to the city for job opportunities but are focused on their children's education. They will even move to areas that have a better school and make financial sacrifices so that their children have the best education possible [...] so that they can pursue careers in medicine and engineering."

How Can I Pray?

✹ Pray for a continued increase in "uptown" mainland Han who find it reasonable to place faith in Christ and that the "downtown" Chinese will cast their cares upon Christ.

Whereas many Chinese in New York cannot speak Mandarin, the Korean-Chinese usually speak Mandarin alongside Korean.

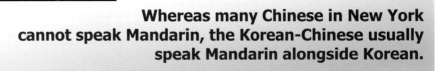

Korean-Chinese

QUICK FACTS:

Place of Origin:
Northeast China (Yanbian Prefecture in Jilin Province, Shenyang in Liaoning Province)

Significant Subgroups:
Largely homogenous (some cultural differences between those from Yanbian and Shenyang)

Location in Metro New York:
Queens (Flushing); New Jersey (Fort Lee)

Population in Metro New York:
20,000 (Community Estimate)

Primary Religion:
Nonreligious

Secondary Religion:
Buddhism

Status of Christian Witness:
Less than 2% evangelical. Initial (localized) church planting within the past two years.

Primary Language:
Korean

Secondary Languages:
Mandarin, English

Registry of Peoples Code:
105225

Significant Notes:
❀ There are an estimated 70,000-80,000 Korean-Chinese in the United States. Los Angeles has the largest concentration with approximately 30,000.[3]
❀ Living in Flushing, Korean-Chinese are exposed to the vibrant Christianity of Korean-Americans.
❀ When public transportation routes are difficult, restaurant and nail salon owners actually send buses to Flushing to pick up and drop off Korean-Chinese workers.
❀ Korean-Chinese immigrants often come to America without their spouses, yet frequently send money home.

In an accent that Koreans immediately identify as Korean-Chinese, Caroline describes the immigrant life, "For the first five years, you really want to go back home. After that, you really want to stay!" With an estimated population of 20 thousand in Metro New York, the Korean-Chinese are an increasing presence in the city.[1] Their ancestors moved to northeast China from what is now North Korea between 1860 and 1945, and they are now known in Chinese as the Chaoxian ("Chosun" in Korean), which is the word for North Korea. As one of China's official ethnic minorities, they have their own autonomous region called the Yanbian Prefecture where they run the schools, hospitals, and local government. Korean-Chinese are allowed to keep their language and cultural traditions, and unlike some other minorities, they are not

harassed by the Chinese government. In Metro New York, the Korean-Chinese are a human bridge between two of the largest and most successful immigrant communities, the Koreans and the Chinese. Influenced, but often overlooked and exploited, by both groups, they belong to neither. As their numbers grow and they gain a foothold in the economy, they are becoming a powerful force in Metro New York. With the ability to speak both Korean

and Mandarin and their connections to China, they have opportunities to attract international business and tap into two large ethnic markets.

When Did They Come to New York?

Even with the difficulties of securing a US visitor visa in China, Korean-Chinese began arriving in Metro New York in the 1990s, with a huge surge since 2000. Almost all have the same goal: to make as much money as possible to send back to family. Some Korean-Chinese came to go to college, but few can afford that today. With visas now harder to obtain, many Korean-Chinese resort to the dangerous option of using "brokers" to bring them in through Mexico.

Where Do They Live?

A walk through "Korean Chinatown" along Northern Boulevard between Union Street and 41st Avenue in Flushing, Queens, reveals a growing number of Korean-Chinese restaurants and shops along with countless nail salons where Korean-Chinese work. Not surprisingly, the largest concentration of Korean-Chinese live right where one might expect—at the intersection of Metro New York's largest Korean and Chinese communities. Groups of Korean-Chinese have moved to Fort Lee, New Jersey, just across the George Washington Bridge, where there is a large Korean community and growing numbers of Chinese.

What Do They Believe?

"Nothing—they believe in nothing," said the pastor of one of the two Korean-Chinese churches in Flushing. Korean-Chinese immigrants in Metro New York grew up under the influence of atheism in China. Some have retained remnants of Buddhism, but very few have any connection to Christianity—totally unlike their South Korean kindred. Having existed in a spiritual vacuum for most of their lives, they are a "blank slate" upon which to write the good news of Jesus Christ, but reaching them is

a challenge. In their desperation to earn money, they work long hours, often seven days a week. One of the Korean-Chinese churches has gained trust in the community by effectively meeting needs through ESL classes and social activities.

What Are Their Lives Like?

"Mr. Xu," a Korean-Chinese from Flushing, made headlines when, with the help of the Korean Workers Project, he successfully obtained back wages from a New York construction company that had refused to pay him.[2] Eager to work, Korean-Chinese are often targets for unscrupulous employers who pay low wages and demand long hours. While men have a choice between restaurant work and construction, Korean-Chinese women work almost exclusively in nail salons. Most Korean-Chinese come to Metro New York alone, so work becomes their life, and loneliness is a constant companion. Some turn to alcohol and gambling to fill the emptiness.

How Can I Pray?

✳ As most Korean-Chinese have little time outside of work, pray that a vision will develop and a way will be made to share the gospel with the Korean-Chinese community at their workplace.

✳ Pray that the evangelistically minded Korean Christian community will embrace the mission of reaching Korean-Chinese in their neighborhoods and workplaces.

The Korean-Chinese have retained their Korean language and many customs even though they started migrating to China well over a century ago.

Koreans

QUICK FACTS:

Place of Origin:
South Korea (mainly in and around Seoul)

Significant Subgroups:
Largely homogenous (most significant difference exists between those from the Gyeongsang and Jeolla regions)

Location in Metro New York:
Queens (Flushing, Douglaston, Little Neck, Bayside); New Jersey (Palisades Park, Fort Lee)

Population in Metro New York:
183,249 (ACS 2008 Koreans who selected Asian alone as race); 154,176 (ACS 2008 Born in Korea)

Population in New York City:
84,309 (ACS 2008 Koreans who selected Asian alone as race); 69,099 (ACS 2008 Born in Korea)

Primary Religion:
Christianity (evangelical)

Secondary Religions:
Buddhism, Christianity (Roman Catholic)

Status of Christian Witness:
Greater than or equal to 10% evangelical.

Primary Language:
Korean

Secondary Language:
English (1.5 and 2nd generations)

Registry of Peoples Code:
105225

Significant Notes:
❉ Koreans in Metro New York are known for operating their own businesses. The most popular are grocery stores, nail salons, and dry cleaners.
❉ Around 70% of Koreans in Metro New York are evangelical Christian, compared to 18% evangelical in South Korea.

Armed with tracts and cassette tapes of her pastor's sermons, Young* plunged into conversation with the man at the next table at the busy Koryodang Bakery on Northern Boulevard in Flushing. "Jesus died for your sins," she told him. He didn't say much but nodded repeatedly and accepted a tape and schedule of church events. When the conversation ended, she announced, "He promised to come to church." Young's encounter with her fellow bakery customer exemplifies a defining characteristic of the Korean immigrant culture—an incomparable evangelistic zeal. In fact, it is impossible to understand Korean immigrants apart from their Christian identity. While only twenty-nine percent of Korea's population is Christian, a remarkable seventy-five percent of Koreans in the US are Christians, and the vast

majority are evangelical Protestants.[1] The New York Metro area is home to over 180 thousand Koreans (ACS 2008) and has over one thousand Korean churches, ranging from house churches, to small congregations that rent space from other churches, to churches with multi-million dollar budgets and facilities.[2] Korean Christians have established dozens of religious organizations and theological schools in Metro New York that teach Christians how to evangelize and prepare for missionary work. Korean churches also play a vital

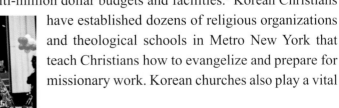

role in the community; their weekly activities include not only worship services and prayer meetings but also music programs for kids, activities for senior citizens, and ESL classes for new immigrants.

When Did They Come to New York?

Koreans started arriving in large numbers in the late 1970s. The 1990s saw the biggest influx, with Metro New York's Korean population growing by thirty percent.[3] Most are from areas around Seoul, and a top reason for emigrating is to provide good education for their children. With many children coming to America with their parents, a large group of 1.5 generation Korean-Americans has developed with its feet in both cultures. Nearly eight out of ten Korean-Americans in Metro New York are immigrants.[4]

Where Do They Live?

Once limited to Koreatown in downtown Flushing, Korean shops and restaurants are now fixtures on the main streets of many Metro New York suburbs. Since 2000, one-third of Flushing's Koreans have moved out, primarily to find better schools for their children. In Douglaston, Queens, Koreans are the fastest-growing ethnic group, while Palisades Park, New Jersey, has the highest concentration of Koreans (thirty-six percent) of any community in the US.[5] Korean churches can now be found throughout Metro New York from Westbury, Long Island, to Norwood, New Jersey.

What Do They Believe?

Known for all-night prayer vigils, month-long fasts, and a passion for missions, the Korean church is not for wimps. However, concerns about a growing "silent exit" from church among the 1.5 and second generations have motivated leaders to let younger Korean-Americans put their own stamp on church, whether it means using English or including hip-hop routines during worship. While evangelicals dominate in numbers, Korean Catholics—although just a fraction of Christians in Metro New York—are also very devout and active. Small numbers of Buddhists and a few syncretistic religious groups are also found in Metro New York's Korean communities.

What Are Their Lives Like?

No Saturday morning cartoon watching for Korean kids! Most spend Saturdays at a *hagwon*, a "cram school" (sometimes run by churches) designed to get them into prestigious high schools, Ivy League colleges, and eventually a lucrative career. Korean parents work long hours to provide opportunities for their children. In return, they expect children to honor them by fulfilling their own view of success. Nevertheless, the children often adopt American individualism, which leads to family conflict over weighty issues such as the meaning of success and Christianity.

How Can I Pray?

✳ Pray for God to continue to bless the prayers and evangelistic efforts of Koreans who seek to bring the gospel to the lost in their communities and around the world.

✳ Although the first generation has much zeal, they have trouble relating to others cross-culturally. Pray that the 1.5 and second generations will take the missionary baton from their parents and run with it.

Downtown Flushing, Queens, is known as both Little Korea and Little Taiwan.

69

Taiwanese

QUICK FACTS:

Place of Origin:
Republic of China (Taiwan)

Significant Subgroups:
Ethnic Taiwanese (60%); ex-mainlander (40%)

Location in Metro New York:
Queens (Flushing, Oakland Gardens, Bayside, Fresh Meadows); New Jersey (Crawford Corners, Hanover, Gililandtown, Newport)

Population in Metro New York:
42,947 (ACS 2008 Born in Taiwan)

Population in New York City:
19,575 (ACS 2008 Born in Taiwan)

Primary Religion:
Buddhism

Secondary Religion:
Christianity (mainline Protestant, evangelical)

Status of Christian Witness:
Greater than or equal to 10% evangelical.

Primary Languages:
Mandarin, Taiwanese

Registry of Peoples Code:
102140

Significant Notes:

✳ The four main ethnic groups in Taiwan today are the Aborigine, the Hoklo, the Hakka, and the mainlander. While the Aborigines are indigenous to Taiwan, the Hoklo and Hakka started migrating to Taiwan in the 17th century from China. Due to their long history on the island, the Hoklo and Hakka are labeled in this profile alongside the Aborigines as "native to Taiwan."

✳ In Taiwan, Christians are about 4% of the population, but in Metro New York, more than 25% of Taiwanese are Christians.

✳ Over 80% of Taiwanese have had some college education, compared to around 55% for Metro New Yorkers as a whole.

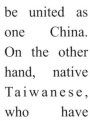

A children's book published by the Republic of China (ROC, better-known as Taiwan) graphically depicts Taiwan as a child being shoved off the globe by other children (international organizations) and another child cowering from the fire of a dragon-headed companion (China). Above the drawing, a Chinese official is quoted as saying to Taiwan, "No one cares about you."[1] These caricatures accurately reflect the sentiment of many Taiwanese in Metro New York. The Kuomintang (KMT)—the ruling political party of the ROC—ruled much of mainland China from 1928 until their retreat to Taiwan in 1949 after being defeated by the Communist Party in a civil war. Despite the defeat, the United Nations (UN) still recognized the ROC as sovereign over all of China until 1971, even though it ruled only Taiwan. At that point, political momentum shifted, and the UN transferred China's one seat in the UN from the ROC in Taipei to the communist government in Beijing. The whole fiasco has left people from Taiwan in a politically turbulent position. On the one hand, the ex-mainlanders who were exiled to Taiwan with the KMT identify themselves as Chinese and still desire to be united as one China. On the other hand, native Taiwanese, who have

existed for centuries on the island, forming their own identity, long to be fully recognized as an independent country. Both desire to participate in and be recognized by the international community. For decades, New York City has been at the center of this political web. Dr. Hong-Tien Lai, a dentist by day, has long been active in the struggle for independence and democracy in Taiwan. He leads yearly rallies and demonstrations at the UN, Times Square, Chinese Consulate, and wherever else he can gain attention for the cause. Dr. Lai claims that ex-mainlanders are proportionately more numerous in New York than in Taiwan. Out of the 43 thousand people in Metro New York who were born in Taiwan (ACS 2008), up to forty percent are ex-mainlanders, and the rest are Taiwanese who are native to Taiwan.

When Did They Come To New York?

Growing up under the authoritarian rule of the KMT, young students such as Dr. Lai often went to the movies to dream of living in America. From the 1950s to '70s, many dreams were realized, as studying abroad was practically the only way Taiwanese could leave the country, and American universities were eager to accept students trained in the sciences. Because of martial law in their homeland, many Taiwanese students stayed in America after completing their studies. In the early 1980s, another surge of migration from Taiwan occurred because US visa quotas were raised to 20 thousand a year. However, with the democratization and economic stabilization of Taiwan developing in the mid-1980s, immigration to America quickly tapered off.

Where Do They Live?

Flushing's Chinatown rivals that of its better-known counterpart in Manhattan. However, the one in Flushing has a large Taiwanese influence, even though Taiwanese continue to spread into neighboring Oakland Gardens, Bayside, and Fresh Meadows as well as central and northern New Jersey.

What Do They Believe?

Even though Christians number about four percent of the population in Taiwan, they number over twenty-five percent in Metro New York.[2] There are at least two reasons. First, New York Taiwanese are more educated than their compatriots back home, and East Asian intellectuals have high conversion rates to Christianity. Second, the Taiwanese church has long been active in social justice, which creates an outlet for politically active Taiwanese Americans. Overall, Taiwanese are more religious in America, which applies to the majority's Buddhist practices as well.

What Are Their Lives Like?

Due to the nature of early emigration from Taiwan, Taiwanese New Yorkers are highly educated and predominantly involved in business and the medical industry. Furthermore, many use their platform in New York to advocate for Taiwanese political concerns.

How Can I Pray?

☀ Pray for social justice and international inclusion for Taiwan but also that the enthusiasm Taiwanese Christians exhibit for political concerns will carry over into their relationship with Christ in every aspect.

Both Taiwanese and Tibetans have a rocky relationship with China, which has politically united them in New York.

Tibetans

QUICK FACTS:

Place of Origin:
Tibet (China) via India (mainly Dharamsala) and Nepal

Significant Subgroups:
Tibetans often organize along the four main schools of Tibetan Buddhism (Gelugpas, Nyingmas, Sakyas, and Kagyus)[2]

Location in Metro New York:
Queens (Jackson Heights, Astoria); Brooklyn (Crown Heights); Manhattan (Morningside, Tudor City, Murray Hill, Gramercy, East Village); New Jersey (Newark)

Population in Metro New York:
3,000 (Community Estimate)

Primary Religion:
Buddhism (Tibetan)

Status of Christian Witness:
Less than 2% evangelical. Some evangelical resources available, but no active church planting within the past two years.

Primary Language:
Tibetan

Secondary Languages:
Multiple dialects of Tibetan, English, Ladakhi, Nepali

Registry of Peoples Code:
110033

Significant Notes:
❈ The largest number of Tibetans outside of China, India, and Nepal is in Metro New York, and around one-third of Tibetans in the United States live in Metro New York.
❈ The Tibet House is a non-profit organization in New York devoted to the preservation of Tibetan culture. Its president is Robert Thurman, an author and academic who is the father of actress Uma Thurman.

Sonam Tashi, a Tibetan man whose father was killed by Chinese border patrol when he was three years old, comes on March 10th of every year to a plaza by the UN building, rallying on behalf of a free Tibet. He solemnly claims, "Every people need a freedom [....] Lot of people in China are not free." It has been about fifty years since the Chinese occupied Tibet, and the sting is still felt by the estimated three thousand Tibetans who now live in the New York Metro area.[1] On the March 10th National Tibetan Uprising Day, hundreds of Tibetans and sympathizers march to the UN and Chinese Consulate, shouting such cries as, "China lie, people die," and, "China out of Tibet now." While New York is where they live, it is certainly not their home.

When Did They Come To New York?

For centuries, Tibet was an isolated country. Very few came in. Very few went out. All of that changed in 1949 when the Chinese took control of Tibet—an act that led tens of thousands of Tibetans to resettle in India and Nepal. The Tibetans' struggle for their homeland has continued ever since. During the following decades, immigration slowly began to the US, but it was a 1990 immigration visa opportunity for one thousand displaced

Tibetans that initiated a large immigration. From the late 1990s to the current time, Tibetans have been streaming into New York City on family reunification visas or tourist visas that they overstay. The city

retains most of these immigrants due to the abundance of service jobs available and its friendliness towards the undocumented.

Where Do They Live?

While there is no overt "Little Tibet" in Metro New York, many Tibetans and Tibetan businesses are clustered in Jackson Heights (Queens) and other South Asian neighborhoods. Tibetans can also be found in Astoria (Queens), Crown Heights (Brooklyn), south and east of Midtown Manhattan, and in Newark, New Jersey.

What Do They Believe?

Tibetans have largely resisted attempts of evangelization by Christians, as they see their identity as inextricably linked with their religion of Tibetan Buddhism. The much-publicized Dalai Lama is considered a "god-king," a political and religious leader to the Tibetans. Tibetan Buddhism also encompasses the Bon religion, which contains elements of witchcraft and the occult. Although Americans and other Westerners practice Buddhism at increasingly popular "Tibetan" meditation centers, Tibetans are more likely to practice Buddhist rituals in front of their shrines at home. Some say they find it difficult to find time to pray and meditate because of the demands of work and daily life in their new country. Some believe Buddhist monks do the spiritual work for them.

What Are Their Lives Like?

Tibetans in Metro New York enthusiastically attend cultural events such as the Tibetan New Year and Buddha's birthday party. Cultural events also receive support and publicity from American groups who feel sympathetic towards the Tibetan exile situation. In October 2007, a huge celebration took place in Manhattan's Union Square in honor of the Dalai Lama's visit and his selection for the US Congressional Gold Medal. With many Tibetans undocumented in the city, the women tend to work as babysitters and housekeepers. Ironically, many Tibetan men work in Chinese restaurants! Tibetans hope to advance economically, provide education for their children, and send remittances to their families in India and Nepal. Besides sending money, some Tibetans also send their children to India in order to learn Tibetan language and culture.

How Can I Pray?

✵ Due to the plight of their people, Tibetans are very open and willing to talk to outsiders about their culture and struggles. Pray that God would create opportunities for conversations between Christians and Tibetans that would lead to sharing the gospel.

✵ Behind the façade of serenity and peace that often typifies Buddhism, doubts and superstitions prevail. Pray that Tibetans would yearn for the peace that only God can give.

✵ Many Tibetans migrated first to India, where there are Christians, and then to the US. Pray for Indian and other South Asian churches in New York to reach out to the Tibetan community.

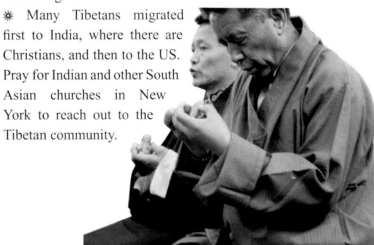

Because many of the Tibetan immigrants in Metro New York were actually born and raised in India or Nepal, they tend to settle alongside others from these countries.

Indo-Caribbeans

QUICK FACTS:

Place of Origin:
India, then Guyana, Trinidad and Tobago, Suriname, Jamaica

Significant Subgroups:
Indo-Guyanese (70%); Indo-Trinidadian (20%); Indo-Surinamese (5%); Indo-Jamaican (5%)

Location in Metro New York:
Queens (Richmond Hill, South Ozone Park, Hollis); Bronx (Eastchester, Parkchester); New Jersey (Jersey City)

Population in Metro New York:
Up to 300,000 (Community Estimate)

Primary Religion:
Hinduism

Secondary Religions:
Islam, Christianity

Status of Christian Witness:
Greater than or equal to 5% evangelical.
Less than 10% evangelical.

Primary Language:
English Creole (Patois)

Secondary Languages:
English, Hindustani

Registry of Peoples Code:
108730

Significant Notes:
※ The largest populations of Indo-Caribbeans outside the Caribbean and Guyanese outside of Guyana are in Metro New York.
※ The former mayor of Schenectady—in upstate New York close to Albany—actively recruited Indo-Guyanese from Richmond Hill to move to his town. At times even leading tours and launching a website geared towards seducing the immigrant group to the town "where housing is cheap and people are nice," the mayor convinced several thousand Indo-Caribbeans to make the move.

The earth, sky, and individuals were enshrouded in baby powder and the fluorescent colors of blue, yellow, pink, and purple dyes. Children and adults alike participated as Indo-Caribbeans from Guyana, Trinidad, Suriname, and Jamaica gleefully threw the dyes and powder at each other in a Hindu celebration they call Phagwah (called Holi in Hindi). Taking place at a rather drab-looking park in a drab-looking neighborhood in Queens, the Indo-Caribbeans use the annual event to do what immigrant groups are renowned for doing in New York City—adding color to an otherwise gray palette! The large attendance at the Phagwah event reflects the fact that a significant portion of the Hindu population in Metro New York did not emigrate directly from South Asia but from the Caribbean. In 1838, the first indentured laborers set sail from India to British Guiana (Guyana) in order to work on sugar plantations. These Indian laborers were from the lower and working classes, and migration continued into Guyana, Trinidad, Suriname, and Jamaica up until the 1920s.[1] Today, around fifty percent of Guyana's population and forty percent of Trinidad's have East Indian ancestry.[2] Just as these Indians brought their culture, language, religion, and influence to the Caribbean in the 1800s and early 1900s, up to 300 thousand Indo-Caribbeans are doing the same today in Metro New York.[3]

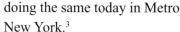

When Did They Come To New York?

When Britain enacted a law in 1962 to restrict unregulated immigration, and the United

74

States conversely opened its doors in 1965 to a wider immigrant pool, Indo-Caribbeans began pouring into New York. Immigration continued to escalate in the 1970s and '80s when the economy and political situation in Guyana worsened under the socialist government of Forbes Burnham. As a result, the majority of Indo-Caribbeans in Metro New York (around seventy percent) are Guyanese.

Where Do They Live?

Danny, an Indo-Guyanese who moved to New York over thirty years ago, spoke proudly about the community that Indo-Caribbeans have formed in the Richmond Hill neighborhood of Queens. In an accent tinged with patois, Danny boasts, "Have you been to Liberty Avenue here? Have you been? It has everything! Temples, shops, restaurants—everything! It is like a 'Little Guyana,' you know." While Richmond Hill is their main neighborhood in New York, Indo-Caribbeans can also be found in other Caribbean neighborhoods in Brooklyn, Queens, the Bronx, and New Jersey.

What Do They Believe?

When the first East Indians came into the Caribbean in the 1800s, they were almost exclusively Hindu or Muslim. Years of exposure to other religions, most notably Christianity, has altered the religious dynamics of Indo-Caribbeans to a point where no dogmatic claims can be made on what they believe. However, the majority of Indo-Caribbeans are still Hindu (perhaps sixty percent), while Muslims make up about twenty percent, Christians around ten percent, and agnostics and adherents of other religions make up the rest. Sometimes the religious dynamics shift tremendously depending on the country of origin, such as Jamaica, where most Indo-Caribbeans are now Christians.

What Are Their Lives Like?

The Indo-Caribbean migration, from its inception in India, has always been a story of working-class people with little opportunity making a way for themselves, despite difficult circumstances and conditions. Their lives in New York are no different. Although Indo-Caribbeans often work at service jobs that pay little and take a lot, their hard work has paid off with neatly kept houses, a neighborhood they call their own, and organizations that sprinkle the year with lively parades, festivities, and events. On the weekends, a unique Indo-Guyanese pastime can be observed at Phil Rizzuto Park in Queens, where morning whistling matches between black finches from Guyana garner reactions from spectators who resemble those at a horse race. The "chirp-offs" are so popular in the local community that finches are even smuggled into the country and sold for up to $1,500.

How Can I Pray?

✳ Pray for the existing Indo-Caribbean churches to continue having an impact on their community, especially through providing opportunities for their people to respond to the gospel.

✳ Pray that, with a much higher percentage of Christians than their Punjabi Indian neighbors in Richmond Hill, Indo-Caribbean Christians will take advantage of their unique opportunity to share the gospel with unreached immigrants from their original homeland of India.

While Indo-Caribbeans have an Indian identity without having lived in India, many Tibetans have migrated from India and live in Indian neighborhoods throughout Metro New York.

Punjabis

QUICK FACTS:

Place of Origin:
India (Punjab State)

Significant Subgroups:
Sikh, primarily Chamar and Jat (70%);
Hindu (28-29%); Christian (1-2%)

Location in Metro New York:
Queens (Richmond Hill)

Population in Metro New York:
110,000 (Community Estimate)

Primary Religion:
Sikhism

Secondary Religions:
Hinduism, Christianity

Status of Christian Witness:
Less than 2% evangelical. Initial (localized)
church planting within the past two years.

Primary Language:
Punjabi

Secondary Languages:
Hindi, English

Significant Notes:

❋ The five K's, or articles of faith that
baptized Sikhs are required to wear:
Kesh: uncut hair (men wrap theirs
in a turban),
Kanga: a wooden comb to hold the hair,
Kara: an iron bracelet to remind them
to do good,
Kachera: a long cotton undergarment that
promotes modesty and self-control,
Kirpan: a small sword kept at the waist, to
be used only in self-defense or
protecting others.

❋ Upon baptism, Sikhs take a religious
name. Men are called Singh ("lion")
while women are Kaur ("princess"). This
explains why Singh is the most common
Punjabi surname.

❋ The first Asian American to serve in the
US Congress was a Sikh from California
named Dalip Singh Saund, elected in 1956.

"We just want people to know who we are. We are Sikhs, and we are Americans!" This comment characterizes the collective frustration of Punjabi Sikhs, whose ethnic and religious identity has been a mystery to many Americans. Sikhs are the majority ethno-religious group among Indians from the state of Punjab in northern India. In 1947, the Punjab region was divided along religious lines between India and Pakistan, forcing Muslims into Pakistan and Sikhs and Hindus into India. Although Hindus and Sikhs have traditionally lived in relative harmony for generations, demands that Punjab be a Sikh-ruled state sparked a decade of violence. Between 1984 and 1993, clashes between extremists on both sides as well as between Sikhs and the Indian government killed more than 25 thousand people.[1] There are 27 million Sikhs, most of whom live in Punjab, making it the world's fifth-largest religion.[2] Because the Sikh faith requires men to wear turbans and have long beards, they are often mistaken for Muslim fundamentalists. Consequently, Sikhs have been victims of more

than two hundred hate crimes nationally since the 9/11 attacks.[3] Punjabis, who number approximately 110 thousand people, are one of the top three Indian ethnic groups in Metro New York along with Gujaratis (p. 24) and Keralites (p. 58).[4] A majority of the Punjabis in Metro New York are Sikhs.

When Did They Come to New York?

Medical students and professionals were the first Punjabis to come to Metro New

York in the 1960s and '70s. However, it was the aftermath of the 1984 assassination of Indian Prime Minister Indira Gandhi that drove Sikhs to come in large numbers. The Prime Minister was killed in retaliation for ordering an attack on extremists who were hiding in a Sikh temple, which in turn led to anti-Sikh riots that resulted in three thousand deaths. Fearing for their lives, thousands of Sikhs sought a new home in the small Sikh community in Metro New York. Punjabi immigration has been steady since the mid-1980s, with no signs of stopping.

Where Do They Live?

"I know half the Punjabis in Richmond Hill," joked Inder, a waiter in Manhattan. Because Sikh life revolves around the *gurdwara*, their places of worship, Sikhs live in close proximity to them. Richmond Hill, Queens—home to the first *gurdwara* in Metro New York—remains the epicenter of the Sikh community. While the largest concentration of Sikhs is in the area surrounding the Sikh Cultural Center at 118th Street and 97th Avenue in Richmond Hill, *gurdwaras* can be found throughout Metro New York, from Glen Cove, Long Island, to Glen Rock, New Jersey, reflecting a growing affluence among Sikhs and a desire to live in the suburbs.

What Do They Believe?

"A person who leaves the Sikh faith is considered a traitor to their nation," explained Pastor Gill, who leads a Punjabi church in Richmond Hill. While Sikhs are open to learning about other faiths—the word "Sikh" means "one who seeks truth"—those who embrace other religions are typically cut off from family and community. Sikhism has many parallels to Christianity, such as belief in one creator God, named *Waheguru*, who is revealed in a sacred scripture called *Guru Granth*. Sikhism has three primary principles: continual meditation and prayer, making an honest living, and sharing with others. Sikhs are encouraged to be baptized, and after baptism they are required to wear the "five K's" (see Significant Notes). The four Sikh commandments prohibit tobacco and alcohol usage, cutting hair, eating meat that has been sacrificed, and committing adultery. Besides at Pastor Gill's church, Bethlehem Punjabi Church in Richmond Hill, Punjabi Christians worship at many Indian and Pakistani churches in Metro New York. Punjabi Hindus worship alongside Hindus from all over India in temples across the Metro area.

What Are Their Lives Like?

"When I need advice, I go to my parents," Inder stated. Family is the core of Punjabi life, with several generations typically living under one roof. Being involved in a *gurdwara* is essential for Sikhs, and it serves as their main social network. While most first-generation Punjabis own or work at small businesses, such as gas stations, taxi services, or construction, they want their children to be professionals. The medical field is the number one choice for the second generation.

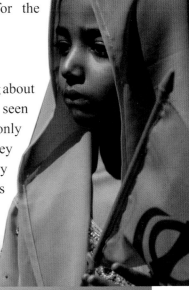

How Can I Pray?

❋ Sikhs are very open to learning about Christianity. Pastor Gill has seen several come to know Christ, only to return to Sikhism because they could not handle the rejection by family. Pray for these seekers and that the Punjabi church will be a source of strength and community for them.

Over one-half of Nepal borders India, and the two countries share a regional South Asian identity.

Nepalis

QUICK FACTS:

Place of Origin:
Nepal

Significant Subgroups:
Janajati (60%, mainly Sherpa, Gurung, Rai, Limbu, Tamang, Newar); Bahun-Chhetri (40%); Madhesi (less than 1%)

Location in Metro New York:
Queens (Woodside, Ridgewood, Sunnyside, Jackson Heights)

Population in Metro New York:
30,000 (Community Estimate)

Primary Religions:
Hinduism, Buddhism

Status of Christian Witness:
Less than 2% evangelical. Initial (localized) church planting within the past two years.

Primary Languages:
Nepali, indigenous languages

Secondary Languages:
Nepali (secondary language for Janajati and Madhesi)

Registry of Peoples Codes:
111785, 103752, 110781, 113409, 113409, 114697, 113733, 107217

Significant Notes:

❊ Over 17,000 ethnic Nepali refugees who lived in neighboring Bhutan for generations have arrived in the US in recent years.[4] Many around the country are showing interest in the gospel.

❊ Nepal's cultural diversity is evident in the physical characteristics of Nepalis. The Janajati mainly descend from Tibeto-Mongolians and have similar features to Chinese or Mongolians. The Bahun-Chhetri and Madhesi both trace their ancestry back to Indo-Aryan people and look much like Asian Indians.

❊ In June 2001, Nepal's Crown Prince Dipendra shot and killed his parents and 11 family members before taking his own life.

Back home in Nepal, Tsering used to guide mountain climbers attempting the ultimate test of human survival: conquering Mount Everest. Some might argue his current job—driving a taxi in downtown Manhattan—can be equally as hazardous![1] It is a long way from the clear thin air of the Himalayas to the smog-filled streets of Queens, but a growing number of Nepali Sherpas have chosen to make Metro New York their home. In fact, New York's Sherpa population is the largest outside Nepal and India.[2] The Sherpa are just one of many ethnic groups that comprise Metro New York's Nepali community of approximately 30 thousand.[3] Nepal, a monarchy for most of its history, forced its king to abdicate in 2008 after twelve years of civil war led by the communist party. At the crux of the conflict were centuries of pervasive ethnic and religious discrimination. Since the mid-1800s, the Bahun-Chhetri, a high-caste Hindu group, has held power over Nepal's sixty-five indigenous, primarily Buddhist groups known collectively as Janajati, as well as the Madhesi, who live in the southern plains of Nepal. These groups are currently fighting to secure rights and power in the new government of Nepal, which is still very unstable and on the brink of financial collapse.

When Did They Come To New York?

Very few Nepalis came to Metro New York until the 1990s, when political tensions began brewing in Nepal. Most arrived after the 1996 communist

insurgency began and during the resulting civil war, which scared off tourists from the Himalayas and forced thousands such as Tsering to search for work elsewhere. Ongoing turmoil and repeated strikes in the cities shut down universities and businesses, driving students and professionals to the US to finish their education or find steady work. Nepalis are continuing to arrive to escape the political chaos at home.

Where Do They Live?

Queens is Nepali central! In Ridgewood, there are a few apartment complexes near Wyckoff Avenue comprised almost entirely of Nepali people. In Sunnyside, Nepalis live between 37th and 52nd Streets. A few Nepali stores and restaurants can be found close to Roosevelt Avenue and 74th Street in Jackson Heights, the heart of the "Little India" commercial district. Woodside also has many Nepalis living among the Indian and Bangladeshi communities.

What Do They Believe?

Nepal had been a Hindu monarchy for over 250 years until

the government declared it a secular state in 2006. The Hindu kings who united Nepal in the late 1700s forced many of the indigenous Janajati groups—who mostly followed Buddhism, animism, or ancestor worship—to convert to Hinduism. As a result, many Janajati practice a mixture of Buddhism and Hinduism, while also retaining their animistic core. Nepali Hindus (mainly the Bahun-Chhetri and Madhesi) are far more connected to their religion, and many attend temples in Ridgewood, Elmhurst, and Jackson Heights. The Janajati have proven to be quite receptive to Christianity in Nepal, and one church that focuses on the Nepali community has recently been founded in Woodside, Queens. There is also an organization in the same area that has Nepalis involved in ESL classes and Bible studies.

What Are Their Lives Like?

"For us, New York is not a melting pot. It's a money pot," explained Paramendra, a young Nepali man. Since Nepal is one of the poorest countries in the world, Nepalis who come to Metro New York have one goal: make as much money as possible. Most work twelve to fifteen hours a day, six or seven days a week. Men are typically taxi drivers or work in restaurants or grocery stores, while women find jobs as housekeepers and nannies. They often live in groups, crowding as many as eight people into an apartment to save money. Their lives are built around relationships within the culture of their ethnic community. Nepalis in Metro New York are very active, with dozens of cultural and political associations that keep them connected to each other and engaged in Nepal's political situation. As one man said, "Nepalis may not know who the mayor of New York is, but they know everything happening back in Nepal!"

How Can I Pray?

✳ Many Nepalis are insulated in their communities, having little contact with Christians. Pray for greater opportunities to minister to some of their specific needs, such as learning English, as ways to build relationships and introduce them to Jesus Christ.

While Nepal is home to the world's largest mountains, the Gorsky-Kavkazi are called the "Mountain Jews" due to their Caucasus Mountains origin.

Gorsky-Kavkazi Jews

QUICK FACTS:

Place of Origin:
Caucasus Mountain region (former Soviet Republics of Dagestan, Chechnya, Azerbaijan)

Location in Metro New York:
Brooklyn (Flatbush)

Population in Metro New York:
10,000 (Community Estimate)

Primary Religion:
Judaism (Sephardic)

Status of Christian Witness:
Less than 2% evangelical. Some evangelical resources available, but no active church planting within the past 2 years.

Primary Language:
Russian

Secondary Languages:
Judeo-Tat, English

Registry of Peoples Code:
101431

Significant Notes:
✹ There are approximately 100,000 Gorsky-Kavkazi people in the world. Half live in Israel and 25% in the US.[4]
✹ The Gorsky-Kavkazi are Mizrahi Jews, or "Eastern Jews." Because they practice rites similar to Sephardic Jews, they are usually identified under the term "Sephardim."[5]
✹ While owning and farming land was forbidden for most of the Jewish Diaspora, the Gorsky-Kavkazi were renowned farmers, growing rice and tobacco, and raising silkworms. The Jewish vineyards were famous, even though their Muslim neighbors were prohibited from consuming wine. The Soviets forced the Gorsky-Kavkazi onto collective farms but allowed them to keep their traditional ways of growing grapes and making wine.[6]

"**Y**ou know you're Gorsky when…."[1] This lighthearted entry on a Gorsky-Kavkazi Facebook page provides some humorous insights about this community of ten thousand living in Flatbush, Brooklyn.[2] Answers include such tidbits as "You have thirty cousins" and "Your parents drink six cups of tea a day." For those who have never heard of the Gorsky-Kavkazi, just figuring out what to call them is an achievement! In the US they are typically known as "Mountain Jews," a loose translation of the Russian name "Gorsky-Kavkazi." As the Facebook page shows, they often simply go by "Gorsky" or "Kavkazi," the word for their ancestral homeland in the Caucasus Mountains. To add to the confusion, they call themselves "Juhuro" in their native language, Judeo-Tat, which is a version of ancient Persian with Hebrew mixed in. The Gorsky-Kavkazi claim to be descendents of the

Jews taken captive by the Babylonian Empire in 586 BC. The Babylonians were later conquered by the Medo-Persians. In the sixth century AD, a Persian king sent many Jews to reinforce his northern border in the rugged Caucasus, where they settled among the native Aryan and Muslim tribes. In 1869, the Gorsky-Kavkazi helped the Russians defeat Islamic armies that wanted an independent Shari'a state in the Caucasus. In return, they were spared the anti-Semitic persecution experienced by the Russian Jews. When the Soviets took over the Caucasus region in 1926, the Gorsky-Kavkazi were incorporated into the Soviet republics of Dagestan, Chechnya, and Azerbaijan. Since the Soviet Union's collapse, most of the Gorsky-Kavkazi population has left the Caucasus for Moscow, Israel, or the US.

When Did They Come To New York?

While they could have chosen to live in Israel, the group of Gorsky-Kavkazis who came to Metro New York in the mid-1990s was seeking a safe place for their children to grow up. The break-up of the Soviet Union brought conflict to the Caucasus. By the early 1990s, Azerbaijan was at war with Armenia, Chechnya was fighting for independence, and Dagestan was a hotbed of crime and kidnapping. Deciding to come to Metro New York instead of Israel was a choice for peace. As one man said, "Why leave one war zone for another?"

Where Do They Live?

"You know you are Gorsky when...you have relatives who live on Ocean Parkway!" The largest Gorsky-Kavkazi community in the US is in Flatbush, Brooklyn, between Beverly Road and Avenue I along Ocean Parkway. Metro New York's only Gorsky-Kavkazi cultural center and synagogue, named Beit Knesset Ohr Hamizrah, is at the intersection of Avenue C and Ocean Parkway.

What Do They Believe?

"All our customs come straight from the Torah," most Gorsky-Kavkazis claim although scholars

see influences of Zoroastrianism in some of their superstitions, stemming from their roots in ancient Persia.[3] The Gorsky-Kavkazis occupy an interesting place on the continuum of Jewish communities in Metro New York. With their mystical approach to Judaism, they are much like Hasidim, but living under Soviet secularism made them less rigid about following all the *mitzvots* (commandments) and more accepting of the nonreligious in their community. However, because they held fast to their religious traditions during the Soviet years, they retained far more of their faith and culture than the Russian Jews. Only a handful of Messianic believers are known.

What Are Their Lives Like?

"You know you are a Gorsky when...at least one person in your family is a taxi driver!" Like many new immigrants, Gorsky-Kavkazis take any job available to provide for their families, expecting their hard work to be rewarded when their children become doctors, lawyers, and accountants. The Gorsky-Kavkazi are an extremely tight-knit community, where "everyone knows each other and each other's business," said Diana, who works at the Gorsky-Kavkazi Cultural Center. "We take care of one another," she continued. "When I need advice, I can ask anyone."

How Can I Pray?

✳ The Gorsky-Kavkazi are largely unnoticed by Christians in Metro New York, even among ministries to Jewish people. Pray for believers to befriend and tell them of Jesus, the Messiah.

While Israel and New York have received many Gorsky-Kavkazi immigrants, Germany is also a top destination.

Germans

QUICK FACTS:

Place of Origin:
Germany

Significant Subgroups:
Mainly religious

Location in Metro New York:
Queens (Ridgewood); Brooklyn (Gerritsen Beach);
Manhattan (Washington Heights, Yorkville);
Westchester (White Plains)

Population in Metro New York:
1,867,089 (ACS 2008 Total Ancestry Reported);
67,508 (ACS 2008 Born in Germany)

Population in New York City:
281,762 (ACS 2008 Total Ancestry Reported);
21,076 (ACS 2008 Born in Germany)

Primary Religion:
Christianity (Roman Catholic, Lutheran)

Secondary Religions:
Nonreligious, Judaism

Status of Christian Witness:
Greater than or equal to 2% evangelical. Less than
5% evangelical.

Primary Language:
German

Secondary Language:
English

Registry of Peoples Code:
103305

Significant Notes:
❋ One in seven Americans claims German
ancestry.
❋ Included in Pope Benedict XVI's New York
itinerary in 2008 was a visit to St. Joseph's
Church, established in 1873 to serve the German
community.
❋ In the mid-1800s, German Jews started the
Reform movement, the most liberal form of
Judaism.
❋ The German-American Steuben Parade is held
each September in Manhattan. The parade honors
General von Steuben, a German who fought
alongside the Americans in the Revolutionary War.

On a sunny Wednesday in June 1904, 1,300 church members of St. Mark's Evangelical Lutheran Church in Manhattan's Little Germany—mostly mothers and children—boarded the steamship *The General Slocum* to travel to their annual Sunday school picnic. Forty minutes into the trip, fire broke out, and the ship burned to the water line. Just over one thousand were killed. It was the deadliest disaster in New York City's history until the 9/11 terrorist attacks on the World Trade Center, and it devastated New York's German community.[1] At the time, many believed New York to be the third-largest German-speaking city in the world after Berlin and Vienna.[2] Following the disaster, shattered families fled the German enclave on the Lower East Side, trying to escape sad memories. In the next few decades, the role of Germany in the two World Wars and the Holocaust brought further pain and shame upon German-Americans. Although Metro New York has the largest concentration of people of German descent in the US, currently estimated to be 1.9 million (ACS 2008), the German population has steadily declined as few newcomers arrive and the older generation passes away. Between 2000 and 2008, the number of German-born residents decreased by 17,500.[3] Pastor Muenich, who recently retired from a German Lutheran church in Manhattan, saw this firsthand. "In the 1990s, we had fifty to sixty people coming to our German services. It shrank to only ten to fifteen in the last few years," he explained.

When Did They Come To New York?

Germans have been coming to Metro New York since colonial times. Those who died on *The General Slocum* were part of the massive influx of nearly six million Germans who arrived in the US between 1820 and 1920. The last major wave was in the 1950s and '60s, when over 750 thousand came to the US to escape bleak post-war Germany.[4] With Germany's current prosperity, few are immigrating to the US although thousands come on temporary work assignments with German or multinational corporations.

Where Do They Live?

It is difficult to find a German enclave in Metro New York today, as most Germans are fully assimilated. After their exit from the Lower East Side following *The General Slocum* disaster, many Germans settled along 2nd Avenue in Yorkville on the Upper East Side. Others migrated out to Ridgewood, Queens, joining a large community of Germans who worked in Brooklyn's breweries. Around the same time, German Jews left the ghettos of the Lower East Side for Washington Heights. Ridgewood soon became the new German center of Metro New York, remaining seventy percent German until the 1960s.[5] Today, Gerritsen Beach in Brooklyn and White Plains in Westchester—home to the German School of New York—have small concentrations of Germans.

What Do They Believe?

"In the past, going to church and believing in God was just second nature for Germans," explained Pastor Wasserman, who serves one of the remaining German Lutheran churches in New York. "But younger Germans are very secular and materialistic—they have no need for church in their lives." Since the Reformation, the German population has been evenly divided between Protestants and Catholics, plus a small Jewish minority, but Pastor Muenich believes one-third of Germans in Metro New York today adhere to no religion. A few churches hold German services and reach out to the German community, including St. Joseph's Roman Catholic Church in Yorkville and the German Evangelical Lutheran Church of St. Paul on West 22nd Street.

What Are Their Lives Like?

Most New Yorkers know at least one German word—"Oktoberfest!"—the annual celebration of German food, beer, and music. Metro New York still has dozens of German cultural clubs, even though many are fading from lack of interest. "Germans who came in the fifties and sixties really needed these clubs to stay connected. The younger generations don't need it as much," said Pastor Wasserman. Fewer families enroll children in German language and dance classes, and most of these activities are viewed as recreational rather than intense training in language and culture.

How Can I Pray?

✳ Although Germans such as Martin Luther played a pivotal role in re-establishing biblical Christianity, Germans today are disassociating themselves from the Christian faith. Pray that the spirit of the Reformation would be rekindled and draw many Germans back to Christ.

Due to a long history of German migration to Argentina, Argentina has one of the largest German-speaking populations in the world.

Argentines

QUICK FACTS:

Place of Origin:
Argentina

Location in Metro New York:
Queens (Elmhurst)

Population in Metro New York:
50,000 (Community Estimate); 37,643 (ACS 2008 Specific Origin Argentina); 28,788 (ACS 2008 Born in Argentina)

Population in New York City:
14,601 (ACS 2008 Specific Origin Argentina); 11,391 (ACS 2008 Born in Argentina)

Primary Religion:
Christianity (Roman Catholic)

Secondary Religions:
Christianity (evangelical), Judaism

Status of Christian Witness:
Greater than or equal to 5% evangelical. Less than 10% evangelical.

Primary Language:
Spanish

Secondary Language:
English

Registry of Peoples Code:
100492

Significant Notes:
❋ Argentina's famous cattle are grass fed, which makes them less fatty than cattle raised on corn. The average Argentine eats 150 pounds of beef each year![6]
❋ Argentina has Latin America's largest Jewish population—over 250,000 people. They are descended from European refugees who fled the Nazis during World War II.[7]

"If there is one thing you should know about Argentines, it's that we love our meat and soccer! Our lives are centered on these things," exclaimed Jonathan. His fellow Argentine friends, Steven and Christian, happily confirmed this. "Soccer is a huge part of Argentine culture," said Christian. "We play it every week. We watch it on television. We are always talking about it! It connects us together and reminds us of home." As for the meat-loving aspect of Argentine culture, Steven explained that Argentines get together every Sunday for a traditional *asado*, a finger-licking barbeque featuring different types of grilled meat. A recent study estimates there are as many as 50 thousand Argentines in Metro New York.[1] Significant numbers of recent arrivals are undocumented, like Steven and Christian, who came to visit family members but found jobs and decided to stay. Like the US, Argentina is a nation of immigrants. Once a country of silver mines and prosperous cattle ranches, it attracted millions of Europeans seeking to make their fortune in the early twentieth century. Ninety percent of Argentines are descendants of those Italian and Spanish immigrants.

When Did They Come to New York?

While Metro New York has been welcoming Argentines since the 1960s, around half of the current population arrived in the 1980s and '90s.[2] Early Argentine

immigrants followed the classic "brain drain" pattern of highly educated professionals seeking better opportunities in the US. Later waves were less educated. Most were fleeing persecution at the hands of a military dictatorship that was waging a "dirty war" against its opponents. An estimated 30 thousand people were killed or simply disappeared between 1976 and 1983. In 2001, after years of government corruption, Argentina's economy collapsed, driving half of the population into poverty and destroying the country's middle class.[3]

Where Do They Live?

"The New York center for all things Argentine" is how *The New York Times* described the intersection of Junction Boulevard and Corona Avenue in Elmhurst, Queens, in 2001.[4] Less than ten years later, just a few restaurants and bakeries remain of what was Metro New York's main Argentine community. With their European features and high levels of education and skills, Argentines assimilate more easily than other Hispanic immigrants. Argentines themselves have a difficult time identifying where their compatriots live. As Marciella, a waitress at one of the remaining Argentine restaurants in Elmhurst, said, "Everyone is so spread out now."

What Do They Believe?

"I pray every night," Steven explained, "but I don't go to church anymore. I just don't think I need a priest to talk to God." Much like Italy and Spain, to which most Argentines trace their roots, Argentina is a historically Roman Catholic country that has become post-Christian. Although over ninety percent of Argentines are Catholic, only an estimated twenty percent practice their faith.[5] Unlike other parts of Latin America where evangelical Christianity is exploding, Argentina is again more similar to Europe, with just a small minority of evangelicals. Only two churches in Queens are known to be actively ministering to Argentines. One church started a soccer outreach, tapping into passion for the sport to build relationships and open doors.

What Are Their Lives Like?

"I have no plans to return to Argentina," Steven said. "This is my home. I've been through 9/11 and the Iraq War. I feel connected to this country." Jonathan chimed in, "Life is good here. I can make lots of money and things are easier." With big smiles, they described the best part of their week: "Sundays! We always have barbecues and play soccer!"

How Can I Pray?

✴ Many Argentines do not think they need church, but they want God. Pray that outreaches such as soccer ministries will open doors and help them pursue a relationship with Jesus.

Argentina and Portugal are both coastal countries known for their soccer (better known as *fútbol*) prowess.

Portuguese

QUICK FACTS:

Place of Origin:
Portugal (primarily from Murtosa and the northern countryside)

Location in Metro New York:
New Jersey (Newark, Hillside, Crane Square); Nassau (Mineola); Westchester (Mount Vernon, Yonkers, Ossining, Tarrytown)

Population in Metro New York:
150,000 (Community Estimate); 137,743 (ACS 2008 Total Ancestry); 47,636 (ACS 2008 Born in Portugal)

Population in New York City:
20,000 (Community Estimate); 13,037 (ACS 2008 Total Ancestry); 1,969 (ACS 2008 Born in Portugal)

Primary Religion:
Christianity (Roman Catholic)

Status of Christian Witness:
Greater than or equal to 2% evangelical. Less than 5% evangelical.

Primary Language:
Portuguese

Registry of Peoples Code:
108129

Significant Note:
✳ Over 90% of the Portuguese in Metro New York live outside of New York City.

When immigrants in Metro New York are discussed, New York City seems to receive all the attention. However, there are some immigrant groups that practically shun the city to build their ethnic enclaves elsewhere. For instance, the Salvadoran enclave is in Long Island; the Peruvian, Turkish, and main Arab enclaves are in Paterson, New Jersey; and the Ironbound District of Newark has long been host to the "Little Portugal" of Metro New York. Along Ferry Street in North Ironbound, Portuguese restaurants, cafes, bakeries, and other stores are thriving. Even when Newark has suffered economically, the Ironbound section has hardly been affected due to the bustling Portuguese businesses. Within a decade of the first Portuguese immigrants arriving in the 1910s, the Ironbound District had a large enough Portuguese population to form its first social club. The Sport Club Portuguese, formed in 1920, served as a precursor to the dozens of social organizations now in existence that cater to the Portuguese community.[1] The 2008 American Community Survey estimates that there are 137,743 people with Portuguese ancestry and 47,636 Portugal-born in the New York Metro area. Over one-third of those born in Portugal live in the Newark area, and under five percent live in New York City itself. The Portuguese community estimates their population to be around 150 thousand in the Metro area.[2]

When Did They Come To New York?

Portuguese have a long history of emigration. They have emigrated for centuries to Brazil and their colonies in Africa and, in the late eighteenth and early nineteenth centuries, mainly left the Azores (Portuguese islands in the Atlantic) to work on whaling ships in Massachusetts, California, and Hawaii. The large Portuguese immigration wave to New York, however, mainly occurred after America changed visa policies in 1965. Under the dictatorship of António de Oliveira Salazar, the country's poor became poorer and, after Salazar's death in 1970, the country experienced high inflation, economic turmoil, and high emigration. While the Portuguese government stabilized in the mid-1970s, the negative economic repercussions were felt into the early-1980s.[3] During this period, many poor people from around Murtosa and elsewhere emigrated out of Portugal into Newark. After Portugal joined the European Economic Community in 1986, immigration to Metro New York subsided tremendously.

Where Do They Live?

The Ironbound District of Newark undoubtedly remains the center of Portuguese activity in Metro New York. However, a Portuguese presence also exists in Mineola, Long Island, and parts of Westchester County.

What Do They Believe?

With four Portuguese Masses and one English Mass on Sunday, as well as a bilingual Mass on Saturday, Our Lady of Fatima Catholic Church in Newark reflects the strong

Portuguese devotion to Catholicism. Built in the 1950s as the first Catholic church in Newark devoted to the Portuguese community, it has been joined by several others in the last few decades. Around ninety-five percent of the Portuguese identify themselves as Catholic, while up to five percent are Protestant. However, there are hardly any Protestant churches that have a predominantly Portuguese congregation.

What Are Their Lives Like?

From Magellan to the whaling industry in New Bedford, Massachusetts, Portuguese success has long been linked to the sea. In Metro New York, though, the Portuguese have had to branch out into other industries such as carpentry, construction, and the restaurant and bakery businesses to be successful. Mainly coming from the peasant class, the Portuguese are less organized, educated, political, and professionally ambitious than some other immigrant groups. Nevertheless, they have built and sustained a successful community in Newark, and the Ironside seafood industry they have specialized in has kept them anchored to their maritime roots.

How Can I Pray?

✳ Pray that churches will be started that focus on reaching Portuguese people and culture, as almost all "Portuguese" evangelical churches in Metro New York are predominantly Brazilian.

Brazilians and Portuguese identify with one another as Luso-Americans (people whose culture consists of Portuguese traditions or language).

Brazilians

QUICK FACTS:

Place of Origin:
Brazil (Minas Gerais, Rio de Janeiro, Sao Paulo)

Significant Subgroups:
By region or city of origin: Minas Gerais (50%); Rio de Janeiro (30%); Sao Paulo (10%); Espírito Santo Paraná and other states (10%)[6]

Location in Metro New York:
New Jersey (Newark, Harrison, Linden, Kearney, Long Branch); Queens (Astoria); Westchester (Mount Vernon)

Population in Metro New York:
300,000 (Community Estimate); 75,067 (ACS 2008 Total Ancestry Reported); 67,777 (ACS 2008 Born in Brazil)[7]

Population in New York City:
17,323 (ACS 2008 Total Ancestry Reported); 17,467 (ACS 2008 Born in Brazil)

Primary Religion:
Christianity (Roman Catholic)

Secondary Religion:
Christianity (evangelical)

Status of Christian Witness:
Greater than or equal to 10% evangelical.

Primary Language:
Portuguese

Secondary Language:
English

Registry of Peoples Code:
101657

Significant Notes:
☀ Brazil, colonized by the Portuguese, is South America's melting pot—a blend of European, African, and indigenous peoples.
☀ New York City's Brazilian Day is the largest Brazilian event outside of Brazil, drawing more than one million people.

Ask a Brazilian living in the Ironbound section of Newark, New Jersey, where he comes from, and the likely answer will be "Governador Valadares," a city in the state of Minas Gerais in southeastern Brazil. Asking the same question of a Brazilian in Mount Vernon in Westchester County will probably elicit the response, "Poços de Caldas," a resort town also located in Minas Gerais. The response of "Minas Gerais" will also be heard in Astoria, Queens, where almost half of Brazilians trace their origins back to the large coffee- and emigrant-producing state of Brazil. Indeed, out of an estimated 75 thousand people with Brazilian ancestry in Metro New York (ACS 2008), a majority hail from this one state. The connection was made when US companies went to Minas Gerais in the 1940s to obtain mica, a mineral needed for the defense industry. When Brazil's economy collapsed in the 1980s, thousands of Brazilians made their way to Metro New York. Although many were middle-class professionals, they took any job available and began sending money back home. At one point, five million dollars a month was sent into Governador Valadares, and most of the new housing in Poços de Caldas was financed with Mount Vernon money.[1] While the US economy is now faltering, Brazil's is growing, causing the dollar's influence in Brazil to wane. These factors, along with the burden of being undocumented, are leading many Brazilians to return home.

When Did They Come to New York?

In the 1980s and '90s, thousands of Brazilians desperate for financial security made their way to Metro New York. Brazil's inflation was so extreme that people would race through the supermarket to beat the constant price increases.[2] Most came on tourist visas, found under-the-table jobs, and stayed. Community leaders agree the vast majority of Brazilians are undocumented.[3]

Where Do They Live?

Only a few Brazilian merchants remain in "Little Brazil" on West 46th Street in Manhattan, once a thriving commercial center. The largest Brazilian community in Metro New York is in the Ironbound section of Newark. Brazilians have revitalized this historically Portuguese neighborhood, with shops, bakeries, and restaurants lining Ferry Street. In Astoria, Brazilians live and work in a thriving multi-ethnic community concentrated around 36th Avenue and 31st Street. In Mount Vernon, a city of 70 thousand in Westchester County just north of the Bronx, an estimated one in ten residents is from Brazil.[4]

What Do They Believe?

Since Brazil is the world's largest Catholic country, the majority of Brazilians in Metro New York are Catholics although most are nominal believers. Many active Brazilian Catholics are finding a new spiritual home in Pentecostal churches, where the vibrant worship style is similar to the lively Masses they had in Brazil, and abundant social activities help them make friends and feel at home. Counting other evangelical churches such as Presbyterian and Baptist, there are now around forty-five evangelical Brazilian churches in Metro New York.[5] Brazilian Catholicism, though, has been heavily infiltrated by occult practices and spiritist religions, most notably Santería, which was brought to the New World by African slaves and involves animal sacrifices and communication with the dead.

What Are Their Lives Like?

When Brazil's economy went into free fall, Brazilian money was useless. Since having American dollars was key to economic survival in Minas Gerais, thousands of people left family and friends to come to Metro New York. Hoping to earn as much money as they could as housekeepers, dishwashers, and shoe-shiners, only to return to Brazil once the economy recovered, Brazilians have not laid down roots in the US. As a result, Brazilians have little socio-political clout. Their uniqueness as non-Spanish speaking Latinos of mixed European, African, and American Indian ancestry means they have struggled to fit into America's prescribed ethnic categories. With an improved economy back home, along with the lure of family and a much more relaxed Brazilian pace, many Brazilians are moving back home or beginning to seriously consider the possibility.

How Can I Pray?

✳ Brazilian Christians are leading a new wave of South American missionaries that is spreading the gospel in Muslim countries around the world. Pray that their sociable personalities will assist them in crossing cultural lines in Metro New York to share the joy of Christ with Muslims and others.

One of the staples of New York City street food vending is the Nuts4Nuts industry, which makes and sells candied nuts. Most of these are run by Brazilians and Colombians.

Colombians

QUICK FACTS:

Place of Origin:
Colombia

Location in Metro New York:
Queens (Jackson Heights, Woodside, Corona, Flushing); New Jersey (Victory Gardens, Dover, Morristown, Lake View, Hackensack, Englewood, West New York, North Bergen, El Mora, Crane Square); Connecticut (South Norwalk)

Population in Metro New York:
255,592 (ACS 2008 Specific Origin Colombia); 180,683 (ACS 2008 Born in Colombia)

Population in New York City:
95,972 (ACS 2008 Specific Origin Colombia); 69,515 (ACS 2008 Born in Colombia)

Primary Religion:
Christianity (Roman Catholic)

Secondary Religion:
Christianity (evangelical)

Status of Christian Witness:
Greater than or equal to 5% evangelical. Less than 10% evangelical.

Primary Language:
Spanish

Registry of Peoples Code:
102261

Significant Note:
☀ 10% of Colombians (around 4 million) live outside of their country.

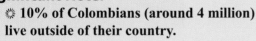

S ince the mid-twentieth century, the New York Metro area has become a choice destination for the crime-weary, war-weary, and financial-weary emigrants from Colombia. Maria Gomez, a New York City ethnographer, documented the story of a Colombian immigrant named Rocio in her Colombia Migration Project.[1] Rocio, like many other Colombian immigrants, is well educated and left behind a well-respected occupation for an entry-level job in New York. In describing her journey and life in the city, Rocio finds it difficult to explain why she has stayed in New York so long, yet she always finds some compelling reason to stay. "If I came here and took all this risk," she says, "I have to see it through to the end." With determination and a sense of mission, many of the 255 thousand Colombians in Metro New York (ACS 2008) are seeking to see it through.

When Did They Come to New York?

Colombians first started having a noticeable presence in New York City after World War I, when several hundred professionals and students formed a community in Jackson Heights. This little Colombia became known as Chapinerito, after a middle-class suburb of Bogota. However, it was not until the onset of "La Violencia"—the Colombian Civil War that started in 1948—that the Colombian community in New York started to swell. Even when order was restored in Colombia, emigration increased, and a recession in the 1960s further increased the outpouring of Colombians into the Big Apple. This new wave of

immigration brought a working-class majority that quickly outnumbered the pioneering professionals. As chaos continued in Colombia due to the activities of drug cartels and a corrupt government in the 1980s, the Colombian population in Queens expanded. A carryover of violence and cartel activity into Chapinerito then led some Colombians to extend their settlements to areas in New Jersey and Connecticut.[2]

Where Do They Live?

From the inception of their search for order, safety, and opportunity in New York, the lifeblood of Colombians has been along Roosevelt Avenue in Jackson Heights, Queens. From this center, they have spread out to Corona, Elmhurst, Woodside, and Flushing, while also branching out into areas in New Jersey such as Dover, Victory Gardens, Morristown, Englewood, and North Bergen and in Connecticut cities such as South Norwalk and Stamford.

What Do They Believe?

Like many South Americans, Colombians have a cultural adherence to Catholicism. Dotting the landscape of Roosevelt Avenue, however, are a myriad of *botanicas* that reflect the tendency of Colombians to consult spiritual counselors, fortune tellers, and saints for guidance in their lives. Perhaps ninety percent of Colombians are Catholic, with a significant portion of the rest adhering to an evangelical Christian faith. Some Colombians feel like they should assimilate into American life, viewing Catholicism as cultural baggage they should shed. They still believe that Jesus is an important part of their lives, though, so they search out evangelical churches to join.

What are Their Lives Like?

Whereas the first Colombian immigrants to New York found jobs that suited their professional interests, the wave of immigrants since the 1980s has come to a New York where they typically find only low-paying service jobs. Rocio, quoted above, reflected on New York life by saying, "The depression, the loneliness, in this country is incredible. Here you live to work, and in Colombia we work to live. That gives us a different perspective on all this, this supposed country of—'country of the gods.'"[3]

How Can I Pray?

✳ Pray that Colombians will continue the process of shedding cultural baggage that is not pleasing to Christ, while maintaining and developing their strong devotion to Jesus.
✳ Pray that God alone (instead of saints or fortune tellers) will be the One Colombians seek for the spiritual direction of their lives.

Colombians are the dominant presence along Roosevelt Avenue in Jackson Heights, but a short walk eastward reveals that neighboring Corona is dominated by Ecuadorians.

Ecuadorians

QUICK FACTS:

Place of Origin:
Ecuador (the *sierra*, with many from the El Austro region; the *costa*)

Significant Subgroups:
Serranos (majority); *costeños* (minority); Quichua treated in their own profile (p. 94)

Location in Metro New York:
Queens (Corona, Jackson Heights, Elmhurst, Woodside, Ridgewood); Bronx (Morris Hills, Highbridge); New Jersey (Hackensack, Jersey City); Westchester (Ossining, Mariandale, Sparta); Connecticut (Danbury)

Population in Metro New York:
375,599 (ACS 2008 Specific Origin Ecuador); 268,546 (ACS 2008 Born in Ecuador)

Population in New York City:
190,831 (ACS 2008 Specific Origin Ecuador); 135,438 (ACS 2008 Born in Ecuador)

Primary Religion:
Christianity (67% Roman Catholic, 33% Protestant)

Status of Christian Witness:
Greater than or equal to 10% evangelical.

Primary Language:
Spanish

Registry of Peoples Code:
102869

Significant Notes:
❊ Over 60% of Ecuadorians in the United States live in the New York Metro area.
❊ Metro New York neighborhoods or towns with Ecuadorian concentrations are often dominated by people from one particular region or town in Ecuador. For instance, in New York City itself, *serranos* are predominant in Queens while *costeños* are more populous in the Bronx.
❊ Ecuadorians possibly have the largest number of undocumented immigrants in New York City.

Ask an Ecuadorian to name the largest Ecuadorian cities, and one is likely to receive the following answer: "Guayaquil, Quito […] then New York City." At least in popular opinion, New York City has become the third-largest "Ecuadorian" city in the world.[1] Compared to other South Americans, Ecuadorians in the New York Metro area are incredibly diverse. They are service workers, entrepreneurs, and professionals. They are mestizo and Indian. They are even from regions in Ecuador so distinct they could be their own countries. As a result, many Ecuadorians in Metro New York identify themselves first with their city, then by their region, and only then by their country. The country of Ecuador, located on the coast of northwest South America, is divided by the Andes into three regions. The area by the coast and west of the mountains is called the *costa*. The *costeños* almost exclusively speak Spanish and are known for being politically liberal. Although not the largest group, there are many *costeños* in New York. The crowded, mountainous central area of the country is called the *sierra*, and *serranos* make up a majority of Ecuadorians in Metro New York. The *serranos* consist of both mestizo and Quichuan Indians and are known for being politically conservative. Finally, the region to the east of the Andes is called the *oriente*, a sparsely populated rain forest with a large variety of Indian ethnicities. While people from the *oriente* make up two percent of Ecuador's population, they are even less represented in New York. Overall, Ecuadorians are now the fourth-largest Hispanic group in Metro New York behind Puerto Ricans, Dominicans, and Mexicans. However, their population in Metro New York has

been growing at a faster rate than any demographically significant (more than 20 thousand people) Hispanic group in the area, more than doubling in eight years from 173,966 (Census 2000) to 375,599 (ACS 2008).

When Did They Come To New York?

Perhaps it all started with the Panama hat, which is actually made in Ecuador. In the southern region of the *sierra* known as El Austro, almost a quarter of the workforce lost their jobs due to the collapse of the Panama hat trade in 1947. Former hat merchants and middlemen, who had become familiar with New York City due to the trade, started immigrating to the city in the 1960s. In 1964, land reform in Ecuador ended the centuries-old feudal system, but many peasants, who were not experienced in owning land, also left for New York. Later on in the 1980s and '90s, plummeting oil prices in an economy over-dependent on oil caused an economic recession that placed seventy percent of Ecuadorians below the poverty line in 1997.[2] As a result, a mass emigration of Ecuadorians occurred, which was made up of both *serranos* and *costeños*, as well as all strata of society. The primary immigrant destination became New York City although Madrid has also become a favored spot since the late 1990s.

Where Do They Live?

As evidenced by the countless Ecuadorian businesses along Roosevelt Avenue in Jackson Heights and Corona, around one-third of Ecuadorians in Metro

New York live in Queens. Pockets of Ecuadorians also exist in the Bronx, New Jersey, Westchester County, and Connecticut.

What Do They Believe?

While Ecuador is almost exclusively Catholic, the El Austro region in the southern *sierra* has a disproportionate number of Protestants. In 1980, for instance, the Chimborazo province was nearly forty percent Protestant. With a large representation from El Austro, it is not a total surprise that some community leaders estimate one-third of Ecuadorians in New York Metro to be Protestant.[3]

What Are Their Lives Like?

Due to the diversity of Ecuadorian New Yorkers, their occupations range from white-collar jobs to jobs in garment shops and sweatshops. Astonishingly, the New York City Department of City Planning estimated that, in 2004, twenty-seven percent of the 490 thousand undocumented immigrants in the city were Ecuadorian.[4] For many, the economic instability of living in Ecuador has simply been traded for that of another kind.

How Can I Pray?

✳ When immigrants from several areas in a country settle together in a place like New York City, the change can often forge a relationship between people who would never have set foot in each other's territories back home. With a large number of evangelicals from the El Austro region, pray that their newfound relationship with other Ecuadorians will be used as an opportunity to expand the reach of the gospel.

Although the Quichua live in several different South American countries, most Quichua in Metro New York are from Ecuador.

Quichua

QUICK FACTS:

Place of Origin:
Andes Mountains (Ecuador, Peru, Bolivia)

Significant Subgroups:
Cañari Quichua (large majority); Otavalo (small minority); other Quichua groups (small minority)

Location in Metro New York:
Queens (Jackson Heights, Corona, Ridgewood); Rockland (Spring Valley); New Jersey (Newark); Bronx (Morrisania); Westchester (Sleepy Hollow)

Population in Metro New York:
10,000 (Community Estimate)

Primary Religion:
Christianity (Catholicism syncretized with Inca traditional beliefs and rituals)

Secondary Religion:
Christianity (evangelical)

Status of Christian Witness:
Greater than or equal to 10% evangelical.

Primary Languages:
Spanish, Quichua

Registry of Peoples Codes:
107703, 101871

Significant Notes:
❄ Due to racism that Quichua experienced in their home countries, many Quichua hide their identity in the US.
❄ Most of the Quichua evangelical churches in Metro New York are made up of people from Cañar, but there is at least one Chimborazo-Quichua church.
❄ In Ecuador, the word "Quichua" is used to describe this ethnic group, while in countries like Peru and Bolivia, the word "Quechua" is used.
❄ Many Quichua in Metro New York do not have proper documentation to be in the country.

Sharing Times Square street space with the likes of the "The Naked Cowboy" and "subway musician" space with the likes of musical saw players, Quichua musicians have established themselves as part of New York's tourist trade with their popular Andean folk music. The Quichua, or Quechua, Indians from the Andes Mountains in South America are the largest remaining American Indian group in the world. Hailing from mountain ranges throughout Ecuador, Bolivia, Peru, Argentina, Chile, and Colombia, the Quechuan language and identity spread due to the influence of the Quechua-speaking Inca Empire. It was the Incas who brought Peruvian populations into Ecuador to consolidate their territory, making Quechua the language of government and trade. Although Quechua is still spoken throughout the Andes, some dialects are no longer mutually comprehensible, such as the one spoken in Ecuador—where "Quichua" is the preferred spelling—and the one spoken in Peru.[1] In Metro New York, most Quichua are from either the Otavalo or Cañari highlands of Ecuador. Community leaders estimate that there are ten thousand Quichua in Metro New York, with most of these Cañari.[2] Anthropologist Jason Pribilsky, who wrote an ethnography on Andean Ecuadorian immigration to New York, estimates that there are 1,500 Quichua in Rockland County alone.[3]

When Did They Come To New York?

Quichua from Otavalo started making their way to New York in the late 1970s and early '80s due to economic problems in their homeland. Initially, they primarily sold textiles their people had made in Ecuador and were involved in other small commercial activities between the two countries. The population has grown steadily until today, when most Otavalo Quichua immigrate and specialize in a particular construction industry, such as siding, roofing, or cement. Shortly after the Otavalo Quichua carved a niche for themselves in the New York economy, Quichua from the Ecuadorian provinces of Cañar and Chimborazo immigrated and followed suit in the construction business.

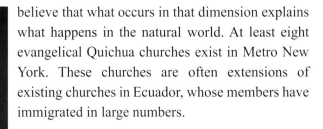

Where Do They Live?

The main concentration of the Quichua is in the Jackson Heights, Corona, and Ridgewood areas of Queens. With little free time apart from work, however, new Quichua communities have developed throughout the Metro area as they settle close to their work sites. They can be found along Westchester Avenue in the Morrisania area of the Bronx, Newark, New Jersey, and north of New York City in Rockland County—particularly in Spring Valley.

What Do They Believe?

Quichua people almost exclusively identify themselves as Christians. Most of these, however, are Catholics who have syncretized traditional Inca beliefs and rituals with Catholicism. Many Quichua have a strong sense of the reality of the supernatural world and

believe that what occurs in that dimension explains what happens in the natural world. At least eight evangelical Quichua churches exist in Metro New York. These churches are often extensions of existing churches in Ecuador, whose members have immigrated in large numbers.

What Are Their Lives Like?

Apart from the obvious economic reasons, many Quichua and other Ecuadorians immigrate to New York for what it represents. Using their own colloquialism, they seek to adopt the *iony* way. *Iony*, derived from the ubiquitous phrase, "I ♥ NY,"

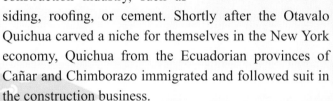

has come to represent a way that is more modern, progressive, and developed.[4] The *iony* way can be used to describe anything from fashion to evolved attitudes on gender equality, and many Quichua begin to adopt the *iony* lifestyle. With male immigrants often leaving their families behind in their home countries, the acute changes that take place in both locations at the hands of *iony* have had both positive and negative effects. While both sides are often excited about the "progress" their family is making because of *iony*, the same force is usually responsible for tearing apart marriages, customs, and traditional values.

How Can I Pray?

✳ There are several Quichua evangelical churches in Metro New York. Pray that God would use them to prevent their people from falling prey to the negatives aspects of the *iony* way.
✳ The Quichua are often looked down upon by Hispanics from Central and South America. Pray that the Quichua would love these people with a Christ-like love, persuading them to investigate the Source of such humility.

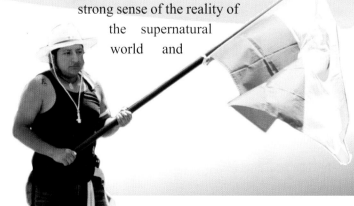

Many Ecuadorians started migrating to Metro New York due to the decline of the Panama hat trade, and most Quichua are from Ecuador.

Panamanians

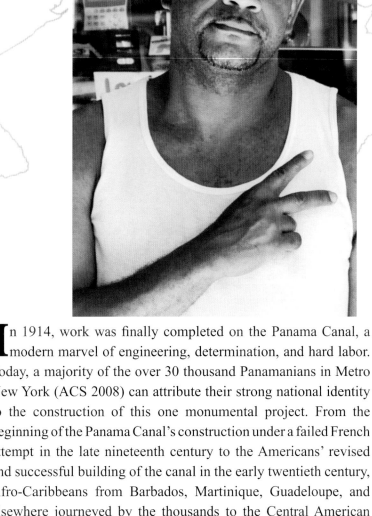

QUICK FACTS:

Place of Origin:
Panama (mainly Panama City and areas around the former Panama Canal Zone)

Significant Subgroups:
Afro-Panamanians (large majority); mestizo Panamanians (small minority)

Location in Metro New York:
Brooklyn (Flatbush, Eastern Parkway, Crown Heights, East Flatbush)

Population in Metro New York:
33,489 (ACS 2008 Specific Origin Panama); 24,959 (ACS 2008 Born in Panama)

Population in New York City:
24,103 (ACS 2008 Specific Origin Panama); 19,043 (ACS 2008 Born in Panama)

Primary Religions:
Christianity (Roman Catholic, evangelical, mainline Protestant)

Status of Christian Witness:
Greater than or equal to 10% evangelical.

Primary Languages:
English, Spanish

Registry of Peoples Codes:
110760, 107814, 107816

Significant Notes:
❀ The largest Panamanian population in the United States is in Metro New York. It is well over twice the size of Metro Miami's Panamanian population, which is the 2nd largest.
❀ Around 50% of Panamanians in Metro New York live in Brooklyn.
❀ Around 60% of Panamanians in Metro New York are women.

In 1914, work was finally completed on the Panama Canal, a modern marvel of engineering, determination, and hard labor. Today, a majority of the over 30 thousand Panamanians in Metro New York (ACS 2008) can attribute their strong national identity to the construction of this one monumental project. From the beginning of the Panama Canal's construction under a failed French attempt in the late nineteenth century to the Americans' revised and successful building of the canal in the early twentieth century, Afro-Caribbeans from Barbados, Martinique, Guadeloupe, and elsewhere journeyed by the thousands to the Central American isthmus for the promise of steady work. After the canal was built, many workers stayed, and now Afro-Caribbeans and mulattos make up fourteen percent of Panama's population.[1] Despite the country's largely mestizo and Spanish-speaking population, many Afro-Caribbean immigrants continued to speak English, mainly settling in Panama City, which bordered the American-controlled Panama Canal Zone. Their familiarity with English and the urban environment later made New York City a popular immigration destination and partially explains why seventy-five percent of Panamanians in Metro New York are Afro-Panamanians. While the remaining mestizos almost exclusively speak Spanish upon arrival, the Afro-Panamanians vary widely in their linguistic ability. Some speak only Spanish or English, while others are bilingual. With

Spanish the official language of Panama, many Afro-Panamanians spoke English at home while learning Spanish at school. Having settled primarily among other English-speaking Caribbeans in New York, however, most second- and third-generation Panamanians speak only English. No matter what their background, as one Panamanian community leader claims, "There is a certain something that Panamanians have—a pride that each Panamanian possesses that unites all Panamanians together. Panamanians are *paisanos* [...] and we greet one another by calling out, '*Paisa!*'"[2]

When Did They Come To New York?

Panamanian migration to New York began in the late 1800s with immigrants first settling in Harlem, later moving to Brooklyn.[3] Almost twenty percent of Panama-born immigrants in Metro New York arrived in the United States before 1965, most of whom arrived in the 1950s and early '60s. Immigration steadily continued in the late 1960s up until the 1980s before slowing in the 1990s. Almost all immigrants have come from in and around Panama City or the former Panama Canal Zone.

Where Do They Live?

While walking along Franklin Avenue from the southeast end of Prospect Park in Brooklyn to the far northeastern end of the park, one can hear a chorus of West Indians chattering in English Creole, hinting at the preferred identity of the neighborhood's Panamanian residents. It is here in Brooklyn's Flatbush and Crown Heights neighborhoods—the center of America's Afro-Caribbean population—that an overwhelming percentage of Metro New York Panamanians

reside, clearly embracing an Afro-Caribbean identity over their Hispanic national heritage.

What Do They Believe?

Panamanians in Metro New York are almost exclusively Christian. Perhaps eighty-five to ninety percent of Latino-Panamanians are Catholic, while about half of Afro-Panamanians are either evangelical or mainline Protestant and forty percent, Catholic.[4] The largest evangelical church in New York City, the Christian Cultural Center in Brooklyn, is pastored by Panama-born A.R. Bernard. Despite a strong Christian identity, some Panamanian Catholics incorporate elements of Pocomania into their religious practice, which involves spirit possession and other religious elements inherited from Africa.

What Are Their Lives Like?

When the pioneers of Panamanian immigration came to New York City, they envisioned a bright future for their children. These first-generation immigrants were disproportionately professionals and highly educated. In a cruel twist of immigration fate, their children and especially their grandchildren have often adopted the worst aspects of New York culture, with few graduating from high school and more than a few involving themselves in illicit activities and occupations.

How Can I Pray?

✳ Pray that wayward Panamanian youth would have their lives transformed by the gospel.

Many men from Barbados left their country to work on the Panama Canal. As a result, many Panamanians with Barbadian ancestry live in Metro New York.

97

Barbadians

QUICK FACTS:

Place of Origin:
  Barbados

Location in Metro New York:
  Brooklyn (Bedford-Stuyvesant, Brownsville, East Flatbush, Eastern Parkway, Flatbush, Crown Heights); Bronx (Huguenot Park, Vernon Park); Queens (North Woodmere, Laurelton, Far Rockaway)

Population in Metro New York:
  150,000 (Community Estimate); 30,206 (ACS 2008 Born in Barbados); 29,813 (ACS 2008 Total Ancestry Reported)

Population in New York City:
  23,515 (ACS 2008 Born in Barbados); 22,386 (ACS 2008 Total Ancestry Reported)

Primary Religion:
  Christianity (Anglican, Pentecostal)

Status of Christian Witness:
  Greater than or equal to 10% evangelical.

Primary Languages:
  Bajan, English

Registry of Peoples Code:
  101047

Significant Notes:
  ❊ The Barbadian population in Metro New York is at least one-tenth the size of the population of Barbados.
  ❊ 60% of the Barbadians in the US live in Metro New York (ACS 2008).
  ❊ 80% of the Barbadians in Metro New York live in New York City (ACS 2008).
  ❊ When slaves were freed throughout the West Indian British colonies from 1833-1834, the number of Africa-born slaves in Barbados was significantly smaller than in other colonies.

Although the British have left their trail throughout the Caribbean, nowhere is it seen more than in the easternmost island of the West Indies. The country of Barbados, which hosts more British tourists than American, has long been known as "Little England." The British settled the uninhabited island in 1605, developed it into one of its most successful colonies with sugar production, and ruled without interruption for 350 years. In 1966, Barbados gained its independence, but Britain's mark remains strong. The Queen of England is still the country's head of state, the government is patterned after the British Parliament, British people and place names abound, and even high court judges wore white horsehair wigs until recently.[1] Furthermore, the people of Barbados are known for their refined accent and manner, and African influences are much more subdued in Barbados than in other Caribbean countries with populations of African ancestry. Almost all Barbadians, known as "Bajans," are of African descent and speak a unique Creole English also called "Bajan." While over 30 thousand Metro New Yorkers were counted as born in Barbados (ACS 2008), the Barbados Consul General in New York estimated their population to number 150 thousand in the Metro area.[2] Only 284,589 people currently live in Barbados.[3]

When Did They Come To New York?

In the first two decades of the twentieth century, a West Indian immigrant community that included Barbadians began to develop in New York City. Stalled by restrictive policies, immigration did not pick up again until the 1950s. However, it was a US policy change in 1965 that ensured a steady inflow of Bajans searching for opportunities.[4] Apart from being one of the most densely populated places on earth, Barbados has presented no major reasons for its people to emigrate. The country is stable economically, politically, and socially. Because of this, most Bajan New Yorkers come for educational or economic opportunities and retain close ties to their country. One Bajan New Yorker shrugged off the difference between his home country and New York by saying, "When you come to New York, you've gone to Barbados."

Where Do They Live?

There is only one place in Metro New York where people might feel that they are in Barbados, and that is East Flatbush, Brooklyn, and the surrounding neighborhoods. The area has a high concentration of English-speaking West Indians, and fifty-four percent of Metro New Yorkers born in Barbados live in Brooklyn, primarily in this one area.

What Do They Believe?

"Clergy throughout the West Indies go to Barbados to study," a Bajan Episcopalian priest in Brooklyn claimed. The first documented religion in Barbados was the Anglican Church, which is the Church of England, and its influence remains to this day. A majority of Bajans have some sort of connection with the Anglican Church (Episcopal is the American equivalent), and Bajan priests are disproportionately represented among the Episcopalian clergy in Brooklyn. The Pentecostal movement also claims a large number of adherents, and their number only continues to grow. Strikingly absent is the presence of an Afro-centric Caribbean religion such as voodoo, Shango, or Pocomania, reflecting the limited influence African traditions have had in Barbados compared to other Caribbean countries.[5]

What Are Their Lives Like?

Bajan professionals certainly exist, but most Bajans have what is the common lot for immigrants: domestic, construction, and service jobs. Bajans usually aspire to buy a house, and part of the attraction of Brooklyn is the abundance of houses suitable for large families. Once they buy a house, extended family members often live under one roof, sharing cooking responsibilities in their own "little island" in New York. One of their favorite dishes is an African carryover Barbadians call "cou-cou," which is firm cornmeal, usually served with slimy okra sauce and steamed or fried flying fish. The politics of Barbados is a favorite conversation topic over dinner.

How Can I Pray?

✳ With the long Anglican history in Barbados, many Bajans associate the faith with tradition, and some even consider it a colonial leftover. Pray that God would bring them fresh understanding and faith in the timeless message of salvation from sin through the death and resurrection of Christ.

Many of the popular fried chicken places in Afro-Caribbean neighborhoods are owned by Afghans.

Afghans

QUICK FACTS:

Place of Origin:
Afghanistan (Kabul, Kandahar, Jalalabad)

Significant Subgroups:
Muslims (16,000: Pashtun, over 50%; Tajik, less than 50%); Hindu-Sikhs (3,000); Jews (1,000)

Location in Metro New York:
Muslims: Queens (Kew Gardens Hills, Flushing, Jackson Heights); New Jersey (Parsippany, Newark); Hindu-Sikhs: Queens (Flushing, Fresh Meadows); Nassau (Hicksville); Suffolk (Lindenhurst, Babylon); New Jersey (Manalapan); Jews: Queens (Flushing, Forest Hills, Jamaica)

Population in Metro New York:
20,000 (Community Estimate); 11,888 (ACS 2008 Total Ancestry); 8,204 (ACS 2008 Born in Afghanistan)

Population in New York City:
7,317 (ACS 2008 Total Ancestry); 5,213 (ACS 2008 Born in Afghanistan)

Primary Religions:
Islam, Hinduism, Sikhism, Judaism

Status of Christian Witness:
Less than 2% evangelical. Some evangelical resources available, but no active church planting within the past two years.

Primary Languages:
Dari (Muslims, Jews); Pashto (Muslims); Kandhari/Multani and Punjabi (Hindu-Sikhs)

Significant Notes:
❋ As of 2008, there are four predominantly Afghan mosques in the Flushing area of Queens.
❋ There is only one Afghan Jew left in Afghanistan.
❋ Under Taliban rule, both Hindus and Sikhs were forced to wear yellow cloth to identify themselves.
❋ The Hindu-Sikh temples teach Hindi to the children, as opposed to their parents' languages.
❋ There is no one known who is focusing on evangelism and church planting among Afghans in Metro New York, and only a handful of Afghan Christians exist in the Metro area.

Having fled Soviet invasion, war, and even Taliban terror, an estimated 20 thousand Afghans have grown accustomed to calling Metro New York their home.[1] However, due to the Taliban's involvement in the destruction of the World Trade Center, the world Afghan New Yorkers left behind has invaded their world once again. In the aftermath of 9/11, this once inconspicuous group faced increased persecution, scrutiny, and inter-ethnic tensions. Beforehand, the exquisite Hazrat-i-Abu Bakr mosque in Flushing, Queens, served as a religious respite for the largely Tajik- and Pashtun-Afghan Muslim population. Within a few days of the attack, though, the mosque was already dividing itself along ethnic and political allegiances. The imam at the time, ethnically Tajik Mohammed Sherzad, had long spoken out against the Taliban. Nevertheless, over half of the Afghan population in New York is Pashtun, and Imam Sherzad accused many Pashtun leaders in the mosque of being pro-Taliban. These accusations almost immediately split the congregation, and a largely Pashtun group eventually left the mosque. In 2004, however, the State Supreme Court decided that the ousted group was the mosque's rightful owners. In effect, Imam Sherzad and his largely Tajik following were forced to leave.[2] In 2009, when it finally seemed that the dust had settled, most of Metro New York's 16 thousand Afghan Muslims were shocked to hear that Afghan coffee-cart vendor Najibullah Zazi was arrested for allegedly planning to bomb the city's transit system. The Taliban influence in Afghanistan has also driven out Afghanistan's minority groups, such as the Hindus, Sikhs, and Jews. With a decline in worship space due to arson, many Hindus and Sikhs started worshiping together and—despite their religious differences—formed a unique common identity. This forged identity has carried over into Metro New York, where an estimated three thousand Afghan Hindus and Sikhs live, organize, and worship together.[3] With over two hundred families, Queens is also host to the largest Afghan Jewish community outside of Israel.[4]

When Did They Come To New York?

Allowed to leave the country in the early 1950s, most Afghan Jews emigrated in the following years to Israel and New York. It was the years following the 1979 Soviet invasion of Afghanistan, however, that brought the majority of today's diverse Afghan community to Queens. Another round of safety-seekers came after the Taliban took control of the country in 1996, and these immigrants tend to be either more secular than their average compatriots or Hindus and Sikhs who were fleeing Taliban oppression. A smaller round of immigrants came to Metro New York after America started bombing Afghanistan in 2001.

Where Do They Live?

Despite the ethnic tensions, Afghans primarily live, shop, and worship in the same areas. The largest concentration is in the Kew Gardens Hills area of Queens between Main Street and Kissena Boulevard. Just north of this area in Flushing, Afghans are concentrated south of downtown, as well as in the area of their main mosque, which is east of Union Street and north of Northern Boulevard. The Hindu-Sikh population also has a large concentration in Hicksville, Long Island, and Afghan Jews are concentrated in the Jamaica neighborhood of Queens.

What Do They Believe?

At the entrance of the aforementioned Hazrat-i-Abu Bakr mosque, an inscription reads, "In the name of Allah, Most Gracious, Most Merciful, enter

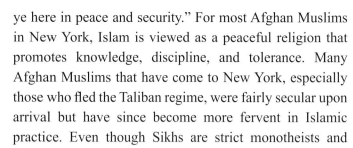

ye here in peace and security." For most Afghan Muslims in New York, Islam is viewed as a peaceful religion that promotes knowledge, discipline, and tolerance. Many Afghan Muslims that have come to New York, especially those who fled the Taliban regime, were fairly secular upon arrival but have since become more fervent in Islamic practice. Even though Sikhs are strict monotheists and Hindus are not, their shared oppression at the hands of religious radicals has created a fusion of tolerant religious practice and identity. They worship together at a small temple in Flushing and a large one in Hicksville. In Jamaica Estates, Queens, Congregation Anshei Shalom is considered the only Afghan-Jewish synagogue in the United States.

What Are Their Lives Like?

The average Manhattanite mainly crosses paths with Afghans through their ubiquitous coffee and bagel carts. Often setting up before dawn breaks, Afghans have had a corner on this market since the 1980s. If not at their coffee carts, Metro New Yorkers brush paths with Afghans at one of their several hundred fried chicken restaurants, with names such as Kennedy Fried Chicken and Crown Fried Chicken. Afghan men work hard, usually stopping only for prayers, and many Afghan women remain at home to take care of what are often large families.

How Can I Pray?

✳ Pray that Christian laborers would begin work among Afghans in the city. As of now, there is no one focused on reaching them with the gospel in Metro New York.

✳ Pray that the actions of Muslim fundamentalists will create doubts about the truth of Islam in Afghan hearts and minds, leading them to seek truth from Christians and the Bible.

Afghans and Persian Jews both speak Persian, with Western Persian (spoken in Iran) known as Farsi and Eastern Persian (spoken in Afghanistan) known as Dari.

Persian Jews

QUICK FACTS:

Place of Origin:
Iran (Tehran, Mashad)

Significant Subgroups:
Mashadi (4,000); Tehrani (11,000)

Location in Metro New York:
Long Island (Great Neck, Kings Point, Manhasset); Queens (Kew Gardens)

Population in Metro New York:
15,000 (Community Estimate)

Primary Religion:
Judaism (Sephardic)

Status of Christian Witness:
Less than 2% evangelical. Some evangelical resources available, but no active church planting within the past two years.

Primary Language:
Farsi

Secondary Language:
English

Registry of Peoples Code:
102808

Significant Notes:
❋ Around 25% of the Mashadi Jews in the world live in Metro New York. Around 10,000 live in Israel, while Milan, London, and Hamburg also have concentrations.
❋ The largest Tehrani-Jewish population in the United States is in California, particularly in Los Angeles and Beverly Hills. Although Persian Jews in Metro New York are not very involved politically, those in California have become increasingly involved in politics and the media. In 2007, a Persian Jew named Jimmy Delshad was elected mayor of Beverly Hills.
❋ There are no known organized ministries in Metro New York that regularly engage the Persian Jews with the gospel.

Although Persian Jews had lived relatively peacefully and successfully for a century in Mashad—one of the largest cities in Iran and a holy site for Shi'ah Muslims—the Shi'ite community suddenly revolted against the Persian Jews in March 1839, storming the synagogues, destroying sacred Torah scrolls, and killing dozens of people. A few of the Jews managed to escape, pleading with the local imam to stop the violence. The imam agreed, on condition that the Jews immediately convert to Islam. Knowing that this was the only way to preserve their lives, the "Mashadi Jews," as they came to be known, agreed to convert. For eighty-six years, the Mashadi Jews openly practiced Islam. They adopted Muslim names, learned the Muslim prayers, attended mosque regularly, sent their children to Qur'anic school, and even took pilgrimages to Mecca. However, from the beginning of the "conversion," the Mashadi Jews made a secret pact to preserve their heritage and religion. In order not to draw suspicion, meat would be bought from the open market only to be given to the dogs while kosher meat was prepared in the confines of Jewish households and distributed secretly from courtyard to courtyard. Although outwardly the members of the community had Muslim names, they were also given secret Hebrew names. Upon return from the Friday prayers at the mosque, the Jewish community would gather in secret meeting rooms to

welcome the Sabbath. Stores remained open on the Sabbath, but children would often work on these days instead of their fathers. Even with these precautionary measures, the community would have been exposed and possibly destroyed if intermarriage had taken place. Therefore, the community methodically arranged the marriages of their members to each other at an early age, ensuring that their secret heritage would be spared. To this day, the Mashadi Jews remain one of the most insular Jewish groups in the world, and the four thousand-member Mashadi Jewish community in Metro New York preserves their Mashadi heritage more than any other in the world today.[1] Living alongside the Mashadis are a larger number of "Tehrani Jews," who are simply Persian Jews who are not Mashadi. They number around 11 thousand and are more open to intermarrying and associating with other Jewish groups.[2]

When Did They Come To New York?

Although the Mashadi Jews were able to begin practicing their religion openly again in 1925, the spread of anti-Semitism in the 1940s and '50s forced the Mashadi Jews to gradually leave Mashad for Tehran. Some made their way to Israel and America during this time. However, the onset of Iran's Islamic Revolution in the late 1970s sparked the largest wave of immigration, with Persian Jews of all types seeking refuge outside the country. Whereas the largest Mashadi-Jewish population in the world outside of Israel is in Metro New York, the largest Tehrani-Jewish population in the US is in California.

Where Do They Live?

Great Neck, the inspiration for F. Scott Fitzgerald's new-money peninsula of "West Egg" in *The Great Gatsby*, is a Long Island town that has become the setting for "new Persian-Jewish immigrants with money." With gaudy mansions and modern synagogues along Steamboat Road and Middle Neck Road, the Persian Jews' seemingly ostentatious style has been a point of conflict with American

Jews and others in the small town. Persian Jews have spread into neighboring Kings Point and Manhasset and still have a presence in their original enclave in Kew Gardens, Queens.

What Do They Believe?

Even though their Judaic rituals are similar to each other, as well as to those of other Sephardic Jews, the Mashadi and Tehrani Jews maintain their own distinct synagogues. The Mashadi Jews, with their long history of resilience and faithfulness in preserving their religion, have forged their religious and ethnic identity together and continue to be guarded towards those outside their community.

What Are Their Lives Like?

Persian Jews have long been known for being adept at commerce. They are immigrants who have primarily come to Metro New York with money and have only increased their fortune since being here, largely through jewelry and rug businesses. The Mashadi and Tehrani Jews do not particularly like each other, and whereas the Mashadis are very insular, the Tehranis are a little more open to associating with other Jewish groups.

How Can I Pray?

✳ With most of the other Mashadis in the world slowly losing their ethnic identity in Israel, New York provides the best opportunity to engage Mashadi Jews with the gospel. College campuses and the business world provide the most natural opportunities for Christians to interact with Mashadis. Pray for students and businesspersons to walk through the doors God opens.

✳ Drug and alcohol abuse by Persian-Jewish youth has become a major community issue. Pray that God would reveal Himself to the Persian Jews by healing broken lives and communities.

Persian Jews and Salvadorans are the most noticeable ethnic groups that have chosen Long Island as their primary Metro New York residence.

Salvadorans

QUICK FACTS:

Place of Origin:
El Salvador

Location in Metro New York:
Nassau and Suffolk Counties in Long Island (Hempstead, Brentwood, New Cassel); New Jersey (Union City, West New York)

Population in Metro New York:
175,373 (ACS 2008 Specific Origin El Salvador); 126,538 (ACS 2008 Born in El Salvador)

Population in New York City:
35,026 (ACS 2008 Specific Origin El Salvador); 25,516 (ACS 2008 Born in El Salvador)

Primary Religion:
Christianity (Roman Catholic)

Secondary Religion:
Christianity (evangelical)

Status of Christian Witness:
Greater than or equal to 5% evangelical. Less than 10% evangelical.

Primary Language:
Spanish

Registry of Peoples Code:
108560

Significant Notes:
✷ About 25% of the population of El Salvador left the country during the civil war.
✷ An estimated one million Salvadorans fled to the US during the war. Today, the total number is thought to be 3.2 million.[5]
✷ Approximately one-third of Salvadorans in the US are undocumented.[6]
✷ Pentecostal and Catholic churches are the most active in ministry among Salvadorans in Metro New York.

"**P**ick me! Pick me!" the men shout at the building contractors circling the Home Depot parking lot in Hempstead, Long Island. Because of their limited English and undocumented status, working as day laborers is one of the few ways Salvadoran immigrants can earn money. When the economy was booming, they were picked every day and made up to $800 a week. Now they are lucky to get a couple of work days per week.[1] Most of the money goes to family in El Salvador. In 2008, $3.8 billion was sent, the highest amount ever recorded.[2] While the Long Island suburbs may seem like an unusual place to find a community of 100 thousand Salvadorans, Hempstead became a magnet for them in the 1980s, mainly because rural Salvadorans preferred it to the city and it offered an abundance of service jobs.[3] However, life in the suburbs has not been easy. Anti-immigrant sentiment is prevalent, and there is significant racial conflict. With the US economy faltering, stress and difficulties have only increased for the "suburban" Salvadorans.

When Did They Come To New York?

A large number of Salvadorans began arriving in Metro New York in 1980 with the start of El Salvador's civil war. As death squads roamed the countryside, kidnapping and murdering thousands, a steady influx of Salvadorans made their way to the United States. Since US policy did not allow them to enter legally, they came secretly. Most of the early arrivals were men fleeing these death squads. After these immigrants were legalized by the 1986 Amnesty Act, they brought their families. With El Salvador's economy still struggling, thousands of people risk entering the US illegally for the chance to earn money to support their families back home.

Where Do They Live?

Long Island has the largest concentration of Salvadorans in Metro New York. This is unique because the vast majority bypassed the city—the typical entry place for immigrants—to settle in the suburbs. Hempstead in Nassau County is Metro New York's "Little El Salvador." Salvadoran businesses line Franklin Avenue in Hempstead and Suffolk Avenue in Brentwood, which is located in Suffolk County. Union City and West New York in New Jersey form the second-largest

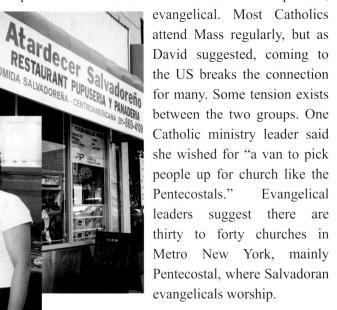

community in the New York Metro area, with an estimated 20 thousand Salvadorans clustered around Bergenline Avenue. Smaller numbers have assimilated into other Latino neighborhoods, such as Washington Heights and East New York, Brooklyn.

What Do They Believe?

"People are searching for something different when they come here," said David, a long-time Salvadoran resident of Brentwood. El Salvador, named for "Christ the Savior," has historically been a Catholic country. Today, evangelicals are a third of the population.[4] In Metro New York, an estimated seventy-five percent of Salvadorans are Catholic and five percent, evangelical. Most Catholics attend Mass regularly, but as David suggested, coming to the US breaks the connection for many. Some tension exists between the two groups. One Catholic ministry leader said she wished for "a van to pick people up for church like the Pentecostals." Evangelical leaders suggest there are thirty to forty churches in Metro New York, mainly Pentecostal, where Salvadoran evangelicals worship.

What Are Their Lives Like?

"Potentially, there could be a lot of homeless in this community—but no," said one local church leader. "Salvadorans take care of each other, even when it is inconvenient for them." Salvadorans are known for being hardworking, reserved people, whose lives revolve around their community. Typically, several families will share one house together, while single men will crowd into an apartment, working and sleeping in shifts. Because so many Salvadorans are undocumented, they are often suspicious of outsiders. Gangs, led by former Salvadoran militia leaders, have become a problem on Long Island, as they aggressively recruit high school students and start violent turf wars in the neighborhoods.

How Can I Pray?

✷ Salvadorans have basic needs such as learning English and finding work. Pray that Christians will join outreach ministries to help, build friendships, and share the love of Christ.

✷ Many Salvadorans associate immigration with starting a new life. Pray that those who do not know Christ would start a new life with Him.

Both Salvadoran and Cuban migrations started because of political upheaval in their countries.

Cubans

QUICK FACTS:

Place of Origin:
Cuba

Location in Metro New York:
New Jersey (West New York, Union City, North Bergen)

Population in Metro New York:
145,546 (ACS 2008 Specific Origin Cuba);
78,707 (ACS 2008 Born in Cuba)

Population in New York City:
41,436 (ACS 2008 Specific Origin Cuba);
21,039 (ACS 2008 Born in Cuba)

Primary Religion:
Christianity (Roman Catholic)

Secondary Religions:
Santería, atheism, Christianity (evangelical)

Status of Christian Witness:
Greater than or equal to 5% evangelical.
Less than 10% evangelical.

Primary Language:
Spanish

Secondary Language:
English

Registry of Peoples Code:
102324

Significant Notes:
❋ Cuba was declared an atheistic state after the 1959 revolution. In 1992, the constitution was revised to read "secularist" and guarantee freedom of religion.
❋ Bergenline Avenue, which was revitalized by Cuban immigrants in the 1970s to '80s, is currently the longest commercial avenue in the state of New Jersey, with over 300 stores.[4]
❋ The 2nd-largest Cuban population in the United States is located in the New York Metro area.

"The most important thing to understand about Cubans is that we came here for political reasons," explained Ana, a woman in her sixties who came to Metro New York in 1964. "We are different from other Hispanic immigrants, who come for economic reasons." Ana wanted this important distinction noted. Unlike Central Americans or other Caribbean migrants, Cubans are refugees, forced to flee their homeland because of persecution. With no option to return home, Cubans are determined to achieve the American dream. When they came, they put down roots, educated their children, and built businesses, radically transforming the communities they settled in. The antagonistic relationship between the US and Cuba's leader Fidel Castro has made Cuban-Americans a politicized group that wields significant influence on US-Cuban relations. Most Cubans supported US policies that were designed to weaken Castro, even those that would affect them personally, such as restricting travel to Cuba and limiting the amount of money that could be sent to relatives. Metro New York's Cuban-American community numbers around 145 thousand people. Roughly half were born in Cuba, and half are the second- and third-generation born in the US (ACS 2008).

When Did They Come To New York?

Once a paradise for the wealthy, Cuba fell into the hands of revolutionaries in 1959, who promised equality and social justice.

This quickly devolved into a repressive communist regime that imprisoned and killed thousands. Cuban immigration to Metro New York has had several waves. The first group came immediately following the revolution. Another wave arrived between 1965 and 1973 when Cubans were permitted to join family in the US. In 1980, Castro opened the port of Mariel, prompting over 100 thousand "Marielitos" to board rickety boats and come to the US. Since the 1990s, the US has allowed a set number of Cubans to enter as refugees each year.

Where Do They Live?

"When I first started in Union City, nineteen out of twenty students were Cuban. Now, there are one or two," said Maria, who has been teaching for thirty years. With their strong desire for upward mobility, Cubans have been steadily moving out of the old neighborhoods into more affluent suburbs. The northern New Jersey communities of Union City and West New York, known as "Havana on the Hudson," were two-thirds Cuban in the 1970s.[1] Today, Cubans make up less than twenty percent, even though these communities remain as entry points for other Latino immigrants. Despite the decline, Metro New York still has the world's third-largest population of Cubans outside of Cuba and Miami.[2]

What Do They Believe?

"I grew up when religion was not allowed in Cuba," Louisa said, "and I don't feel a need for it now." Once a Catholic nation, decades of persecution has taken a toll on Christianity in Cuba. When the Soviet Union collapsed in 1991 and Cuba lost its economic

support, many Cubans began to seek God. A reawakening of faith among nominal believers, coupled with passionate evangelism efforts, has brought many to new life in Christ. In Metro New York, however, most Cubans seem content with a nominal Catholic identity. Some dabble in Santería practices as well. Around five percent of Metro New York's Cubans are evangelical Protestants.[3] Most have been Christians for a few generations and are actively involved in a number of established churches in Metro New York.

What Are Their Lives Like?

Education + hard work = success. Most Cubans live by this formula. "It is simply understood by all Cubans that they will get an education and better themselves," said Maria, who came to the US as a child in 1962. Strong family connections and community solidarity have helped Cubans reach their goals. Cubans have left an indelible mark in Metro New York, building thriving businesses, restoring once-neglected communities, and paving the way for new Latino groups.

How Can I Pray?

✳ Pray that the reawakening of true Christian faith in Cuba will have an impact on Cuban-Americans in Metro New York and bring many to new life in Christ.

✳ Pray that Cuban Christians in Metro New York will embrace a new mission to minister to other Latino immigrants who need friendship and spiritual direction.

One of the most interesting restaurant phenomena in Metro New York is the preponderance of Latino-Chinese restaurants, many of which are owned by Chinese-Cubans.

Wenzhounese

QUICK FACTS:

Place of Origin:
China (Wenzhou and Qingtian in Zhejiang Province)

Significant Subgroups:
Strong hometown identity, with the largest number coming from Wenzhou (majority) and Qingtian (up to 10%)

Location in Metro New York:
Queens (Flushing, Corona, Elmhurst, Woodside, Whitestone)

Population in Metro New York:
50,000 (Community Estimate)

Primary Religion:
Nonreligious

Secondary Religions:
Christianity, Chinese Popular Religion, Buddhism, Taoism

Status of Christian Witness:
Greater than or equal to 10% evangelical.

Primary Language:
Wu (southern dialect/Wenzhounese)

Secondary Languages:
Mandarin, English

Registry of Peoples Code:
102143

Significant Notes:
✸ Wenzhou is the 2nd-largest Chinese source of illegal immigration to America. Fuzhou is the largest (p. 30).
✸ Even though Wenzhou is located in socialist China, almost all industry in the city is privately run.
✸ Many of the first Wenzhounese emigrants were from Qingtian, and they mainly settled in Europe, especially in Paris. The percentage of Wenzhounese that are from Qingtian is much greater in Europe than it is in America, where they make up about 10%.
✸ In general, Chinese love to gamble, and many associations organize gambling over *mahjong*.

There is a Jerusalem in China, and its name is Wenzhou. The Wenzhounese, who hail from the large city of Wenzhou and its environs off the east coast of China in Zhejiang Province, are known as the "Jews of China" because of their shrewdness in business. However, Wenzhou did not become known as the "Jerusalem of China" because of its economy. Rather, the name can be attributed to the reputation Wenzhou has garnered as the heart of Christianity in China. Throughout socialist reign in China, efforts have been made to stamp out Christianity and capitalism throughout the country. Despite these efforts, Wenzhou has become even more of an enigma, as capitalism and Christianity have only increased throughout communist rule! In fact, during China's Cultural Revolution, which sought to remove capitalistic elements from the country, Jiang Qing, the wife of Mao Zedong, launched an attack on Wenzhou, saying, "If you want to see capitalism, visit Wenzhou."[1] Their efforts did not work, though, and the "Wenzhou Model" of private-owned industry has made an impact throughout the country and beyond. Nevertheless, the entrepreneurial spirit that the Wenzhounese developed created a longing to taste the economic fertility of the Western world, and this has led many Wenzhounese from Wenzhou and the surrounding areas to Metro New York. United by the southern dialect of the Wu language, which is unintelligible to Wu speakers from Shanghai or to Mandarin speakers, the Wenzhounese are tightly knit socially and

commercially. Even though community estimates differ widely, Wenzhounese most likely number around 50 thousand in Metro New York.[2]

When Did They Come To New York?

Although a Wenzhou townspeople association existed in New York City by 1977, most immigrants from Wenzhou came after 1979 when the United States and China resumed diplomatic relations. At that point, a wave of both legal and illegal immigration started, with the 1990s witnessing the greatest influx of the "Chinese capitalists." A Wenzhounese immigrant in Queens claimed, "It was popular to go overseas because it was said that you

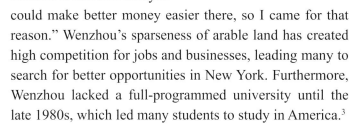

could make better money easier there, so I came for that reason." Wenzhou's sparseness of arable land has created high competition for jobs and businesses, leading many to search for better opportunities in New York. Furthermore, Wenzhou lacked a full-programmed university until the late 1980s, which led many students to study in America.[3]

Where Do They Live?

Due to their location in mainland China, Wenzhounese often learned Mandarin in school or through their business experience. As a result, they most often settle among other Mandarin speakers in Flushing and Corona in Queens, or in the suburbs where they have bought homes.

What Do They Believe?

In 1989, the Chinese government claimed that ten percent of all Christians in China come from Wenzhou.[4] This 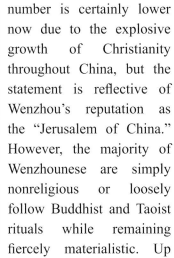 number is certainly lower now due to the explosive growth of Christianity throughout China, but the statement is reflective of Wenzhou's reputation as the "Jerusalem of China." However, the majority of Wenzhounese are simply nonreligious or loosely follow Buddhist and Taoist rituals while remaining fiercely materialistic. Up to thirty percent of the Wenzhounese in New York might consider themselves Christian, but as a Wenzhounese pastor in Queens explained, "A lot say they are Christian but do not go to church or practice the religion." Whereas there are over 160 Chinese churches in Metro New York, there are only two known worship services in the Wenzhou language. However, many Wenzhounese Christians attend Mandarin worship services.

What Are Their Lives Like?

Many visitors to New York frequent Canal Street in Manhattan for bargains on souvenirs or handbags. Because of the Wenzou propensity to operate light industrial enterprises, the Wenzhounese dominate this souvenir industry from production to point of sale. They are also involved in the garment business, and most Chinese supermarkets in Queens are owned and operated by Wenzhounese. While some return home to visit, almost all Wenzhounese plan on staying in America.

How Can I Pray?

✸ Most Wenzhounese, including Christians, find little time to "practice religion" in New York. Pray that Christians would live for Christ throughout the week and prioritize fellowship.

Whereas Wenzhounese are known for their business acumen among the Chinese, the Syrian Jews might be the wealthiest Jewish population in the world.

Syrian Jews

QUICK FACTS:

Place of Origin:
Syria (Aleppo, Damascus); Lebanon; Egypt

Significant Subgroups:
Aleppan (majority); Damascene (minority); Lebanese Jews (several hundred families); Egyptian Jews (several hundred families)

Location in Metro New York:
Brooklyn (Ocean Parkway, Flatbush, Gravesend); New Jersey (Deal, Asbury Park, Bradley Beach)

Population in Metro New York:
75,000 (Community Estimate)

Primary Religion:
Judaism (Sephardic)

Status of Christian Witness:
Less than 2% evangelical. Some evangelical resources available, but no active church planting within the past two years.

Primary Language:
English

Secondary Languages:
Arabic, Hebrew

Registry of Peoples Code:
109665

Significant Notes:
❋ The largest Syrian-Jewish community in the world is in Metro New York.
❋ Concentrated in the apparel industry, Syrian Jews own, operate, or manufacture for companies such as Jordache, Champion, Esprit, Reebok, Starter, Levi's, and Gap.[4]
❋ In July 2009, the Syrian-Jewish community received unwanted publicity when 44 people were arrested, including prominent New Jersey politicians and, from the Syrian Jewish community, several leading rabbis. The rabbis were arrested on money laundering charges.
❋ Damascene and Aleppan Jews come from different traditions although distinctions have dissipated.

In the early twentieth century, when America's educational policies focused on assimilating and "Americanizing" immigrants into an idealized "melting pot," the Syrian Jews of Metro New York took measures to ensure that they would retain their ethnic, cultural, and religious identity. In 1935, a *takkanah*, or rabbinical edict, was signed by several leading Syrian rabbis, declaring that Syrian Jews could marry neither non-Jews nor those who had converted to Judaism solely for the purpose of marriage. Since that time, the edict has been reaffirmed in 1946, 1972, 1984, and again in 2006.[1] The edict has also been strengthened, so that Syrian Jews are now forbidden to marry any convert to Judaism, even if the conversion has been validated by other Orthodox rabbis.[2] Intermarriage with non-Syrian Jews is at a very low rate, and even contact with non-Jews is minimal. While most immigrant groups in the last century have lost their ethnic identity through subsequent generations, the measures taken by Syrian Jews have actually strengthened ethnic and religious identity through each generation, creating a more cohesive Syrian Jewish community today than the one that first arrived in America! While Syrian Jews typically trace their family's migration to America directly from Aleppo or Damascus, many Lebanese and Egyptian Jews are also of Syrian descent and tend to assimilate into the larger Syrian-Jewish community, which numbers around 75 thousand in Metro New York.[3]

When Did They Come To New York?

Avoiding compulsory military service under the Ottoman Empire and seeking economic opportunity, Syrian Jews started leaving their country and arriving in New York City around 1908. Most of the Syrian Jews in Metro New York are descendants of those who arrived between 1908 and 1924. These Syrian Jews were primarily from Aleppo although there was a minority from Damascus. The Suez Crisis in 1956 sparked Egyptian Jewish emigration, and retaliation against Jews in Lebanon—due to the 1967 Six-Day War—incited Lebanese Jews to leave for New York. When Syria lifted a travel ban in 1992 on its remaining Jewish citizens, almost all of them left for New York City.

Where Do They Live?

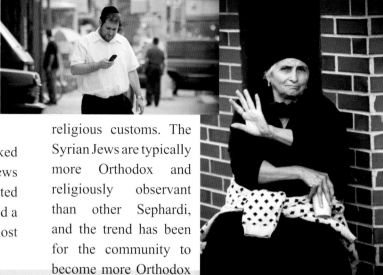

New York City's Syrian Jews live almost exclusively around Brooklyn's Ocean Parkway between Avenues O and X. However, when Syrian Jews started prospering economically, the wealthy started building summer homes in Bradley Beach, New Jersey, and later in nearby Deal. While several thousand Syrian Jews eventually settled in the Deal area year-round, the Syrian-Jewish population still swells exponentially each summer with seasonal residents.

What Do They Believe?

Syrian Jews are Sephardic, which is a term that specifically refers to those who follow the traditions of Jews who once lived in the Iberian peninsula but has broadened to designate all non-Ashkenazi Jews, including Mizrahi Jews, who are those that descend from communities in the Middle East, Central Asia, and the Caucasus. Whether they come from Morocco, Syria, or Iran, Sephardic Jews have similar religious customs. The Syrian Jews are typically more Orthodox and religiously observant than other Sephardi, and the trend has been for the community to become more Orthodox with each subsequent generation. While dozens of *yeshivas* have been started to educate their children, there are also over fifty Syrian-Jewish synagogues in Metro New York.

What Are Their Lives Like?

Unlike the Ashkenazi, the Syrian Jews have typically believed that trade rather than education is the path to success. Although Syrian Jews did not have much money upon arrival in America, they have been largely successful in the apparel, electronics, and real estate industries and are now one of the wealthiest Jewish communities in the world. Whether at their large households in Brooklyn or their Mediterranean-style mansions in Deal, Syrian Jews are constantly celebrating weddings, circumcisions, bar and bat mitzvahs, and the regular Jewish holidays together.

How Can I Pray?

✴ Due to the Syrian Jews' insular community, it is difficult for Christians to have access to them. Pray that through business, college, or other means, this access would be made possible.

✴ Pray that Syrian Jews would see an emptiness in their deep materialism and turn to Christ.

Just north of the Syrian Jewish enclave in Brooklyn is a mixed conservative and Orthodox Jewish enclave that borders the Little Pakistan of New York.

Pakistanis

QUICK FACTS:

Place of Origin:
Pakistan (Karachi, Mirpur, Lahore, Islamabad)

Significant Subgroups:
Punjabi/Mirpuri-Kashmiri (50%); Muhajir (30%); Pathan (10%); Balochi (5%); Sindhi (5%)

Location in Metro New York:
Brooklyn (Midwood, Ditmas Park, Brighton Beach); Queens (Flushing, Jackson Heights, Corona); Long Island (North Valley Stream); New Jersey (Jersey City, Edison, Parsippany); Bronx (Bronxdale)

Population in Metro New York:
120,000 (Community Estimate); 65,171 (ACS 2008 Pakistanis who selected Asian alone as race); 66,933 (ACS 2008 Born in Pakistan)

Population in New York City:
39,233 (ACS 2008 Pakistanis who selected Asian alone as race); 34,644 (ACS 2008 Born in Pakistan)

Primary Religion:
Islam (Sunni)

Secondary Religions:
Islam (Shi'ah), Ahmadiyya, Christianity

Status of Christian Witness:
Less than 2% evangelical. Initial (localized) church planting within the past two years.

Primary Languages:
Varies by group (Punjabi, Potwari, Urdu, Sindhi, Balochi, English)

Registry of Peoples Codes:
108182, 108183, 210402, 102830

Significant Note:
❈ In the 1960s, the construction of the Mangla Dam displaced thousands of people in the Mirpur area of Pakistani Kashmir, and many headed to Britain as well as America. Mirpuris, who are counted with Punjabis in this profile, make up around 70% of Britain's Pakistanis.

No immigrant enclave in Metro New York was affected by the aftermath of 9/11 as much as "Little Pakistan" in Midwood, Brooklyn. In the months following the terrorist attacks, enough Pakistanis became victims of verbal and, sometimes, physical abuse that a deep fear swept over the community. In the weeks following 9/11, federal agents stormed Pakistani apartments in Brooklyn and detained hundreds of people. In the fall of 2002, as part of the war on terrorism, the federal government required non-American citizens from twenty-five countries (twenty-four of which were primarily Muslim) to report to the Immigration and Naturalization Service (INS) for "special registration." Those who complied were fingerprinted, photographed, and interrogated. Although many of these immigrants had lived peacefully in the country for years, around sixteen percent were put into deportation proceedings after reporting to the INS, which only increased the fears in the Pakistani community.[1] Over a two-year period, the thriving Pakistani enclave changed drastically. According to Moe Razvi, the director of the Council of Peoples Organization—established to assist the Pakistani community in the aftermath of 9/11—thirty of the 150 Pakistani-owned shops in Little Pakistan have shut down since 9/11.[2] Conservative

estimates claim that 15 thousand Pakistanis left the neighborhood to return to Pakistan or seek refuge in Canada or Western Europe.[3] Pakistanis living elsewhere in Metro New York stopped frequenting Little Pakistan for fear of being deported, and others, especially the younger generation, started changing their appearance to look "more American." The turbulence seems to have finally dissipated, and the Pakistani population has leveled off at an estimated 120 thousand in Metro New York, fifty percent of which are Punjabi, thirty percent Muhajir, and the rest Pathan, Balochi, and Sindhi.[4]

When Did They Come To New York?

A large emigration from Pakistan to New York City began in the late 1960s primarily among the middle- and upper-class professionals of Karachi and Lahore, most of whom were Punjabi or Muhajir (Urdu speakers who migrated to Pakistan after its independence in 1947), as well as from the Mirpur District of Kashmir. These immigrants were followed by their often lower-class family members and less-urbanized compatriots, including other Punjabis, Pathans, Sindhis, and Balochis. Up until 9/11, Pakistanis were one of the fastest-growing immigrant groups in the city.

Where Do They Live?

Even though it seems sedate compared to pre-9/11, the area around Coney Island Avenue between Avenue I and Foster Avenue in Brooklyn still hosts the largest Pakistani population in the Metro area. However, concentrations exist throughout Metro New York where Pakistanis almost fully occupy some apartment complexes in places like Jackson Heights, Queens, and Jersey City.

What Do They Believe?

Pakistan itself is the second-largest Muslim country in the world. In the words of one New York cabbie, "All Pakistanis here are Muslim. Eighty percent are Sunni and twenty percent are Shi'ah." While these numbers are consistent with other community estimates, there are around ten Pakistani-Punjabi churches in Metro New York with around six hundred members, but there are only a handful of Muslim-background Christians in these churches. There are also a small number of Ahmadis, who follow a sect that claims to be Muslim but has been rejected as such by orthodox Muslims.

What Are Their Lives Like?

As the first Pakistani immigrants were largely urban professionals with English skills, the Pakistani community has continued to have many professionals. However, the most visible Pakistanis in the city are those working time-intensive, exhausting jobs, such as those in construction, street vending, owning small businesses, and taxi driving. In the aftermath of 9/11, divisions have accelerated between the first and second generations, with many young Pakistanis eagerly desiring to assimilate. Still, various Pakistani languages such as Punjabi, Potwari (closely related to Punjabi and spoken by Mirpuris), Urdu, Balochi, and Sindhi can be heard among the second generation.

How Can I Pray?

✳ Although several efforts have been made, there are still no churches in Metro New York made of Pakistani Christians from a Muslim background. Pray for a breakthrough in Pakistanis' response to the gospel.

Around 38% of yellow taxi cab drivers in New York are South Asian, with Pakistanis and Bangladeshis accounting for 14% each.

Bangladeshis

QUICK FACTS:

Place of Origin:
Bangladesh (Dhaka, Chittagong, Sylhet)

Significant Subgroups:
Bengali, including Sylheti Bengali (99%); Garo, Santal, Marma (1%)

Location in Metro New York:
Queens (Hillside/Jamaica, Astoria, Elmhurst, Woodside, Jackson Heights, Ozone Park); Brooklyn (Kensington, Cypress Hills); Manhattan (East Village); New Jersey (Paterson, Jersey City)

Population in Metro New York:
100,000 (Community Estimate); 69,968 (ACS 2008 Born in Bangladesh)

Population in New York City:
56,907 (ACS 2008 Born in Bangladesh)

Primary Religion:
Islam (Sunni)

Secondary Religions:
Hinduism, Christianity

Status of Christian Witness:
Less than 2% evangelical. Initial (localized) church planting within the past two years.

Primary Languages:
Bangla, Sylheti

Secondary Language:
English

Registry of Peoples Codes:
111658, 109660

Significant Notes:
※ Bengalis are by far the largest unreached people group in the world, with a worldwide population of over 230 million people.
※ After Bengal was partitioned in 1947, with West Bengal remaining part of India and East Bengal becoming a province in the dominion of Pakistan, many Hindu Bengalis rushed to live in West Bengal while many Muslim Bengalis migrated to East Bengal, which later became Bangladesh.

Biju Matthew, who represents the New York Taxi Alliance and wrote the book *Taxi!: Cabs and Capitalism in New York City*, claims that fifty-five to sixty percent of cab drivers in the city are South Asian.[1] In a recent survey with more conservative estimates, thirty-eight percent of yellow cab drivers are believed to be South Asian, with fourteen percent of those from Bangladesh.[2] By all accounts, Bangladeshis are now the largest cab-driving immigrant group in the city. Despite their overwhelming presence in the most visible job in New York City, many Bangladeshis are often mistaken for Indians, even though their language, religion, and culture are in most cases different. Part of the confusion is that Bangladeshis themselves feed into the misidentification, as many of the "Indian" restaurants in New York City are actually owned, managed, and serviced by Bangladeshis! As one restaurant worker claimed along the row of Bangladeshi-owned "Indian" restaurants on 6th Street in Manhattan, "No one knows Bangladesh. Americans know Indian. It is good for business." There are believed to be over 100 thousand Bangladeshis in Metro New York.[3] Almost all of the Bangladeshis in Metro New York are Bengali, many of whom are from Sylhet. There are also a small number of Garo, Santal, and Marma.

When Did They Come To New York?

For twenty-four years, Bangladesh was known as East Pakistan and, as part of the independence of Pakistan from India, was

ostensibly united with West Pakistan to form one country, even though their borders were over one thousand miles apart and the government was dominated by West Pakistan. In 1971, after much bloodshed, Bangladeshis won their independence, but in the years leading up to this point and the decade following, many professionals and white-collar workers left the country for places like New York. In the 1980s and '90s, many working-class Bangladeshis settled in Metro New York, either on diversity or family reunification visas, or illegally. While Bangladeshis have emigrated from all over their country, most immigrants in Metro New York come from the urban areas of Dhaka and Chittagong as well as Sylhet, whose emigrants make up a significant portion of the world's Bangladeshi diaspora. However, immigrants from urban areas often have further associations with their original hometown, and most Bangladeshis organize along these lines. There are believed to be over sixty of these hometown Bangladeshi associations in Metro New York.

Where Do They Live?

At least seven major concentrations of Bangladeshis have developed around Metro New York. A largely working-class Bangladeshi community lives around McDonald Avenue and Church Avenue in Kensington, Brooklyn. In Queens, Bangladeshis who consider themselves to have a higher standard of living than their Brooklyn counterparts are concentrated in Astoria, Elmhurst, Hillside, and Ozone Park. Bangladeshi Manhattanites reside close to "Curry Row" on 6th Street, between 1st and 2nd Avenues, and the New Jersey contingent is largely in Paterson.

What Do They Believe?

Around ninety-five percent of Bangladeshis in Metro New York are Sunni Muslims, while the rest are primarily Hindu. Catholics and evangelical Christians exist in sparse numbers. There are over a dozen Bangladeshi mosques in Metro New York and at least two Bangladeshi Hindu temples. There are also a few small evangelical Bangladeshi churches in Queens, but only a handful of Muslim-background Christians exist in these congregations. The small numbers of Bangladeshis that have converted to Christianity in New York have almost exclusively come from a Hindu background.

What Are Their Lives Like?

Among the first immigrants from Bangladesh were a disproportionate number of dentists and pharmacists. While other Bangladeshi professionals exist in Metro New York, most Bangladeshis are service workers. Besides cab driving, Bangladeshis also work in such New York institutions as fruit, hot dog, gyro, and newspaper stands, Dunkin' Donuts, and Subway, and Sylhetis run many of the "Indian" restaurants in Metro New York.

How Can I Pray?

✳ In recent years, there has been a movement in Bangladesh of Bengali Muslims responding positively to the gospel and becoming believers. Pray that this movement would carry over to Metro New York, where only a handful of Bangladeshi Muslim-background Christians exist.

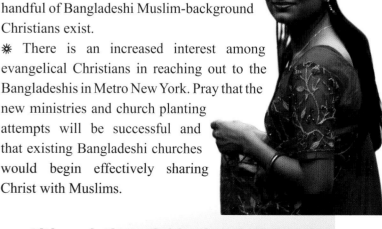

✳ There is an increased interest among evangelical Christians in reaching out to the Bangladeshis in Metro New York. Pray that the new ministries and church planting attempts will be successful and that existing Bangladeshi churches would begin effectively sharing Christ with Muslims.

Although the neighborhood of Jamaica is not named after the country, many Jamaicans, as well as Bangladeshis, live in the neighborhood.

Jamaicans

QUICK FACTS:

Place of Origin:
Jamaica

Significant Subgroups:
None. Indo-Jamaicans covered under Indo-Caribbeans (p. 74)

Location in Metro New York:
Brooklyn (Flatbush, Brownsville, East Flatbush, Crown Heights); Bronx (Eastchester, Wakefield, Baychester); Queens (Laurelton, North Woodmere, Springfield Gardens, Rosedale); Westchester (Mount Vernon)

Population in Metro New York:
377,847 (ACS 2008 Total Ancestry Reported); 271,577 (ACS 2008 Born in Jamaica)

Population in New York City:
232,846 (ACS 2008 Total Ancestry Reported); 178,814 (ACS 2008 Born in Jamaica)

Primary Religion:
Christianity (evangelical, mainline Protestant)

Secondary Religion:
Rastafari movement

Status of Christian Witness:
Greater than or equal to 10% evangelical.

Primary Languages:
Jamaican Patois, English

Registry of Peoples Code:
104168

Significant Notes:
❊ 43% of Jamaicans in the US live in Metro New York (ACS 2008).
❊ Retired four-star general and former Secretary of State Colin Powell was born in Harlem and is the son of Jamaican immigrants.
❊ Harlem's "central park" is named Marcus Garvey Park after the Jamaican hero and activist.
❊ Jamaica is typically counted among the top five countries in the world with the highest per capita murder rate.

"**H**e is the King of Kings, Lord of Lords, and Conquering Lion of Judah." Christians around the world immediately identify this title with Jesus. Among Jamaicans, however, entitlement to these words is equally claimed by the Rastafari movement in reference to former Ethiopian leader, Haile Selassie I. While Christians make up a majority of the Jamaican population in Metro New York, Rastafaris, or Rastas, have a strong voice and presence in the Jamaican community, especially considering that those who follow the Rastafari religion make up less than ten percent of the population.[1] The Rastafari movement began in Jamaica in the 1930s, building upon Africa-influenced religions, Marcus Garvey's "Back to Africa" campaign, and a general disgruntlement with Western oppression. When Ras Tafari Makonnen was crowned emperor of Ethiopia—a country known for resisting Western colonization—he took the title "Haile Selassie I," meaning "Might of the Trinity." Rastafaris believed (and still believe) that Haile Selassie I was God incarnate, and they adopted the Ethiopian ruler's original name as their own. A variety of cultural, social, political, and religious ideologies converged, and soon Rastas gained a large following with their opposition to Babylon (the West) and an apocalyptic cause to repatriate the black diaspora to Zion (Ethiopia).[2] While the Rastafari movement is a religion, its influence extends much more broadly. Reggae music popularized by Bob Marley, dreadlocks and baggy clothes, ritual smoking of ganja (marijuana), and resistance to oppression are elements of Rastafari that have extended beyond religion into a cultural movement with followers all over the world. Although Rastas often decry the materialism of Babylon, many have opted not to "repatriate" to Zion yet and have settled in New

York instead, a city so materialistic that Christians of an apocalyptic bent have labeled it "Babylon" themselves! Jamaicans are the third-largest foreign-born group in New York City, and people of Jamaican ancestry number close to 380 thousand in the Metro area (ACS 2008).

When Did They Come To New York?

Jamaicans led the Caribbean migration to New York throughout the twentieth century, including an initial wave in the first two decades, a small wave from the late 1930s to the early '60s, especially after World War II, and a large surge from the late 1960s to the present. An estimated fifteen percent of Jamaica's population left the country in the 1970s and 1980s, prompted by a failing economy.[3] In the past couple of decades, Jamaica has become notorious for crime and gangs, inciting others to emigrate for safety reasons. Women are usually the first to migrate, and there are fifty-six Jamaican women for every forty-four Jamaican men in the US (Census 2000).

Where Do They Live?

There are three main concentrations of Jamaicans in Metro New York. Apart from the West Indian mecca of East Flatbush and Crown Heights in Brooklyn, Jamaicans have spread out to the Laurelton-Rosedale area of Queens and have a large concentration in the northern tip of the Bronx in the working-class neighborhoods of Eastchester, Wakefield, and Baychester.

What Do They Believe?

On New York subways on Sunday mornings, it is common to see small groups

of Jamaican women wearing colorful hats and conversing about "living for God" on their way to church. Indeed, Jamaicans, as well as other Caribbeans, have infused their evangelistic zeal into the city, reviving "black churches" and others throughout the Metro area. Most Jamaicans adhere to Christianity, with Pentecostal, Baptist, Anglican, and Seventh-day Adventist denominations among the most popular. Although Haile Selassie I "disappeared" in 1975, Rastafaris still worship him as God and King. Other Afrocentric religions such as Pocomania have a small following.

What Are Their Lives Like?

Jamaicans have a reputation for being strong, confident, and hard-working. Many professionals and intellectuals immigrated to New York because they could not find work in Jamaica commensurate with their education. However, Jamaicans in Metro New York are primarily working-class people who socialize in their own networks, through which their native tongue of Patois can flow freely.

How Can I Pray?

✻ Rastafarians have muddled the identity of Christ by claiming that Haile Selassie I was a second incarnation of Jesus. Rastas refer to the Bible regularly, especially Old Testament passages about exodus and restoration, and their congregations hold regular Bible studies. Pray that God would use the Scriptures to point Rastas to a correct understanding of Christ and His Second Coming.

Rastafarianism, with its roots in Jamaica, believes that the Ethiopian ruler Haile Selassie I was God incarnate.

117

Ethiopians

QUICK FACTS:

Place of Origin:
Ethiopia

Significant Subgroups:
Amharic, Oromo, Tigrayan

Location in Metro New York:
Bronx (Parkchester); New Jersey (Jersey City, East Orange)

Population in Metro New York:
7,000 (Community Estimate); 6,458 (ACS 2008 Total Ancestry Reported); 4,111 (ACS 2008 Born in Ethiopia)

Population in New York City:
3,900 (ACS 2008 Total Ancestry Reported); 1,768 (ACS 2008 Born in Ethiopia)

Primary Religion:
Christianity (Ethiopian Orthodox)

Status of Christian Witness:
Greater than 5% evangelical. Less than 10% evangelical.

Primary Languages:
Amharic, Oromo, English

Registry of Peoples Codes:
100293, 110261, 110051

Significant Notes:
❋ Three main theories exist about Ethiopian Jews. One claims they descended from the Queen of Sheba and King Solomon. Another suggests they are the ancient lost Israelite tribe of Dan. A third believes they are descended from Jews who fled to Egypt after the first destruction of the temple in 586 BC.[4]
❋ The Rastafarian religion (practiced primarily among Jamaicans) believed the late Emperor Haile Selassie I was a reincarnation of Jesus who would usher in prosperity and peace for Africans and the African diaspora. Ethiopians, though, do not practice Rastafarianism.
❋ Monophytism states that Christ had a "united nature." This was denounced by the Council of Chalcedon in 451 AD, which claimed Christ had both a human and divine nature, known as the "hypostatic union."

"Ethiopia has been called 'the Island of Christianity' in Africa," explained Tekeste, a translator who works with Ethiopian asylum seekers in New York City. "We were one of the first Christian countries in the world, and we have been surrounded by Muslim nations for centuries." Located in the Horn of Africa, Ethiopia's rich history is a great source of pride for its people. Once known as Abyssinia, Ethiopia is one of the world's ancient countries, and one of two African nations that claim never to have been colonized (although it was occupied by Italy between 1936 and 1941). All three Abrahamic religions have thrived in Ethiopia. How Judaism arrived remains a mystery (see Significant Notes), but Jews have been in Ethiopia for thousands of years. It is believed Christianity was first introduced to Ethiopia by the royal officer who was converted by Philip the Evangelist, as recorded in Acts 8, even though the official adoption of Christianity was in the fourth century. Ethiopia's Islamic history dates back to Mohammed's time in Mecca, when persecuted followers fled to seek refuge in Abyssinia. Modern Ethiopia was shaped by Emperor Haile Selassie, a charismatic leader who came to power in 1930 and made Ethiopia a player on the

world stage. However, recurrent droughts, famines, and an ongoing civil war with Eritrean separatists led to his overthrow in 1974. An oppressive Soviet-backed Marxist regime was in power until 1991, when they were ousted by a coalition of rebel groups who formed a new government. An estimated seven thousand Ethiopians now live in Metro New York.[1]

When Did They Come To New York?

Ethiopians began arriving in Metro New York when the Marxist regime came to power in the 1970s. The 1980 Refugee Act opened the door for thousands who had escaped Ethiopia and were living in Sudan to come to the US as refugees. A border war in the late 1990s with Eritrea created another wave of refugees. While Ethiopians are not currently admitted as refugees, Metro New York's Ethiopian population continues to grow in small numbers through family reunions and a few asylum seekers.

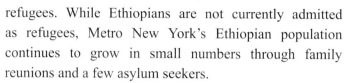

Where Do They Live?

The closest thing Metro New York has to a "Little Ethiopia" is a large concentration of Ethiopians living in the Parkchester condominium complex in southeast Bronx. Smaller groups are located in Jersey City and the St. Cloud section of East Orange, New Jersey, while others are scattered throughout Metro New York. Ethiopian cuisine has gained a foothold among New Yorkers, and at least a dozen restaurants, some quite trendy, can be found throughout the area.

What Do They Believe?

"The service is long, especially when you don't know what they are saying. Then it's extra long!" That is how Adel, a young Ethiopian man, described the three-hour Mass to a visiting *New York Times* reporter.[2] The Ethiopian Orthodox

Tewahedo Church—the spiritual home of the vast majority of Ethiopians in Metro New York—grew out of the Coptic Orthodox Church of Egypt, which split from the Roman Catholic Church over the issue of monophytism (see Significant Notes). There are six Ethiopian Orthodox Churches in Metro New York, and their services are highly ritualistic and often given in Ge'ez, a "dead" liturgical language. The church venerates Mary and places a heavy emphasis on Old Testament teachings, requiring followers to adhere to Jewish dietary laws and other practices. Up to ten percent of Ethiopians in Metro New York, though, are evangelical Christians, and they have churches in the Bronx, Manhattan, and East Orange, New Jersey. While Ethiopia is one-third Muslim, only a small number of Ethiopian Muslims live in Metro New York.[3]

What Are Their Lives Like?

"Even here, we feel the ethnic tensions created by the current Ethiopian government," explained Ms. Asrat, a community leader who works with Ethiopian youth. Ethiopia has recently been divided into "ethnic states," resulting in power imbalances among groups. In Metro New York, the most friction is felt between the Amharic people (Ethiopia's "ruling class" and immigrant majority) and the Oromo (one of the most populous groups in Ethiopia). In fact, some Oromo will not call themselves Ethiopian and refuse to speak Amharic, the national language.

How Can I Pray?

✸ Pray that Ethiopians would go beyond ritualistic faith and seek a personal relationship with Christ. Pray for believers to be strong evangelists like Philip and teach God's Word with power.

Ethiopia is one of two countries in Africa to make claims that they were never colonized (the other being Liberia). This claim is debatable, however, as Italy occupied Ethiopia from 1936-1941.

Italians

QUICK FACTS:

Place of Origin:
Italy (Sicily, Naples, the rest of southern Italy)

Significant Subgroups:
Sicilians, Neapolitans, Calabrians

Location in Metro New York:
Brooklyn (Bensonhurst, New Utrecht, Gravesend, Bath Beach, Dyker Heights); Staten Island (Southern and Eastern Parts); New Jersey (West Paterson); Queens (Howard Beach, Whitestone, Astoria, Fresh Pond, Douglaston, Corona); Bronx (Country Club, Morris Park); Westchester (East White Plains, Tuckahoe, Yonkers); Nassau (Franklin Square, Glen Cove)

Population in Metro New York:
3,477,945 (ACS 2008 Total Ancestry Reported); 1,851,643 (ACS 2008 Single Ancestry Reported); 164,492 (ACS 2008 Born in Italy)

Population in New York City:
697,313 (ACS 2008 Total Ancestry Reported); 452,747 (ACS 2008 Single Ancestry Reported); 63,600 (ACS 2008 Born in Italy)

Primary Religion:
Christianity (Roman Catholic)

Status of Christian Witness:
Greater than or equal to 2% evangelical. Less than 5% evangelical.

Primary Language:
English

Secondary Languages:
Italian, Sicilian, other dialects

Registry of Peoples Codes:
104096, 104102, 107182

Significant Note:
☀ If one were considered Italian by having a single Italian ancestry, over 8% of Metro New York is Italian (ACS 2008).

Italians have left an irrevocable stamp on life in Metro New York. From their food (Lombardi's in Manhattan's Little Italy was the country's first pizzeria) to their vocabulary (new immigrants to New York from all over the world somehow learn to say "fuhgeddaboutit" before being able to hold a regular conversation in English), New York culture has been deeply influenced by the Italians. Today, their presence is fading. Although those reporting a single Italian ancestry in Metro New York still numbered 1,851,643 in 2008, a number similar to the two million reported in 1990, their presence in New York City itself has almost halved in the same time. More striking than these numbers is that large-scale Italian immigration stopped decades ago, meaning that most Italians are second-, third-, fourth-, or fifth-generation. Many of these are "closet ethnics" who embrace their Italian identity only when it is convenient. When New York University students overheard a Little Italy restaurant owner speaking Italian to potential customers, they asked him about his language ability. The man responded, "I don't speak Italian. Not at all. But us Italians have to give the illusion of being alive and well."[1] Almost all Italian immigrants are from the southern part of Italy, with the majority from Sicily, the Naples area, and Calabria. Although these divisions were very sharp in the past, descendants of the first immigrants identify themselves strongly with other Italian-Americans.

When Did They Come To New York?

Facing a multitude of problems in southern Italy, including the aftermath of a civil war, overcrowding, feudal working conditions, natural disasters, heavy taxation from a northern-dominated government, and scarcity of good soil, many Calabrians, Neapolitans, Sicilians, and other southern Italians left in droves to seek relief elsewhere. Between 1876 and 1924 alone, more than 4.5 million Italians came to the United States, with New York City as the top destination. During this time, Italians were generally characterized as dirty, unhealthy, uneducated, and criminal. For the most part, this impression changed after World War II when Italian-Americans joined the US military in large numbers and received a corresponding social acceptance from the larger American community. As economic, social, and educational opportunities expanded, most Italian-Americans became fully acculturated into American life. Another wave of southern Italians came in the late 1960s and early '70s, but the improved Italian economy since 1974 has kept Italian immigration at a minimum.[2]

Where Do They Live?

The "Old World" Italian neighborhoods in New York City are fading and giving life to "New World" neighborhoods in the suburbs. As working-class Italians have become Italian-American professionals, houses in Bensonhurst (Brooklyn) are being traded for those in Staten Island and New Jersey, those in Morris Park (Bronx) for Westchester, those in Corona (Queens) for Whitestone (Queens), and those in Astoria (Queens) for Long Island. Even the most recognizable "Italian" neighborhoods, such as Manhattan's Little Italy, are little more than tourist destinations.

What Do They Believe?

At the turn of the twentieth century, Italians were often viewed by Irish Catholics as practitioners of folk religion, or even as pagans, since their celebration of patron saints and superstitious feasts diverged from orthodox doctrine. With the passing of time, some Italians became more aligned with mainstream Catholicism, while others became less enchanted with formal religion. Today, almost all Italians are at least culturally Catholic although a minority of Italian-Americans have converted to evangelical or mainline Protestant Christianity.

What Are Their Lives Like?

No matter what the generation, Italians' lives center around the family. Big events such as patron saint feasts—which were once religious and are now almost completely cultural—as well as Italian soccer matches, continue to draw large families together and ensure a continued Italian identity.

How Can I Pray?

✹ With some Italian-Americans embracing their Italian culture only in part, identification with inherited Catholicism has also loosened. As a result, pray that a personal hunger and openness to God will occur. Pray that Italians will turn to Christ instead of the church for salvation.

Before immigrating to America, many Albanians spent time in refugee camps in Italy, where they learned the food and language.

Albanians

QUICK FACTS:

Place of Origin:
Albania, Kosovo, Macedonia, Montenegro

Significant Subgroups:
Gheg (65%); Tosk (35%)

Location in Metro New York:
Bronx (Belmont, Morris Park, Fordham, Bedford Park); Queens (Ridgewood, Astoria); Brooklyn (Flatbush, Bath Beach); Staten Island (East Shore); Westchester (Yonkers); Connecticut (Waterbury); New Jersey (Garfield, Prospect Park, Wayne, Paterson)

Population in Metro New York:
200,000 (Community Estimate); 71,311 (ACS 2008 Total Ancestry)

Population in New York City:
40,515 (ACS 2008 Total Ancestry)

Primary Religion:
Islam (Sunni)

Secondary Religions:
Islam (Sufi Bektashi); Christianity (Albanian Orthodox, Roman Catholic)

Status of Christian Witness:
Less than 2% evangelical. Initial (localized) church planting within the past two years.

Primary Language:
Albanian (Gheg and Tosk dialects)

Secondary Languages:
Greek, Italian, English

Registry of Peoples Codes:
100222, 103338

Significant Notes:
❋ There are only 50 known evangelical Christians among the estimated 200,000 Albanians in Metro New York.
❋ Over 50% of all Albanians live outside of Albania.
❋ Famous Famiglia, a well-known "Italian" pizza chain in New York, is run by Albanians.

Ah, New York, a place where great Italian food and mafia activity often go hand-in-hand. However, before picturing a large Italian godfather-type running organized crime out of the basement of an Italian *ristorante*, one should know that times are changing a bit in the Big Apple. Albanians are quickly becoming the "new Italians." They now own over one hundred Italian restaurants in the city and have an organized crime syndicate, called the Rudaj Organization, which rivals the storied Italian organized crime families of the city. The Albanians come from an area of the world where survival has always been the modus operandi. Due to constant unrest and instability in the Balkans, an estimated 200 thousand Albanians have now moved their residence to the New York City Metro area.[1] They consist of two main ethnicities that are divided along geographic and linguistic lines. The Albanian Gheg come from northern Albania, Kosovo, Macedonia, and Montenegro. The Albanian Tosk are primarily from central and southern Albania. Each has its own distinct communities and organizations in Metro New York.

When Did They Come To New York?

The ceaseless political strife in the Balkans led to a constant flow of Albanian immigration to New York in the twentieth century. The first large group came in the early 1900s for political reasons. After Albania came under communist control in

the 1940s, another wave came. A large group of Albanians, mainly from Kosovo, Macedonia, and Montenegro, came in the 1960s after Yugoslavia loosened emigration restrictions. More recently, the fall of communism in the 1990s has led more Albanians to America, some reuniting with families, some coming on diversity visas, and some remaining here illegally on expired temporary visas.

Where Do They Live?

There are six main locations of Albanians in Metro New York, with ethnic backgrounds normally determining settlement patterns. The largest concentration is in the Bronx, particularly around Belmont and Bedford Park. This community is dominated by Gheg Kosovars. Along the eastern shore of Staten Island, a large community of Ghegs from Macedonia and Montenegro can be found. Ridgewood, Queens, is the dwelling place of many Tosk-speakers from southern and central Albania. Waterbury, Connecticut, is the host of Albanian Tosks primarily from one county in southeastern Albania, as well as from southwestern Macedonia. Bath Beach and Flatbush in Brooklyn have Tosk speakers from southern Albania, while Garfield and Paterson, New Jersey, have a Tosk majority from southern and central Albania.

What Do They Believe?

An Albanian blogger, after pointing out the religious adherence of Albanians (seventy percent Muslim of whom twenty percent are Sufi Bektashi; ten percent

Catholic; and twenty percent Albanian Orthodox), summed up the religious sentiment of Albanians by saying, "The only god we have is ourselves. We are in fact agnostic!"[2] Although these statements and figures may be true, the religious demography of Albanians varies widely in each of their communities in Metro New York. The Bronx population, while having some Catholics from northern Albania, consists mostly of Kosovar Muslims. The Gheg in Staten Island are perhaps sixty percent Muslim and forty percent Catholic. The population in Queens, many of whom speak Greek and have been influenced by Greek culture, is about one-half Orthodox Christian and one-half Muslim. Albanians in New Jersey and Brooklyn are around seventy percent Muslim and thirty percent Orthodox Christian, while the population in Connecticut is primarily Muslim.[3]

What Are Their Lives Like?

Not surprisingly, considering the history of their people, Albanians are very suspicious of outsiders, very selective in who they socialize with, and incredibly cliquish with people in their own ethnic group or religious organization. They are pressed for time, as many work long hours in service jobs, while others work hard as owners of stores, restaurants, and buildings.

How Can I Pray?

✷ Three of the main areas where Albanians live (Bronx, Queens, and Waterbury) have no known ministries working among Albanians. Pray that Albanian-Christian leaders will start churches in these areas.

✷ Pray that the two Albanian evangelical churches in Metro New York—the one in Clifton, New Jersey, and the one in Brooklyn—will be fertile fields for raising up Christian leaders and disciples.

✷ Pray that the few Albanian Christians will be able to spread the gospel through relationships.

Albanians and Serbs have had deep conflicts with one another for most of the twentieth century, with fighting erupting on multiple occasions.

Serbs

QUICK FACTS:

Place of Origin:
Serbia (former Yugoslavia, mainly from Belgrade)

Location in Metro New York:
Queens (Ridgewood, Astoria, Glendale, Fresh Pond); New Jersey (Cliffside Park, Fairview, Grantwood)

Population in Metro New York:
40,000 (Community Estimate); 40,511 (ACS 2008 Serbo-Croatian Spoken at Home); 12,829 (ACS 2008 Total Ancestry)

Population in New York City:
21,359 (ACS 2008 Serbo-Croatian Spoken at Home); 7,024 (ACS 2008 Total Ancestry)

Primary Religion:
Christianity (Serbian Orthodox)

Status of Christian Witness:
Less than 2% evangelical. Some evangelical resources available, but no active church planting within the past two years.

Primary Languages:
English, Serbian

Registry of Peoples Code:
108856

Significant Notes:
✺ Over 70% of self-identified Serbs in Metro New York were born in America.
✺ There are no known evangelical Serbian churches in Metro New York.

Life is much different in a land that is not haunted with reoccurrence of war. As a result, many Serbs have left their homeland to live in America, and an estimated 40,000 call Metro New York home.[1] The influence of war on Serbian life is strikingly evident in their major celebration of the year, called Vidovdan, or St. Vitus' Day, which occurs on June 28. Unlike most ethnic groups who reserve their major holidays for celebrating historical conquests of war or political victories, the Serbs celebrate their June 28, 1389, defeat by the Ottoman Empire. The defeat represents the resilience of their people who, tragically, have been central players in the wars of the twentieth century. It was on June 28, 1914, that a Serb killed Franz Ferdinand, heir to the Austro-Hungarian throne, an event that triggered World War I. It was on June 28, 1919, that the Treaty of Versailles was signed, ending World War I. It was on June 28, 1921, that the new constitution of the Kingdom of Serbs, Croats, and Slovenes—more commonly known as the Kingdom of Yugoslavia—was proclaimed. It was also on June 28, in 2001, that Serbian President Slobodan Milošević—whom detractors accused of instigating the Yugoslav Wars in Slovenia, Croatia, Bosnia, and Kosovo, and killing or displacing millions of people—was deported to the Hague to stand trial for war crimes.[2] While New York is sometimes characterized as cold and cruel, it is warm and welcoming to some, especially Serbs who have made it their home.

When Did They Come To New York?

Although almost all Serbs who immigrated in great numbers to America in the late nineteenth century ended up in other industrial cities, a small Serbian community developed in New York City around 9th and 10th Avenues between 21st and 40th Streets. The next significant wave to New York consisted of World War II refugees, who came after 1946, becoming very involved in their country's politics from a distance. In the 1960s, Yugoslavia's loosening emigration policies allowed many

ethnic group, but religion against religion, Christian Orthodox and Serbian identity have blended into one. Even in preparation for this profile, the Serbian Consulate General suggested that St. Sava Cathedral was the best source of information. While there are certainly Serbs of other faiths, the majority of Serbs liken leaving the Orthodox faith to ceasing to be Serb.

Serbian professionals to move to New York City and, most recently, the political turmoil of the 1990s resulting in the Yugoslav Wars provided significant motivation for Serbs to leave their country.[3] While undoubtedly, many Serbs have ended up in the city as a result of war in their homeland, many have come to Metro New York for business, education, to reconnect with their family, and to make money to send back to their family in Serbia. Due to the long history of Serbian immigration, the 2000 Census shows that more than seventy percent of self-identified Serbs are actually American children of their immigrant parents, grandparents, or more distant ancestors.

Where Do They Live?

Whereas the Serbian Orthodox Cathedral of St. Sava on 26th Street in Manhattan provides a historical link to the first Serbian immigrants, these days Serbs are concentrated in Queens, mainly in Astoria and Ridgewood, although the Serbian Club is located on 65th Place in Glendale. Not to be left out, New Jersey has a Serbian concentration in the Cliffside Park area.

What Do They Believe?

Milan Lucic, a Serb who runs a community radio and TV show, says plainly, "If you are Serbian, then you are Christian Orthodox." Following years of wars that pitted not only ethnic group against

What Are Their Lives Like?

With both Serbian men and women highly educated and professionally successful in fields such as engineering, medicine, law, and the hotel industry, assimilation has come easily. Like Serbian immigrants in previous decades, some use New York as a base for political and social activism, and as most Serbs are born in the area, they consider the city their permanent home.

How Can I Pray?

✳ When ethnic and Christian identities are the same, being Christian often means nothing more than practicing one's culture. Instead, pray that Serbs enter into a living relationship with Christ.

✳ There are no known evangelical Serbian churches in Metro New York. Pray for one to start.

Many Ukrainians and almost all Serbs are members of Eastern Orthodox churches.

Ukrainians

QUICK FACTS:

Place of Origin:
Ukraine

Significant Subgroups:
Ukrainian Jews (144,000); Western Ukrainians (75% of non-Jews); Eastern Ukrainians (25% of non-Jews)

Location in Metro New York:
Brooklyn (Brighton Beach, Gravesend, Sheepshead Bay, Bensonhurst, Borough Park, Midwood, Bath Beach, Starrett City, Manhattan Beach); Manhattan (East Village); New Jersey (Parsippany, Passaic, Irvington); Sullivan (Glen Spey); Queens (Ridgewood, Forest Hills, Rego Park)

Population in Metro New York:
Over 180,000 (Community Estimate); 87,138 (ACS 2008 Born in Ukraine)

Population in New York City:
64,256 (ACS 2008 Born in Ukraine)

Primary Religions:
Jews: nonreligious; ethnic Ukrainians: Christianity (Eastern Catholicism in the west, Eastern Orthodox in the east)

Status of Christian Witness:
Greater than or equal to 2% evangelical. Less than 5% evangelical.

Primary Languages:
Ukrainian, Russian

Registry of Peoples Codes:
110376, 108454

Significant Notes:
❋ Most Jews from the Ukraine, and elsewhere throughout the former Soviet Union, have no ties to their homeland. All of their relatives typically live in the United States or Israel.
❋ Up to 50% of Soviet Jews in the United States live in Metro New York.
❋ There has been longstanding tension between western Ukrainians and Russians.

Few immigrant groups have as much of a muddled national identity as Ukrainian-Americans. Throughout the first three waves of ethnic Ukrainian migration to America, Ukrainians left a land controlled by outsiders. Depending on the time and location, Ukraine was controlled by Poland, the Austro-Hungarian Empire, or the Soviet Union. Since the independence of Ukraine in 1991, there has been another large influx of "Ukrainians," but most of these have been ethnic Jews with little national identity. Nevertheless, Ukrainian-Americans have organized and socialized as such for over a century. Out of an estimated 400 thousand Russian-speaking Jews in Metro New York, the largest number (thirty-six percent) hail from Ukraine.[1] Using figures from the same study, one could estimate Metro New York's non-Jewish Ukrainian population to number 36 thousand, but this figure only accounts for Russian-speakers, and many Ukrainians do not speak Russian. The curator of the Ukrainian Museum in New York estimates that there are 70 thousand non-Jewish Ukrainians in Metro New York.[2] Whatever the number, there are divisions in the Ukrainian community much deeper than Jew or non-Jew. Around seventy-five percent of ethnic Ukrainian immigrants come from the western part of the country, and as one of their community leaders claims, "The eastern part is highly influenced by Russian propaganda."[3]

Western Ukrainians primarily speak Ukrainian and might understand Russian, but about half of eastern Ukrainians speak Russian as their primary language.

When Did They Come To New York?

While Pennsylvania was the destination of choice for the first wave of Ukrainian immigrants at the end of the nineteenth century, New York City became a prime destination for the second wave, which came after World War I. After World War II, displaced Ukrainians who were lucky enough to find American sponsors made their way to New York to create a third wave of immigration. Starting in the 1970s but escalating in the '90s, a large fourth wave of immigration has primarily consisted of ethnic Jews. While some were genuinely escaping from anti-Semitism, many found that their Jewish identity, sometimes loosely held, created a unique opportunity to relocate to New York. Around eighty-five percent of these Jews came with full refugee status.[4] Inconsistent and corrupt governments have continued to fuel Ukrainian emigration in the twenty-first century.

Where Do They Live?

Often depicted as Russia or Ukraine in a time capsule, Brighton Beach, Brooklyn—just a short walk from Coney Island—is the "Russian amusement park" for immigrants from the former Soviet Union. With its location by the sea, many Ukrainians from Odessa have settled there to remind them of home. Over the years, it has garnered the reputation as a seedy place only fit for the elderly, illegal, or newly arrived. Neighborhoods north of the area in Brooklyn have become much more desirable. For the less "Russified" western Ukrainians,

East Village in Manhattan has long hosted the largest concentration, even though areas of New Jersey are becoming more popular.

What Do They Believe?

"Everyone practices Christianity," George Gajecky, Vice-President of the Ukrainian Educational Council, boldly claimed in describing Ukrainian religious beliefs. He added, "The Ukrainian culture is based within religion, so to be a part of this culture, you must practice religious things." Obviously, these statements do not take into consideration Jews from Ukraine, who are largely secular but practice Judaism more the longer they are in New York. A generally accepted statistic is that in New York there are up to twice as many Eastern Catholics, who come mostly from the Galicia region of west Ukraine, as Eastern Orthodox adherents, who come mostly from east Ukraine. Of the non-Jewish Ukrainians, Protestants number up to ten percent and, recently, hundreds of Ukrainian Jews have converted to Christianity.

What Are Their Lives Like?

Ukrainian immigrants have a very high level of education. While many are able to continue work in their fields, others with few English skills or with certifications that do not transfer to America, end up working in house cleaning or construction. Restaurants that resemble night clubs are extremely popular, and Saturday Ukrainian-heritage schools have been started to educate the second generation.

How Can I Pray?

✵ Many Jews are averse to Christianity due to the Holocaust, during which Jews were killed by Germans "in the name of Jesus," and many Eastern Orthodox Christians view evangelicals as cult-like. Pray that God would remove these barriers and reveal the true essence of evangelical Christianity through Christ.

Ukrainians and Belarusians make up a majority of the non-Russians from the former Soviet Union who have immigrated to Metro New York.

Belarusians

QUICK FACTS:

Place of Origin:
Belarus

Significant Subgroups:
Belarusian Jews (44,000); Belarusians (11,000)

Location in Metro New York:
New Jersey (South River, New Brunswick); South Brooklyn

Population in Metro New York:
55,000 (Community Estimate)

Primary Religions:
Jews: nonreligious; ethnic Belarusians: Christianity (Russian Orthodox)

Secondary Religions:
Jews: Judaism; ethnic Belarusians: Christianity (Roman Catholic)

Status of Christian Witness:
Less than 2% evangelical. Some evangelical resources available, but no active church planting within the past two years.

Primary Languages:
Belarusian, Russian

Registry of Peoples Codes:
101833, 108454

Significant Notes:
❋ In 1995, Belarus declared that Russian would be added alongside Belarusian as an official language of the country. Since then, support for Belarusian language and culture has dwindled.
❋ Depending on where they lived in Belarus, immigrants from Belarus might identify themselves as Russian, or as the case is with many in Chicago, as Polish.
❋ Some Belarusians object to the names "Byelorussia" or "Byelorussian," because of their association with Russia and Soviet rule.
❋ Historically, Belarusians have been lumped into Russian or Polish categories in official US figures.

"It is the last dictatorship in Europe," a group of Belarusian community leaders claimed before a visiting Belarusian politician spoke out against the current Belarus regime. As are most Belarusian gatherings in Metro New York, the meeting was held in a Belarusian Orthodox Church that doubles as a community center. Here, in basement fellowship halls, Belarusian-Americans gather to raise support for a truly democratic Belarus and seek to retain a culture they feel is slipping away in their homeland. The Republic of Belarus was founded in 1991 as the Soviet Union dissolved, but in 1994, Alexander Lukashenko won the presidential election—a position he still retains—and his regime is now widely regarded as a dictatorship. In 2005, US Secretary of State Condoleezza Rice made a statement that there are "outposts of tyranny" in this world, proceeding to name six countries that fit such a title. Belarus was one of them.[1] Of course, Belarusians are no strangers to oppression. Dating back to the late 1700s, attempts have been made to "Russify" them. Alla Romano, a Belarusian community leader, explained that her parents came to America in 1949 to escape persecution and communism. She added, "My parents had been a part of an effort to organize Belarusian schools and were punished for this. They knew that if they did not leave Belarus, they would be killed." Commenting on the present regime, she stated, "The current dictator came to rule and said, 'I am not going to take Belarus into the civilized world. We will stay with Russia.'" Indeed, that is what has taken place. Belarus has retained closer ties with Russia than any other former Soviet Republic. In

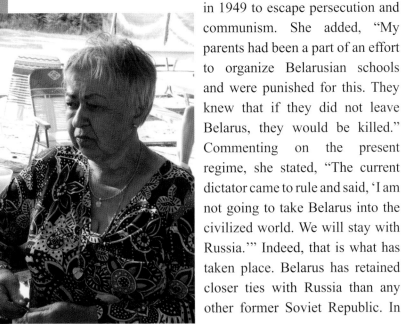

1996, Belarus established a union with Russia in an effort that could lead to the establishment of another miniature Soviet Union. Today, an estimated 11 thousand Belarusians live in Metro New York that identify and organize as such. Jews who immigrated from Belarus have a much larger presence, with around 44 thousand people, but they identify themselves more as Jewish or Russian than Belarusian and have little to do with their compatriots.[2]

When Did They Come To New York?

In the latter part of the nineteenth century until World War I, thousands of Belarusian peasants immigrated to the industrial cities of America for economic reasons. The end of World War II witnessed the immigration of displaced Belarusians who were fervent anti-communists and set up political organizations accordingly. Metro New York was a primary destination for this group. In the 1980s and '90s, a large influx of Belarusian Jews arrived in Metro New York, and a smaller number of ethnic Belarusians continue to immigrate due to conditions in their country.[3]

Where Do They Live?

Dr. Vitaut Kipel, who wrote the book *Belarusans in the United States*, claims that Middlesex County in New Jersey was "primarily Belarusian" in the 1970s. As the first

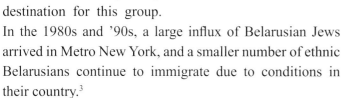

generation gets older and dies off, this presence is less felt, even though the towns of South River and New Brunswick still have a sizeable population. Brooklyn is the other hub for Belarusians, with Brighton Beach and South Brooklyn being the center of the Belarusian-Jewish population.

What Do They Believe?

With the Russian Orthodox Church serving as the backbone of the Belarusian community in Metro New York, up to ninety percent of non-Jewish Belarusians have some sort of affiliation with the Church. The remaining ten percent are mostly Catholic. As Dr. Kipel put it, "A very small percent are Protestant—too small to even count." Despite the central role of the Orthodox Church, the first generation is concerned that their children are no longer interested in religion, as their children seem more concerned about being ridiculed by others than they are about carrying on the faith. Belarusian Jews are mostly nonreligious but tend to practice Judaism the longer they are here.

What Are Their Lives Like?

Metro New York attracts many Belarusians that are independent thinkers and highly educated. With both men and women having high levels of education, Belarusians are involved in a variety of professions. Attracted by the stability in America, they usually seek to assimilate into American life although they cherish their time together at Belarusian churches, festivals, and meetings.

How Can I Pray?

✴ The children of Belarusian immigrants have largely grown disinterested in the church. Pray that they would have encounters with Christ at school and the workplace that would bring fresh meaning and purpose to the gathering of Christians for worship.

The twentieth-century history of Belarus and Romania is largely dominated by the effects communism had on their respective countries.

Romanians

QUICK FACTS:

Place of Origin:
Romania, Moldova, Greece, Albania (Aromanians)

Significant Subgroups:
Ethnic Romanians from Romania, Romanian Moldovans, Hungarian Romanians, Aromanians

Location in Metro New York:
Queens (Ridgewood, Sunnyside, Astoria); Connecticut (Bridgeport)

Population in Metro New York:
66,744 (ACS 2008 Total Ancestry Reported); 22,889 (ACS 2008 Born in Romania)

Population in New York City:
29,330 (ACS 2008 Total Ancestry Reported); 13,234 (ACS 2008 Born in Romania)

Primary Religion:
Christianity (Romanian Orthodox)

Secondary Religions:
Christianity (Roman Catholic, Byzantine Rite, Baptist, Pentecostal); Judaism

Status of Christian Witness:
Less than 2% evangelical. Some evangelical resources available, but no active church planting within the past two years.

Primary Language:
Romanian

Secondary Language:
English

Registry of Peoples Codes:
108398, 108397, 100520, 103918

Significant Notes:
❉ Richard Wurmbrand, a Romanian pastor who was imprisoned and tortured for 14 years under the communists, founded Voice of the Martyrs, a ministry based in America that focuses on aiding persecuted Christians throughout the world. Wurmbrand was born into a Jewish family and converted to Christianity as an adult. He died in 2001.

❉ Ridgewood, Queens, has two Romanian Baptist and two Pentecostal churches.

Got a sweet tooth? Sunnyside, Queens, is a good place to go. The Romanian bakeries clustered around Queens Boulevard are known for their delectable pastries and delicious coffee. Romanians have been in this part of Queens for a couple of generations, supplemented in recent years by a wave of new immigrants who left the former communist country after the 1989 revolution. Like many of its Balkan neighbors, Romania is composed of several people groups from different territories forced together into one country. For centuries it was controlled by foreign powers, including the Ottomans, the Austro-Hungarians, and the Russians. Romania became an independent monarchy with its own king in 1878. After World War II, it was occupied by the Soviets, who overthrew the king and installed one of the most oppressive communist regimes in the world. Forty years later in December 1989, Romanians rose up in revolt. After two weeks of bloody fighting, the ruthless dictator Nicolae Ceausescu was executed on Christmas Day. Today, approximately 67 thousand people in Metro New York identify themselves as having Romanian ancestry (ACS 2008). Besides ethnic Romanians from Romania, other groups with Romanian ties include Romanian Jews; Romanians from Moldova, a former Soviet satellite; ethnic Hungarians from Transylvania, which became part of Romania after World War I; and Aromanians, who are a related group primarily from the Balkans, especially Greece and Albania.

When Did They Come To New York?

Among the crowded Jewish tenements on Manhattan's Lower East Side in the late 1800s, the Romanian quarter stood out as very lively place.[1] Jews were the first Romanians in Metro New York, fleeing the anti-Semitic persecution that swept Eastern Europe in the 1880s. They were followed by Romanians from areas under Austro-Hungarian rule and Aromanians in the early 1900s. Waves of Romanian refugees, mostly educated professionals, arrived during World War II and the Communist Era. After the 1989 revolution, thousands of Romanians and Moldovan Romanians—doubtful of the future at home—chose to start new lives in the US.

Where Do They Live?

The Romanian quarter in the Lower East Side is long gone, and many descendents of Romanian immigrants, eager for upward mobility, moved out of the ethnic neighborhoods. However, Sunnyside, Ridgewood, and Astoria in Queens are still home to thousands of Romanians. Bridgeport, Connecticut, has had a large population of Aromanians since the early 1900s.

What Do They Believe?

"Romanians in Metro New York are difficult to reach. They seem hardened, unwilling to consider the gospel," claims one Romanian church leader. It is not surprising, considering new arrivals grew up in an atheistic state, while many second- and third-generation Romanians deliberately leave the old communities and churches established by their ancestors. Although eighty percent of Romanians belong to the Romanian Orthodox Church, which has six churches in Metro New York, only a fraction are actively involved.[2] Other groups, while much smaller in number, are more devout, such as ethnic Hungarian Romanian Catholics and evangelical Protestants. Catholics and evangelicals (mostly Baptists and Pentecostals) were heavily persecuted by the communists in Romania. In the US, they tend to be more conservative than their American counterparts, and Romanian Jews have essentially assimilated into mainstream Jewish communities by now.

What Are Their Lives Like?

"Long live the king!" Whereas some Romanians in Metro New York are actively working to restore Romania's royal family to power, others are deeply opposed to the monarchy. Romanians are a diverse people with equally diverse views on issues. Many Romanians, newcomers as well as the second and third generations, want to forget about Romania and focus on achieving success here. Others keep a strong connection to their mother country by actively supporting Romanian charities and causes.

How Can I Pray?

✳ Romanians in Metro New York are perceived to be less open to the gospel than Romanians in other parts of the US. Pray for opportunities to break down their distrust and disinterest.

The Aromanians, a group related to Romanians, primarily come from Greece and Albania.

Greeks

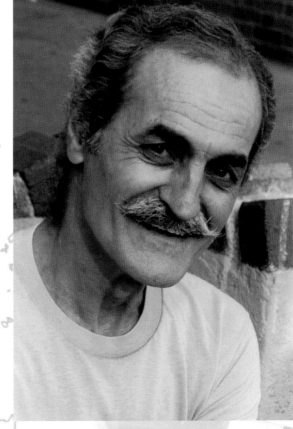

QUICK FACTS:

Place of Origin:
Greece, Cyprus

Location in Metro New York:
Queens (Astoria, Malba, Auburndale, Bayside, Flushing, Whitestone, Jackson Heights, Fresh Meadows); Brooklyn (Fort Hamilton, Bay Ridge); New Jersey (Edgewater)

Population in Metro New York:
131,085 (ACS 2008 Single Ancestry); 47,603 (ACS 2008 Born in Greece)

Population in New York City:
61,621 (ACS 2008 Single Ancestry); 25,686 (ACS 2008 Born in Greece)

Primary Religion:
Christianity (Greek Orthodox)

Status of Christian Witness:
Less than 2% evangelical. Some evangelical resources available, but no active church planting within the past two years.

Primary Languages:
Greek, English

Registry of Peoples Code:
103480

Significant Notes:
☀ Over 500 students are enrolled in the St. Demetrios School in Astoria, making it the largest Greek-American Orthodox school in America.
☀ Astoria, Queens, has the largest concentration of Greeks in America.[2]

In the surprisingly successful 2002 movie *My Big Fat Greek Wedding*, the Greek-centric character Gus Portokalos claimed, "There are two kinds of people—Greeks, and everyone else who wish they was Greek." While this sentiment is not representative of all Greek-Americans, there is nevertheless an exceptional pride that almost all Greeks have in their culture, language, food, religion, history, and country. While the Western world has certainly been shaped historically by Greek philosophy and language, the modern-day Greeks have also left a cultural imprint on the ever-evolving city of New York. As of 2008, there were 131,085 people in the New York Metro area that claimed a single Greek ancestry, with 61,621 of these being in the city itself. A significant number of Greek New Yorkers—47,603 in Metro New York and 25,686 in New York City—were actually born in their beloved country (ACS 2008).

When Did They Come To New York?

The Greek people came to the US in great numbers just before and after the fall of the Ottoman Empire (1922) and the economic crisis following the two world wars and the Greek civil war of the late 1940s. The 1960s also saw an increase of Greek immigration to New York. However, when Greece joined the European Union in the 1980s, emigration fell drastically as the economy surged and people found less reason to venture to America. Today, reverse migration back to Greece is slightly more prevalent than immigration into Metro New York.

Where Do They Live?

Over the years, the neighborhood of Astoria in Queens has earned the title "Little Greece." Although the neighborhood has diversified with an influx of Egyptians, Bangladeshis, Brazilians, Colombians, Ecuadorians, and Peruvians, the

neighborhood is still known as the Greek epicenter of America. As second- and third-generation Greeks become upwardly mobile, though, many are lured away by the more lush surroundings and abodes in Malba, Bayside, and Flushing, Queens, as well as in areas like Edgewater, New Jersey, and Fort Hamilton-Bay Ridge, Brooklyn. No matter where Greeks end up living, Astoria is such a prominent center of the Greek population that it often becomes a weekend destination for people living as far away as New Jersey, Connecticut, Massachusetts, Philadelphia, Baltimore, and Washington, DC.[1]

What Do They Believe?

When the non-Greek Ian falls in love with the Greek Toula in *My Big Fat Greek Wedding*, Ian decides to become Greek Orthodox in order to win over Toula's family. In reaction, Gus Portokalos exclaims, "It is *your lucky day* to be baptized into the Greek Orthodox Church!" The Greek Orthodox Church is practically synonymous with being Greek. Baptisms, weddings, and funerals are linked with the Church as major Greek cultural and social events, affirming the Church's role as the hub of Greek social networking. The churches run large private schools and act as cultural centers for

such activities as Greek language education. Despite many Greek-Americans' being second or third generation, a remarkable number still retain the language due to the influence of the Church. Although some Greek-Americans have become atheists or nonreligious, they almost exclusively retain ties to the Church in which they were raised.

What Are Their Lives Like?

Toula Portokalos tried to explain her people to Ian. "So, you have two cousins. I have twenty-seven first cousins. And my whole family is big and loud. And everybody is in each other's lives and business. All the time!—we're always together, just eating, eating, eating! The only other people we know are Greeks, 'cause Greeks marry Greeks to breed more Greeks." Although some Greek families remain insular through successive generations such as in the description above, the American-born Greeks often intermarry with other ethnic groups and become more Americanized. While certainly retaining some dominant cultural traits, many Greeks work professional jobs, have a high degree of education, and are fully integrated into American life.

How Can I Pray?

✳ Pray that the one Greek evangelical church in New York City will be a light to the Greeks who are not followers of Jesus Christ.

✳ Pray for a Bible-focused renewal to take place within the Orthodox Church.

✳ Pray for more churches to be started among the Greeks in Astoria, Flushing, and Bay Ridge.

While Astoria, Queens, is known as the Greek enclave of Metro New York, other immigrant groups, such as the Croats, are concentrated there as well.

Croats

QUICK FACTS:

Place of Origin:
Croatia

Location in Metro New York:
Queens (Astoria); New Jersey (Fairview, Cliffside Park); Long Island (Syosset, New Hyde Park, Glen Cove); Connecticut (Bridgeport)

Population in Metro New York:
120,000 (Community Estimate); 36,337 (ACS 2008 Total Ancestry Reported); 15,329 (ACS 2008 Born in Croatia)

Population in New York City:
12,126 (ACS 2008 Total Ancestry Reported); 5,930 (ACS 2008 Born in Croatia)

Primary Religion:
Christianity (Roman Catholic)

Status of Christian Witness:
Less than 2% evangelical. Some evangelical resources available, but no active church planting within the past two years.

Primary Language:
Croatian

Secondary Language:
English

Registry of Peoples Code:
102315

Significant Notes:
❋ Croatia's Dalmatian Coast, located on the Adriatic Sea, has become a very popular tourist destination. It boasts crystal clear waters, medieval castles, and fresco-adorned churches and monasteries.
❋ The patron saint of Croatia is St. Jerome, born in Dalmatia around 342 AD. An avid scholar, his translations and revisions of the biblical texts extant in his time formed the foundation of the Latin Vulgate Bible, used by the Church until the Reformation.[3]
❋ Over 8% of the people who claim Croatian ancestry in the United States live in Metro New York (ACS 2008).

"Leaving was very dangerous, and getting political asylum in the United States was very difficult. We were lucky!" Decades later, Father Gio, a Catholic priest in Fairview, New Jersey, still remembers the details of his escape from Croatia, which was then part of Yugoslavia. It was right after World War II, and Eastern Europe had just fallen into communist hands. Fearful of what lay ahead, his family fled to Italy, where they stayed in a refugee camp until asylum was granted and they had a promise of a home and jobs with an uncle in the US. Croats share a difficult history with several other ethnic groups in Metro New York that were part of the former Yugoslavia, including Serbs (p. 124), Bosniaks (p. 136), Macedonians (p. 138) and Albanians (p. 122). While Yugoslavia's communist government succeeded in holding together ethnic groups who were enemies for centuries, it began to lose its grip after the Berlin Wall fell in 1989.

Yugoslavia disintegrated as its republics declared independence, triggering a variety of brutal ethnic conflicts between 1991 and 2001, collectively known as the Yugoslav Wars. The Croatian War of Independence (1991-1995) pitted Croats who wanted a sovereign country against a minority Serbian population, who wanted to remain part of Serb-dominated Yugoslavia. The heaviest fighting occurred in 1991 when ten

thousand people were killed. An estimated 300 thousand people were displaced by the war.[1] Atrocities and ethnic cleansing were alleged on both sides, and suspected perpetrators are still being prosecuted today. Metro New York's Croat population is estimated to number approximately 120 thousand.[2]

When Did They Come To New York?

Croats were definitely among the huge numbers of "Slavs" (as anyone from that part of Europe was known) who came to the US during the great European migration in the late nineteenth century. While most settled in the industrial cities of the Midwest and Pennsylvania, many from Croatia's warm coastal areas kept moving west, ending up in California. Following World War II, a wave of Croats entered the US as displaced persons or seekers of political asylum, as Father Gio did. In the 1960s and '70s, Yugoslavia relaxed its emigration policies, and thousands more were able to leave. The number of Croats coming to the US has been fairly low since then, and Metro New York's population of Croats is starting to decline as the older generation dies off and others leave the area.

Where Do They Live?

Having been in Metro New York for several generations, Croats are well assimilated and spread throughout the area. A few communities stand out, such as Fairview and Cliffside Park in New Jersey, where people from Croatia's Dalmatian Coast primarily settled. Astoria, Queens, one of Metro New York's most diverse communities, is home to many Croats, as are Syosset, Glen Cove, and New Hyde Park in Long Island, and Bridgeport, Connecticut.

What Do They Believe?

"To be Croatian is to be Catholic," explained Father Gio. "But half of them just practice traditions—they don't adhere to church teaching," he continued. "I tell them, 'Just because you come for holidays and funerals doesn't mean you are a Christian!'" A few churches still hold Mass in Croatian, including St. John the Baptist in Fairview and St. Cyril and Methodius in Manhattan. Only a small percentage of Croats identify themselves with other religious traditions.

What Are Their Lives Like?

Father Gio laughed as he explained how Croats are very competitive with each other. "They like to show off, see who can do this or that better." Sports, particularly soccer and basketball, are a popular way to showcase one's talents. Extended family bonds are strong, cemented by frequent get-togethers for Croatian food and music. In addition to using the Internet and satellite television, Croats in Metro New York keep up with news of home by listening to a Croatian radio broadcast from Astoria twice a week and through a newspaper called *The Croatian Chronicle*.

How Can I Pray?

✷ Many Croats see Catholicism as part of their cultural heritage and have little interest in pursuing a personal relationship with God. Pray that their hearts would be moved by the truths of the gospel.

The Yugoslav wars that started in the early 1990s due to ethnic conflict within Yugoslavia resulted in the independence of Croatia in 1991 and Bosnia and Herzegovina in 1992.

135

Bosniaks

QUICK FACTS:

Place of Origin:
Bosnia-Herzegovina

Location in Metro New York:
Queens (Astoria); New Jersey (Lodi, Hackensack, Bound Brook)

Population in Metro New York:
10,000 (Community Estimate); 3,735 (ACS 2008 Born in Bosnia-Herzegovina)

Population in New York City:
1,774 (ACS 2008 Born in Bosnia-Herzegovina)

Primary Religion:
Islam

Status of Christian Witness:
Less than 2% evangelical. Some evangelical resources available, but no active church planting within the past two years.

Primary Language:
Bosnian

Secondary Language:
English

Registry of Peoples Code:
101629

Significant Notes:

⁜ 1.8 million Bosniaks were displaced by the war. Most were resettled in other parts of Bosnia or as refugees in Europe and the United States. Over 20,000 Bosniak men were never accounted for after disappearing in the war.[4]

⁜ The term "ethnic cleansing" was introduced as a result of the Bosnian War to describe the practice of violent forcible removal of a particular ethnic group in order to create an ethnically homogenous area.

⁜ The 1995 Srebrenica massacre, in which 8,000 Bosniak men and boys were killed, was ruled an act of genocide by the International Tribunal for the former Yugoslavia.[5]

"In Bosnia before the war, our children played in the streets and walked miles to school by themselves. Here, we have to watch them every minute, or who knows what will happen. This is not freedom!" complained Adisa, a young Bosniak mother. The historical term "Bosniak" has been resurrected (replacing "Bosnian") to identify Slavic Muslims from the country now known as Bosnia-Herzegovina. Adisa's distress resonates with her fellow Bosniak neighbors in Astoria, Queens, who were torn from their idyllic homeland where they had enjoyed the best lifestyle of any communist bloc country. Multi-ethnic Bosnia was home to Bosniaks, Serbs, and Croats who lived side by side in harmony for generations. However, it was the Bosniaks who suffered the most when Yugoslavia disintegrated during a series of ethnic and religious wars in the 1990s. Of the 100 thousand people killed in the Bosnian War (1992-1995), eighty-three percent were Bosniak civilians, one-third of whom were women and children.[1] During this time, Bosniaks were victims of unfathomable atrocities, including ethnic cleansing, systematic rape, and genocide. Today, an estimated ten thousand Bosniaks, almost all of whom are refugees, live in Metro New York.[2] Most have experienced significant trauma, including the death of family members, loss of home and possessions, torture, and abuse.

When Did They Come To New York?

The US government has resettled 131 thousand Bosniak refugees since 1992. Most arrived between 1995 and 2000. Metro New York was a major resettlement site although the city of Utica, between Albany and Syracuse, received the most Bosniak refugees in the state. While many young adventuresome Bosniaks left their initial resettlement areas for the excitement of New York City, the population is declining as others leave Metro New York to join Bosniak communities in cheaper, quieter places like St. Louis, Missouri and Jacksonville, Florida.

Where Do They Live?

"Cities were like this in Bosnia, but they stopped because of the war. They don't go on forever, like here." That is how Sejad, a young Bosniak man who works at the Cevabdzinica Sarajevo Bakery on 34th Street, described Astoria, Queens, home to the largest Bosniak community in Metro New York. Bosniaks love to gather in the restaurants and shops lining the stretch of 30th Avenue between 34th and 42nd Streets. Smaller numbers of Bosniaks have settled in New Jersey, particularly in Lodi and Hackensack in Bergen County and Bound Brook in Somerset County.

What Do They Believe?

"Before the war, we didn't even know we were Muslims!" Adisa explained. Bosniaks were secular people who enjoyed celebrating different religious holidays with all their neighbors—Christmas with Catholic Croats, Easter with the Serbian Orthodox, and Hanukkah with the Jews. The hatred they experienced during the war awakened them to their heritage and provided a unifying cultural and ethnic identity. As Adnan, a television producer said, "I was born Muslim, my parents are Muslim, I am Bosnian. I cannot be anything else." However, most do not actively practice the Islamic faith. The Bosnian Islamic Center, located at 18th Street and Astoria Boulevard, is typically quiet during the week, as most Bosniaks admit they only go to the mosque for holidays or funerals. Friday prayers are usually attended only by a few older men.

What Are Their Lives Like?

When Bosniaks came to Metro New York, they had two goals: to find family and get a job. "If you could find an aunt, a cousin, anyone, then you could start life over again," one young woman explained. As refugees, Bosniaks had lost everything they owned. Many were victims of unspeakable cruelty or saw their family members victimized. Although most have been able to move ahead with their lives, there is a high prevalence of post-traumatic stress disorder among Bosniaks. Discussion of mental health issues is considered taboo in their culture, so many will not seek help.[3] Adjusting to lower-level jobs was also very difficult for Bosniaks, many of whom were highly educated. "Doctors, lawyers, and high-ranking teachers had to become taxi drivers, janitors, and food service employees to provide for their families," said Selma, a Bosniak woman from New Jersey. Bosniaks typically seek out the best education for their children, pinning their hopes on the next generation to achieve success and "move up the ladder."

How Can I Pray?

✳ Bosniaks have suffered greatly, and there is no known ministry to them in Metro New York. Pray for Christians to befriend and introduce them to the One who heals the brokenhearted.

While Sarajevo in Bosnia and Herzegovina was the scene of the deadliest fighting in the decade-long Yugoslav Wars, Macedonia was relatively peaceful until fighting took place with Albanians in 2001.

Macedonians

QUICK FACTS:

Place of Origin:
Macedonia (former Yugoslavia)

Significant Subgroups:
None. Albanian Macedonians treated in a separate profile, Albanians (p. 122).

Location in Metro New York:
New Jersey (Garfield, Clifton, Paterson); Queens (College Point)

Population in Metro New York:
30,000 (Community Estimate); 9,061 (ACS 2008 Total Ancestry Reported)

Population in New York City:
5,201 (ACS 2008 Total Ancestry Reported)

Primary Religion:
Christianity (Macedonian Orthodox)

Status of Christian Witness:
Less than 2% evangelical. Some evangelical resources available, but no active church planting within the past two years.

Primary Language:
Macedonian

Secondary Language:
English

Registry of Peoples Code:
105968

Significant Notes:
☀ The government of Greece has disputed the validity of the name "Republic of Macedonia" since Macedonia's independence in 1991. Greece insists that naming the country "Macedonia" implies expansionist claims on the northern Greek province historically known as Macedonia.[4]
☀ The Apostle Paul was called by God to preach in Macedonia. Acts 16 records that Paul had a vision of a Macedonian man who pleaded with him to "come over to Macedonia and help us!" Paul "immediately set out for Macedonia," and visited the region again on several occasions.

"**I** don't know a Macedonian who doesn't go to church," said Zvonko, a Macedonia-born real estate broker who lives in New Jersey. "I wouldn't associate with anyone who is not part of the church." Ironically, Macedonians owe their strong religious identity to an unlikely advocate: their former communist rulers, the Yugoslavians. Hoping to win Macedonian loyalty, the Yugoslavian government established Macedonia as an autonomous republic in 1944, actively promoting Macedonian culture, language, and the restoration of the Macedonian Orthodox Church. Up to that time, the Macedonians, a southern Slavic people whose lineage includes Alexander the Great, endured centuries of occupation under the Roman, Byzantine, and Ottoman Empires. After the Ottoman Turks were driven out in 1912, Serbia, Greece, and Bulgaria fought for control of Macedonia. Under the Yugoslavians, Macedonians were finally able to develop a strong ethnic and cultural identity with the Church at the center. In 1991 after Yugoslavia dissolved, Macedonia declared its independence, managing to avoid the horrific ethnic wars that engulfed the other Yugoslav republics in the mid-1990s. However, the 1999 conflict between Serbia and Albanians in Kosovo sparked a nationalist movement among Macedonia's Albanian minority, which makes up twenty-five percent of the population.[1] From January to November 2001, fighting between Albanian insurgents and Macedonian forces killed several dozen people and displaced 174 thousand before a peace agreement was reached in early 2002.[2] Metro New York's

Macedonian population numbers approximately 30 thousand, with the vast majority concentrated in northern New Jersey.[3]

When Did They Come To New York?

The first large wave of Macedonians came in the early 1900s to escape oppression by the Ottoman Turks. They established communities in industrial centers where factory work was available. The next influx of Macedonians to the US came in the 1960s when thousands took advantage of Yugoslavia's decision to relax its emigration policies. Throughout the 1990s after Macedonia's independence, thousands more came to Metro New York hoping to build a better life for their families. As Dimitri, a Macedonian restaurant owner said, "America was the place to go to do well."

Where Do They Live?

Metro New York's main Macedonian communities are found in northern New Jersey. Garfield is the residential and commercial hub, home to several Macedonian businesses, restaurants, a soccer club, and a thriving immigration service. Two Macedonian Orthodox churches are located in the nearby towns of Totowa and Cedar Grove. A much smaller Macedonian community lives in College Point, Queens, where its members have established an Orthodox church and youth center.

What Do They Believe?

"When Macedonians come to the US, they become more religious as a way to stay connected to their culture," explained Gorazd, a Macedonian artist who owns a

gallery in Manhattan. If asked about their faith, most Macedonians would answer as Zvonko did: "We are Christians—Christian Orthodox." Clearly, the Orthodox Church serves as the primary social network and source of cultural identity for the Macedonian community, and most seem content with this type of tradition-based sociocultural Christianity. No evangelical churches exist among Metro New York's Macedonian community, and few Macedonians seem to leave the Orthodox Church.

What Are Their Lives Like?

"We have a stronger Macedonian community here than back in Macedonia," said Dimitri. "We get together more to celebrate and socialize. They cannot afford to do all the things we can," he continued. Macedonians are a very tight-knit group, and they are expected to achieve two specific goals: to take care of their families and "make something" of themselves. Dimitri, who has no children of his own, sponsored five of his nieces and nephews to come to New Jersey. His nephews are in business, and his nieces are professionals. "I am very proud of them! They have really made something of themselves," he exclaimed.

How Can I Pray?

✵ Most Macedonians view church as part of their cultural identity and social life. Pray that the good news of salvation through faith in Christ would be preached in their church, drawing many into a deeper understanding of God's grace.

Garfield, New Jersey, is home to the largest concentration of Macedonians in Metro New York, as well as a large number of Poles.

Poles

QUICK FACTS:

Place of Origin:
Poland

Location in Metro New York:
Brooklyn (Greenpoint); Staten Island (New Brighton, St. George, Rosebank); Queens (Ridgewood); New Jersey (Garfield, Wallington)

Population in Metro New York:
600,000 (Community Estimate); 1,071,428 (ACS 2008 Total Ancestry Reported); 133,974 (ACS 2008 Born in Poland)[4]

Population in New York City:
231,301 (ACS 2008 Total Ancestry Reported); 59,743 (ACS 2008 Born in Poland)

Primary Religion:
Christianity (Roman Catholic)

Secondary Religion:
Christianity (evangelical)

Status of Christian Witness:
Less than 2% evangelical. Some evangelical resources available, but no active church planting within the past two years.

Primary Language:
Polish

Secondary Language:
English

Registry of Peoples Code:
108096

Significant Notes:
❋ The first Polish Baptist Church in the US was founded in Buffalo, New York, in 1907.
❋ The Pulaski Day Parade honoring General Kazimierz Pulaski, a Polish hero of the American Revolution, is one of the largest parades in New York City. It has been held every October since 1937.

Bernadette shared her story with some wistfulness. Several years ago, she abandoned an exciting career as a chef in Poland to be a maid in Greenpoint, Brooklyn. She did it for one reason: to make more money to support her family back in Poland. Such stories are common in Greenpoint, home to Metro New York's largest Polish community, where a walk down Manhattan Avenue looks and sounds like a city in Poland. Signs for stores and offices—and most of the conversations—are in Polish. Over one million people claim Polish ancestry in Metro New York, with Greenpoint and a few other enclaves in northern New Jersey serving as centers of Polish identity and culture (ACS 2008). For generations, these communities were energized by a continual flow of young, hard-working immigrants seeking a better life in America. Today, they are at a crossroads. Poland's entry into the European Union means younger Poles have more opportunities at home or in neighboring countries. The effects are already tangible—many of Greenpoint's Polish stores have closed. LOT, the largest Polish airline, now sells many one-way tickets from New York to Poland. Without fresh immigration, Metro New York's Polish communities will likely lose their distinct ethnic composition and fade away.

When Did They Come To New York?

Major waves of Polish immigrants came to the US between 1860 and 1920. Called *za chlebem*, which means "for bread," they congregated in industrial centers, including

New York, to find work and created the ethnic enclaves that exist today. Thousands more sought freedom here after World War II and during the Soviet Era. With the fall of communism, a fresh wave of young people seeking economic opportunities swelled the ranks of Polish communities throughout the 1990s.

Where Do They Live?

With its distinctly Polish flavor, Greenpoint has long been Metro New York's "Little Polonia." Polish businesses, professional offices, and restaurants dominate Manhattan and Nassau Avenues against the backdrop of the soaring steeple of St. Stanislaus Kostka Roman Catholic Church. Skyrocketing real estate prices have driven many into more affordable communities in Staten Island and Queens. (One Polish Catholic parish in Staten Island doubled in size over the past several years.)[1] Across the Hudson River in northern New Jersey are several large Polish communities, including Wallington, where 51.5 percent of residents claim Polish ancestry.[2] After Chicago, Metro New York has the largest Polish population in the US.

What Do They Believe?

"You believe in the cross, and I believe in the cross. That is all that matters," was Bernadette's take on the differences between Catholics and Protestants. Whether most Poles would agree with her is another story. Approximately eighty percent of Poles in Metro New York are Roman Catholics, and Catholicism is deeply intertwined with their ethnic identity. Church is a huge part of their lives, and tension exists between Catholics and the small evangelical community, who are accused of "abandoning the faith of their fathers." Nevertheless, Metro New York has at least four Polish evangelical churches, including Baptist, Assemblies of God, and Methodist.

What Are Their Lives Like?

For most Poles in Metro New York, life centers on church, work, and family. Known for their strong work ethic, they are no strangers to hard work and long days. For generations, Polish immigrants have lived sacrificially, saving their money to send back to Poland. Among the most recent wave of immigrants are the *wakacjusze*, or vacationers, who come to the US on visitors' visas and work without documentation, intending to save money and return home. As life in Poland improves, this group is dwindling. One of the more remarkable trends is that of established immigrants—including educated professionals, business owners, and retirees—who are pulling up stakes and returning to Poland. For guidance, they can find two bestsellers in Greenpoint bookstores: *Returning to Poland and Retirement of a Re-Immigrant in Poland.*[3]

How Can I Pray?

✳ The Poles are very devout people who will openly talk about their faith. Pray for opportunities to discuss biblical Christianity and what it means to have a relationship with Jesus Christ.

Around four million people in Metro New York claim Polish or Irish ancestry, reflecting the immensity of migration undertaken by these two staunchly Catholic groups.

Irish

QUICK FACTS:

Place of Origin:
Ireland

Location in Metro New York:
Bronx (Woodlawn); Westchester (Lincoln, Yonkers); Queens (Woodside, Sunnyside); Rockland (Pearl River)

Population in Metro New York:
838,154 (ACS 2008 Single Ancestry); 39,604 (ACS 2008 Born in Ireland)

Population in New York City:
161,361 (ACS 2008 Single Ancestry); 15,600 (ACS 2008 Born in Ireland)

Primary Religion:
Christianity (Roman Catholic)

Status of Christian Witness:
Less than 2% evangelical. Some evangelical resources available, but no active church planting within the past two years.

Primary Language:
English

Registry of Peoples Code:
104068

Significant Note:
❋ The New York City Metro area has, by far, the largest Irish-American population in America (ACS 2008).

Even though it was a frigid January evening in New York, the outdoor temperature seemed to have no effect on the merry atmosphere inside Donovan's Pub in Woodside, Queens. For decades, Donovan's has been a bastion of Irish familiarity in a neighborhood of turbulent ethnic turnover, and despite a slight lull from 1965 to 1985, the Irish could always count on a steady inflow of newcomers to add life to the party. Throughout the first decade of the twenty-first century, however, many regulars at Donovan's and other pubs throughout New York City have been returning home to Ireland. This return migration marks a historic shift in the centuries-old relationship between New York and Ireland. New York has always been on the receiving end of the deal, so much so that it is difficult to actually define who is "Irish" today. According to the 2008 American Community Survey, 161,361 people in New York City claimed a single ancestry of Irish, while 838,154 people in the Metro area did the same. However, only 15,600 people in New York City and 39,604 in Metro New York were born in Ireland (ACS 2008).

When Did They Come To New York?

While the Irish were in New York well before, the Irish Potato Famine of the 1840s initiated the first large wave of Catholic Irish immigrants. Emigration from Ireland continued steadily until the 1920s, then picked up again after World War II, and then saw a tremendous decline from 1965 to 1985. In the 1980s, Ireland had one of the largest unemployment rates in Europe, causing many well-educated young people to seek undocumented work in New York.[1] The economic boom of Ireland in the 1990s to the present time, however, has not only encouraged many of these young people to return but also has lured many other Irish to their homeland as well.[2] The time period of 2000 to 2008 saw a remarkable decline of forty-nine percent in the foreign-born Irish population of New York City, and a twenty-five percent decline in Metro New York.[3]

Where Do They Live?

Pubs like Donovan's are both relics and invigorating to the Irish community. Although many traditional Irish neighborhoods have dissipated as the American-born spread throughout the city, such places as Woodhaven, Lincoln, and Yonkers on the Bronx-Westchester border, Pearl River in Rockland County, and Woodside in Queens still have vital signs of Irish life.

What Do They Believe?

The political strife between the largely Catholic Republic of Ireland and the largely Protestant Northern Ireland has only bolstered the sense that Roman Catholic identity is also a national identity. Whereas many have become nonreligious, the Irish have made large contributions to religious New York with such institutions as St. Patrick's Cathedral, the best-known religious building in New York City.

What Are Their Lives Like?

When the executive director of the American Irish Historical Society was asked to describe the Irish people, he adequately described in one word what anyone would have observed at Donovan's Pub. He simply said, "Convivial," which means they are jovial people who are fond of eating, drinking, and good company. Irish are well integrated into New York life and make up a significant portion of the employees of the fire and police departments.

How Can I Pray?

✳ There are no known recent attempts that specifically focus on reaching the Irish with the gospel. Pray that churches in their neighborhoods and others would gain a heart for sharing with them.

✳ The Irish were once responsible for evangelizing England and much of Western Europe. Pray that God would use them once again to create a movement of people turning to Christ.

✳ Pray for churches to be established in Woodlawn, Woodside, and Pearl River that would connect with the Irish over the same values of family and community development.

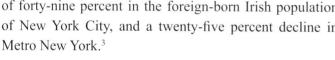

Yonkers, just north of the Bronx, is home to one of the largest concentrations of Irish, as well as Jordanians, in Metro New York.

Jordanians

QUICK FACTS:

Place of Origin:
Jordan

Significant Subgroups:
None. Palestinians treated in a separate profile (p. 50).

Location in Metro New York:
Westchester (Yonkers); Brooklyn (Bay Ridge)

Population in Metro New York:
12,000 (Community Estimate); 7,803 (ACS 2008 Total Ancestry Reported)

Population in New York City:
2,546 (ACS 2008 Total Ancestry Reported)

Primary Religion:
Christianity (Roman Catholic, Melkite Catholic)

Secondary Religion:
Islam (Sunni)

Status of Christian Witness:
Less than 2% evangelical. Some evangelical resources available, but no active church planting within the past two years.

Primary Languages:
English, Arabic

Registry of Peoples Code:
104301

Significant Notes:

✳ Jordan's official name is the Hashemite Kingdom of Jordan. The Hashemite dynasty claims to be direct descendents of the Prophet Muhammad. The current monarch is His Majesty King Abdullah XI.

✳ John 1:28 records that Jesus was baptized by John the Baptist in "Bethany, across the Jordan." This is not the Bethany outside Jerusalem where Jesus visited Mary, Martha, and Lazarus but rather a village on the East Bank of the Jordan River. Jordan has been excavating this area for the past decade and has discovered much evidence supporting the fact that Jesus was baptized on the East Bank, and therefore in Jordan rather than Israel. For more details, visit http://www.baptismsite.com.

"**B**ack in the seventies and eighties, deciding to come to America was easy," explained Mr. Haddad, a former leader of the Arab-American Foundation who has lived in Metro New York for over thirty years. "In Jordan, we were making five thousand dollars a year. If we went to America, we'd make fifty thousand." Today, however, it is a different story. Despite its limited natural resources, Jordan's economy has grown over the past decade, which has reduced the economic incentive to emigrate. Since educated Jordanians are now able to find well-paying jobs at home, emigration from Jordan has slowed considerably. As Mr. Haddad points out, "No one is going to leave for an extra thirty dollars a week!" Situated on the East Bank of the Jordan River across from Israel, Jordan is a young country although its land has been inhabited for thousands of years by such peoples as the Canaanites, Edomites, and Moabites. Jordan was under Ottoman rule for centuries and was then controlled by the British after World War I. Two years after gaining independence in 1946, Jordan seized the West Bank from Israel. The West Bank was recaptured by Israel in the Six Days War of 1967, and in 1988, Jordan formally renounced all claims to the West Bank. Metro New York's Jordanian-Arab community numbers approximately 12 thousand people, even though the number of actual immigrants from Jordan is much greater. Because Jordan is home to nearly two million Palestinian refugees, many Palestinians (p. 50) enter the US carrying Jordanian passports.[1]

When Did They Come To New York?

Compared to their Syrio-Lebanese neighbors, Jordanians are newcomers to Metro New York. The first significant numbers arrived in the 1950s, with the largest waves in the 1970s and '80s. As Mr. Haddad pointed out, most came for better jobs and higher salaries. Jordanians have the distinction of being one of the few Arab groups who have immigrated as whole families.[2]

Where Do They Live?

The city of Yonkers in Westchester County, just north of New York City, has been drawing Jordanians since the 1950s. Many were employed by the Stewart Stamping Company, which operated a factory in Yonkers from the 1940s until 2008. Today, Jordanians are concentrated in the neighborhoods of Park Hill, Dunwoodie Heights, Lowerre, and Lincoln. Smaller numbers also live in the large Arab community in Bay Ridge, Brooklyn. Some third- and fourth-generation Jordanians have moved to other areas of Westchester but maintain strong ties to Yonkers.

What Do They Believe?

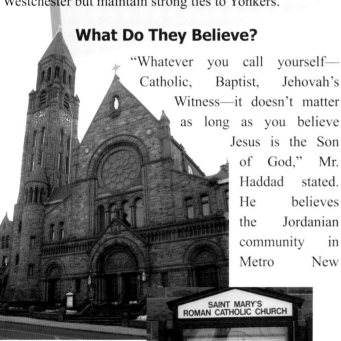

SAINT MARY'S ROMAN CATHOLIC CHURCH

WELCOME TO ALL
CHURCH OPEN 7 AM-3 PM
MASSES ON SUNDAY 5 PM SAT
7:30 AM 9 SPANISH 10:30 12:00
6:15 ARABIC WEEKDAY 8:15 & 12
I WILL GO UP TO THE
ALTAR OF GOD
TO GOD WHO GIVES
JOY TO MY YOUTH PS. 43-4

"Whatever you call yourself—Catholic, Baptist, Jehovah's Witness—it doesn't matter as long as you believe Jesus is the Son of God," Mr. Haddad stated. He believes the Jordanian community in Metro New

York is approximately seventy percent Christian and thirty percent Muslim, a very different breakdown than in Jordan. Largely due to immigration to the US and Europe, Jordan's Christian population has steadily decreased from an estimated thirty percent in 1950 (which included the West Bank) to less than four percent today.[3] Metro New York's Jordanian Christians are primarily from the Roman Catholic and Melkite (Greek Catholic) traditions. In Yonkers, the Church of the Immaculate Conception of St. Mary, known to locals as St. Mary's, has an Arabic Mass for Roman Catholics; Melkites worship at Christ the Savior Church. Yonkers is home to several mosques where Jordanian Muslims worship along with the Andalusia School, a private Islamic school founded in 2004.

What Are Their Lives Like?

"Our churches hold us together," explained Mr. Haddad, speaking for the Christians, "and the Muslims have their mosques." While some first-generation Jordanians live in Metro New York, many families are into their third and fourth generations, and most have fully assimilated. "Like other groups in America, we've adapted," claimed Mr. Haddad. "Later generations only know a little about Jordan. They're Americans now." While Jordanians continue to own shops, delis, and businesses in Yonkers, many are professionals such as doctors, lawyers, and engineers. Education is a high priority, and the vast majority of young people attend college.

How Can I Pray?

✳ The Gospels show that part of John the Baptist's ministry took place in Jordan, and he baptized his disciples in the Jordan River. Pray that Jordanian Christians would build upon their strong Christian heritage and increase their zeal to proclaim Christ—especially to their Muslim neighbors.

Jordanian and Syrio-Lebanese Muslims living in New York City tend to settle in Bay Ridge, Brooklyn, which has the largest pan-Arab concentration in New York City.

Syrio-Lebanese Muslims

QUICK FACTS:

Place of Origin:
Syria, Lebanon

Significant Subgroups:
Lebanese (55%); Syrian (45%)

Location in Metro New York:
Brooklyn (Bay Ridge); New Jersey (Paterson)

Population in Metro New York:
14,000-21,000 (Community Estimate); 63,439 (ACS 2008 Total Ancestry Reported from Lebanon and Syria, including all religions)

Population in New York City:
25,052 (ACS 2008 Total Ancestry Reported from Lebanon and Syria, including all religions)

Primary Religion:
Islam (85% Sunni, 15% Shi'ah)

Secondary Religions:
Alawites, Druze

Status of Christian Witness:
Less than 2% evangelical. Some evangelical resources available, but no active church planting within the past two years.

Primary Languages:
Arabic, English

Registry of Peoples Codes:
105688, 109662

Significant Notes:

✺ While they share the core beliefs of Islam and the Qur'an, Sunnis and Shi'ites split in the 7th century over issues of leadership following the death of the prophet Muhammad. The majority (85%) of the world's Muslims are Sunni.

✺ Alawites are 12% of the Syrian population, including the former and current presidents of Syria.[4]

✺ The Druze do not require ritual prayer or mosque attendance, nor do they allow converts. Only the child of a Druze father and mother can be Druze.[5]

"**I**n Syria, I had many friends, but here I don't have any friends yet—only my family," explained sixteen-year old Rima, who recently arrived from Syria to join her mother and father in Bay Ridge, Brooklyn. For Syrio-Lebanese Muslims such as Rima and her family, who number between 14 thousand and 21 thousand in Metro New York, finding their place in the greater Arab-American community raises a long-standing question: Is there a unified Arab identity?[1] Arabs are fragmented by nationality, ethnicity, religion, and culture. From World War I until the 1960s, several unsuccessful attempts were made to unite the Arab world, such as the pan-Arab and Arab unification movements. These failed in large part because of conflicting political agendas. The drive for Arab unity began to fade in the mid-1970s, and by the 1980s, the concept of pan-Arabism was eclipsed by the increasing influence of Islamist movements. While Muslims are the fastest-growing group in the Arab-American community, Arabic-speaking Muslims constitute a small minority of the 800 thousand-strong Muslim population in Metro New York.[2] A young person such as Rima is likely to witness many changes as Metro New York's Arab-American community evolves and continues to search for its collective identity.

When Did They Come To New York?

Very few Muslims came with the major waves of Christian

and Jewish emigrants from Greater Syria during the late 1800s and early 1900s. The vast majority of Syrio-Lebanese Muslims in Metro New York arrived after 1965. The largest wave began with the arrival of thousands of Lebanese fleeing a sixteen-year-long civil war. An estimated 900 thousand people—twenty percent of Lebanon's pre-war population—were displaced from their homes, and approximately 250 thousand emigrated.[3] Syrians had no similar crisis compelling them to leave, so they have been arriving at a more steady pace than the Lebanese. Most of the Syrians and Lebanese coming today are seeking better educational and job opportunities. As in Rima's situation, often a parent will come first to get established, and the family will join later. While immigration came to a halt after 9/11, the flow has started again but at a lower level than that of the 1990s.

Where Do They Live?

Bay Ridge, Brooklyn, has the largest concentration of Syrio-Lebanese Muslims in New York City. While this neighborhood was once dominated by Arab Christians, the Muslim presence has grown significantly since 1965. The area along 5th Avenue between Senator and 73rd Streets is the main Arab-American thoroughfare, with shops, restaurants, and businesses. The northern New Jersey city of Paterson is also home to a large Arab-Muslim population, including many Syrians and Lebanese. People looking for an outstanding Syrian or Lebanese meal, specialty groceries, or baked goods can find just what they want on South Paterson's Main Street.

What Do They Believe?

The vast majority of Syrio-Lebanese Muslims belong to the Sunni sect although a Shi'ite minority can be found among both Lebanese and Syrians. Also present in small numbers are Alawites, an offshoot of Shi'ah Islam, and the Druze. The Druze faith originated in Islam, but its followers are no longer considered Muslims by the Islamic community. A couple of evangelical ministries are working among the Syrio-Lebanese Muslim community in Brooklyn. One group provides ESL classes and activities for women, and Arabic churches exist that have some outreach to Muslims.

What Are Their Lives Like?

"My father is a chef at a restaurant in Manhattan," Rima said. "He is a very good chef!" Most of the Syrio-Lebanese Muslims in Metro New York are educated, speak English fairly well, and work in professional occupations, businesses, restaurants, and shops. Unlike the early Syrio-Lebanese Christian settlers, who were pressured to conform to Anglo-American culture, the diversity in Metro New York today allows Muslim immigrants to maintain their distinctiveness. However, many still fear their children will become "Americanized" and lose their Arab values.

How Can I Pray?

✳ The Apostle Paul was converted on his way to Damascus (which is in Syria). Pray that evangelical ministries in the Syrio-Lebanese Muslim community will yield powerful converts to Christ.

✳ Pray for an outreach to Arab men to begin, as most current ministries focus on women.

Whereas most Syrio-Lebanese Muslims belong to the Sunni branch of Islam, which is the largest and more orthodox branch of Islam, most Iranian Muslims belong to the second largest branch, called Shi'ah.

Iranians

QUICK FACTS:

Place of Origin:
Iran

Significant Subgroups:
None. Persian Jews treated in a separate profile (p. 102).

Location in Metro New York:
New Jersey (Bergen and Hudson Counties); Long Island (Great Neck); assimilated into affluent suburbs across Metro New York

Population in Metro New York:
60,000-70,000 (Community Estimate); 30,989 (ACS 2008 Total Ancestry Reported); 19,219 (ACS 2008 Born in Iran)

Population in New York City:
8,605 (ACS 2008 Total Ancestry Reported); 4,873 (ACS 2008 Born in Iran)

Primary Religion:
Islam (Shi'ah)

Secondary Religions:
Islam (Sunni), Christianity, Baha'i, Zoroastrianism

Status of Christian Witness:
Less than 2% evangelical. Initial (localized) church planting within the past two years.

Primary Language:
Farsi

Secondary Language:
English

Registry of Peoples Code:
107987

Significant Notes:
❋ Zoroastrianism was the official religion of ancient Persia until the 7th-century Islamic conquest. Zoroastrians believe that there is one supreme creator-God and that the world is a battleground between good and evil.
❋ A small Zoroastrian community still survives in Iran although the 1979 revolution forced many members to flee. The largest Zoroastrian community in the world is now in India. Of those who came to the US, most settled in California. Metro New York's Zoroastrian community is very small.

"When I first came here, I worked at a gas station. A man from Mexico asked me where I was from. When I said 'Iran,' he began yelling, 'Terrorista! Terrorista!' I was so embarrassed." Houshmand, a young Iranian man, shuddered as he related the story. Many Iranians in Metro New York have experienced similar humiliation. Although proud of their heritage—Iran was the heart of the ancient Persian Empire that once controlled territory from North Africa to India—the Iran of today is a cause of sadness and frustration. Fifty years ago, Iran was a secular country and a strong ally of the US. In 1979, Iran's authoritarian Shah was ousted, and the fundamentalist Shi'ite Islamic cleric Ayatollah Khomeini took control, instituting Islamic religious rule. In November 1979, Iranian students seized the US embassy in Tehran, holding fifty-two staff hostage for fifteen months. Since then, the relationship between the US and Iran has been antagonistic, leaving Iranians in the US with the difficult task of forging an identity that values their culture while disassociating themselves from the negative image of their homeland. Metro New York is home to an estimated 30,989 people with Iranian ancestry (ACS 2008), even though community members suggest 60 thousand to 70 thousand is a more accurate number.[1]

When Did They Come To New York?

While small numbers of Iranian students and professionals came to the US in the 1950s and '60s, most left Iran just prior to and

after the Islamic Revolution of 1979. The earliest wave, supporters of the Shah who were wealthy and highly educated cultural Muslims, began arriving in 1977. They were followed by large groups of religious minorities—Jews, Christians, Baha'is and Zoroastrians—who feared persecution by the Islamic Republic. Of those, only Persian Jews (p. 102) settled in significant numbers in Metro New York. Still more fled the devastating Iran-Iraq War (1980-1988). Iranians have arrived steadily since 1979 although it is more difficult to leave Iran now.

Where Do They Live?

"My father read that Nutley, New Jersey, was one of the safest communities in America. So that's where we moved!" said Farah, whose family came in the late 1970s. Apart from the prominent Persian-Jewish community in Great Neck, Long Island, locating Iranians in Metro New York is difficult. Most speak English well, and they do not cluster in groups, preferring instead to assimilate in affluent suburbs populated by professionals with good schools for their children.

What Do They Believe?

"Right now, it seems Iranians are tiring of religion due to the situation in Iran. Many are rejecting all religion and faith in God," explained Bijan,* an Iranian-American who leads a ministry to Muslims in Metro New York. "Iranians are much like other well-educated, successful professionals," he continued. "Many feel they don't have time for God—they are chasing after money and material things." While

Iranian Muslims are not especially devout, they tend to cling to Islamic traditions and holidays as part of their cultural identity. "They are like your Christmas and Easter Christians," explained one young man. In contrast, California's Iranians seem to shed their Islamic identity more easily, and many are turning to Christianity, leading Christian missions experts to hail them as a "budding missional

force of Muslim-background believers."[2] As of now, there is one Farsi-language church in Metro New York with approximately thirty Iranian Christians who are involved in evangelism among their Muslim compatriots.

What Are Their Lives Like?

"There are two essential values embedded in all Iranians: *tarof* and respect," Salman, a college student, explained. *Tarof* is a uniquely Persian social ritual in which offers of hospitality are meant to be refused. "It compels Iranians to fight over who pays for dinner," he continued. "It means you invite people to stay in your home, but they are expected to decline." Since Iranians prize material success, they tend to push their children into prestigious and lucrative professions such as medicine, law, and engineering—described by one young Iranian as the "Holy Trifecta" of careers.[3]

How Can I Pray?

✺ Pray for the spiritual health and outreach of the Farsi-speaking church, as it is one of only a few churches in Metro New York with membership primarily made of Muslim-background believers.

✺ Iran is one of the top three countries where Muslims are coming to Christ, and Christianity is exploding among Iranians in California. Pray for this movement of the Spirit in Metro New York.

Both Iranians and Japanese in Metro New York have some of the highest education levels among first-generation immigrants.

Japanese

QUICK FACTS:

Place of Origin:
Japan (Tokyo, Osaka)

Location in Metro New York:
New Jersey (Fort Lee, Edgewater, Palisades Park); Manhattan (Clinton, Midtown, Murray Hill, NoHo, East Village); Westchester (Scarsdale, Irvington, Harrison, Milton); Connecticut (Cos Cob, Mianus); Long Island (Manorhaven)

Population in Metro New York:
50,000 (Community Estimate); 49,117 (ACS 2008 Japanese who selected Asian alone as race); 39,927 (ACS 2008 Born in Japan)

Population in New York City:
25,000 (ACS 2008 Japanese who selected Asian alone as race); 19,066 (ACS 2008 Born in Japan)

Primary Religions:
Buddhism, nonreligious

Secondary Religion:
Shintoism

Status of Christian Witness:
Less than 2% evangelical. Initial (localized) church planting within the past two years.

Primary Language:
Japanese

Registry of Peoples Code:
104189

Significant Notes:
✦ Percentage-wise, Japanese come to Christ outside of Japan far more often than they do in their homeland.
✦ Almost 60% of the Japanese in Metro New York are women.

The attraction of New York to immigrant groups is almost exclusively based on its being "the Financial Capital of the World," with its universities offering immigrants ample opportunity to connect with successful businesses. Japanese New Yorkers are no exception, as their constituents include a large number of businessmen and their families, as well as a large number of students. However, unique among immigrant groups in the city, many Japanese were lured to Manhattan by arts, culture, and freedom of expression. Nearly sixty percent of the Japanese in New York are women. While some of this may be attributed to frequent marriages between Japanese women and American men, the disparity also reflects the attraction of the city to young Japanese women in search of social and creative freedom. Coming from a male-dominated society with rigid social, educational, and occupational expectations, the journey to New York for many Japanese women, as well as men, is a search for identity.[1] According to the Consulate General of Japan and the 2008 American Community Survey, the Japanese population numbers around 50 thousand in Metro New York.

When Did They Come To New York?

Although the Japanese have had a large presence in Hawaii and California for a long time, their presence in Metro New York is a recent phenomenon. A steady

immigration of Japanese businessmen and students to New York started with increased visa allotments in 1965. This immigration continues, yet Japanese businessmen and their families often stay no more than five years before returning to Japan. With Japan having the second-largest gross domestic product in the world, America does not provide the economic incentive for immigration for Japanese that it offers to other groups. Nevertheless, after three decades of booming economic growth, Japan's economy slowed down tremendously in the 1990s, causing more interest in New York among businessmen. The 2000 Census revealed that close to seventy percent of the Japanese in Metro New York arrived in the previous decade. Adventurous, creative, and free-spirited Japanese young people started arriving during this time as well, many of whom felt stifled by the traditions of Japan. Their immigration continues until this day.

Where Do They Live?

Once a welcoming locale for "huddled masses," Manhattan's East Village is now host to New York City's largest "Little Tokyo," located at St. Marks Place and 9th Street between 1st and 2nd Avenues. While nearly thirty percent of the Japanese in Metro New York live in Manhattan, there are also large concentrations in the Fort Lee area of New Jersey and in Westchester County.

What Do They Believe?

Japanese have long treated religion like a buffet. For instance, it is not uncommon in Japan for a person to have a Shinto wedding, celebrate Christmas, and observe a Buddhist funeral. Over the past few decades, though, materialism has become the pervading ethos of society, causing the influence of organized religion to diminish tremendously.[2] Whereas many descendants of Japanese immigrants on the West Coast have become Christians, a majority of the Japanese in Metro New York are nonreligious, even though almost all would claim to

be Buddhist. For most, religious rituals are only performed at major life events, such as weddings and funerals.

What Are Their Lives Like?

After thousands of Japanese-Americans were put into internment camps in the 1940s, they made a conscious effort to assimilate into mainstream American culture. In one sense, Japanese New Yorkers today act the same. They want to know and befriend Americans, experiencing and learning American culture. On the other hand, most Japanese have a profound Japanese identity and simply desire to experience the arts, universities, or business world in New York before moving back home.

How Can I Pray?

✳ Pray that Japanese will see the futility of materialism and will find meaning in Christ.

✳ Many young people from Japan have come to America in search of their identity and often struggle with depression. Pray that God will reveal to them in Christ what they really need.

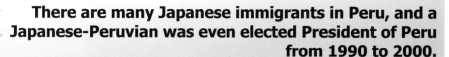

There are many Japanese immigrants in Peru, and a Japanese-Peruvian was even elected President of Peru from 1990 to 2000.

151

Peruvians

QUICK FACTS:

Place of Origin:
Peru (primarily Lima)

Location in Metro New York:
New Jersey (Paterson, Lake View, Riverside, Passaic, Newark, Union City, Orange); Queens (Corona, Jackson Heights, Elmhurst); Westchester (White Plains); Nassau (Glen Cove)

Population in Metro New York:
200,000 (Community Estimate); 135,323 (ACS 2008 Specific Origin Peru); 101,293 (ACS 2008 Born in Peru)

Population in New York City:
55,000 (Community Estimate); 40,382 (ACS 2008 Specific Origin Peru); 33,072 (ACS 2008 Born in Peru)

Primary Religion:
Christianity (Roman Catholic)

Status of Christian Witness:
Greater than or equal to 5% evangelical. Less than 10% evangelical.

Primary Language:
Spanish

Registry of Peoples Code:
107993

Significant Note:
❊ Metro New York, and particularly the Paterson area of New Jersey, has the largest concentration of Peruvians outside of Peru.

"**H**ave you ever eaten Peruvian food?" a Peruvian man living in Paterson, New Jersey, asked, "It is the best in the world. The best in the world! The only food that can compare is French. I am telling you, they say that French cuisine is good, but Peruvian is the best in the world!" How many casual diners would list Peruvian food among their top ten favorite ethnic cuisines? Nevertheless, the seemingly hyperbolic claims of this Peruvian man are not unfounded. For the gastronomically informed, Peruvian food is indeed considered in the top tier of its class.[1] With influences from the Inca, Spanish, African slaves, and immigrants from China, Japan, and Italy, Peruvians mastered the art of fusion cuisine long before it was featured in haute cuisine restaurants across Metro New York. Today, Peruvian food is being recognized even more around the city, as restaurants are frequently opened by constituents of the most concentrated Peruvian population outside of Peru. Community estimates place their population around 200 thousand in Metro New York, while the 2008 American Community Survey estimates around 135 thousand in the same area.[2]

When Did They Come To New York?

At the turn of the twentieth century, Paterson, New Jersey had established itself as America's "Silk City," and had expanded its textile production to Lima, Peru. This relationship fostered a slow immigration of working-class Peruvian families to Paterson, creating a beachhead for later Peruvian immigrants. Immigration increased gradually throughout the century until the 1970s when economic conditions and political turmoil in Peru sparked a large influx of the Peruvian middle class, including many doctors and engineers.[3] Conditions worsened in the 1980s, as inflation rose to over two thousand percent and political violence was rampant. A 1989 *TIME Magazine* article claimed, "On an average day in Peru, six people die by political violence. One day it is a government agent organizing peasant cooperatives. One day it is a ruling-party mayor. One day it is a government-aligned journalist. Most days it is peasants who get in the way."[4] With the country in disarray, the working class immigrated in large numbers to places like Paterson and Jackson Heights, doubling Metro New York's Peruvian population in the 1980s and then again

in the decade that followed. With the Peruvian economy becoming more stabilized in the twenty-first century, immigration has slowed, yet Metro New York's Peruvian population has continued to increase.

Where Do They Live?

The Peruvians are one of the few ethnic groups in Metro New York that have never had their main immigration area located in New York City. Instead, this honor belongs to Paterson, New Jersey, an industrial city that Peruvians have been immigrating to for over a century. The site of the Peruvian Annual Parade is not Madison Avenue; it is Main Street in Paterson. The location of the Consulate General of Peru is not the Upper East Side; it is Paterson, and if one wants to journey to "Little Lima," it can only be

found on western Market Street in downtown Paterson. While New Jersey is host to over fifty percent of the Peruvians in Metro New York, New York City has

a smaller concentration of Peruvians along Roosevelt Avenue in Jackson Heights, Queens.

What Do They Believe?

Over ninety percent of Peruvians claim to be Catholic, and Catholic churches play a central role in helping Peruvian immigrants adjust to America by providing social and religious services, a place to socialize with other Peruvians, and a link to their lives back home. One such connection is a large street celebration held every October that celebrates the symbolic Señor de los Milagros (Lord of Miracles), a mural of Jesus that survived a devastating earthquake in Peru.

What Are Their Lives Like?

Like their predecessors nearly a century before, many Peruvian men and women find work in the textile industry or other factories in the Paterson area. However, as Peruvians have become more established, they are opening more restaurants, travel agencies, and retail stores.

How Can I Pray?

✳ There is a large movement in America of Hispanics adopting the evangelical faith. Pray that Peruvians in Metro New York would do the same.
✳ Pray that the Lord of Miracles celebration would glorify Jesus Himself and not the mural.

Only a small percentage of Peruvians in Metro New York are Quichuan, an indigenous ethnic group, but around one-half of the Guatemalans in Metro New York are indigenous peoples.

Guatemalans

QUICK FACTS:

Place of Origin:
Guatemala

Significant Subgroups:
Amerindian (mainly Quiche, Mam, Cakchiquel 50%); Mestizo (50%)

Location in Metro New York:
Queens (Jamaica, Jackson Heights, Flushing, Far Rockaway); New Jersey (Fairview, Palisades Park, Morristown, Trenton); Rockland (Spring Valley); Westchester (Mt. Kisco, Port Chester, Yonkers); Connecticut (Stamford)

Population in Metro New York:
119,063 (ACS 2008 Specific Origin Guatemala); 91,202 (ACS 2008 Born in Guatemala)

Population in New York City:
32,095 (ACS 2008 Specific Origin Guatemala); 23,334 (ACS 2008 Born in Guatemala)

Primary Religions:
Christianity (Roman Catholic, evangelical)

Status of Christian Witness:
Greater than or equal to 10% evangelical.

Primary Languages:
Spanish, indigenous languages (e.g., K'iche', Mam, Kaqchikel)

Registry of Peoples Codes:
103510, 109736, 108669, 102244

Significant Notes:
❊ Guatemala's Fraternidad Cristiana de Guatemala in Ciudad San Cristóbal (also known as MegaFrater) is one of the largest evangelical churches in Latin America.
❊ Hundreds of thousands of pilgrims annually visit the shrine of the "Black Christ" at the Basilica of Esquipulas in Guatemala. The pilgrimages started shortly after the statue of Christ on the cross arrived in Esquipulas over 400 years ago, as reports of healings attributed to the "Black Christ" increased.

"**S**ince Guatemalans are so spread out, we have to go to them," explained Rosa Maria, the Guatemalan Consul General. "Eight years ago we started the Consaldo Movil [Mobile Consulate]," she continued. "One weekend a month, we travel to a Guatemalan community, offering our services in churches and schools. We recently saw one thousand people in one day!" While official data suggests Metro New York's Guatemalan population is approximately 120 thousand (ACS 2008), community leaders believe it could be up to three times higher, as many are undocumented. Guatemala has a very diverse population, with the largest concentration of indigenous people in Central America—mostly descended from the Mayan Indians.[1] There are twenty-one ethnic subgroups among the Mayan population, each with its own language.[2] Metro New York has become home to many of these groups, collectively called Amerindians, as well as mestizo Guatemalans, who have mixed Amerindian and Spanish ancestry. The Amerindians suffered profoundly during Guatemala's long civil war (1960-1996), which pitted the government and wealthy landowners against middle-class activists and rural Amerindians. Over four hundred massacres of Amerindians were documented, with tens of thousands murdered and hundreds of villages destroyed.[3] As a result of the war, Guatemala is extremely poor, with over 50 percent of the total population and seventy-five percent of Amerindians living in poverty.[4]

When Did They Come To New York?

Throughout the first part of the war during the 1960s and '70s, small numbers of middle-class activists, targeted by the Guatemalan government, began arriving. As attacks against Amerindians intensified during the 1980s, thousands fled to the US although

they were never granted refugee status. Guatemalans have arrived steadily since the 1980s, mostly to escape the civil war and chronic poverty.

Where Do They Live?

While Guatemalans are spread across Metro New York, they have settled in distinct ethnic communities based on where they came from in Guatemala. "New Jersey's Guatemalans are mainly Amerindians from rural areas in the north and west of Guatemala. Brooklyn, Queens, Connecticut, and Westchester have more mestizo people from the cities and suburbs in the south and east," explained Rosita, president of a Guatemalan cultural association. Mestizo Guatemalans in Brooklyn and Queens typically blend in with other Central Americans while the Amerindians in New Jersey, many of whom do not speak Spanish, are more isolated.

What Do They Believe?

Like many of its Central American neighbors, Guatemala is a historically Catholic country that has experienced a dramatic explosion of evangelical Christianity in the last twenty years. Guatemala's evangelical population is now around forty percent.[5] Community leaders suggest

sixty to seventy percent of Guatemalans in Metro New York are Catholics and thirty to forty percent are evangelicals,

with mestizo and Amerindian evangelical percentages roughly the same. Despite the growing number of evangelicals, Catholic roots run very deep. Every year, Guatemalans at Presentation of the Blessed Virgin Mary Church in Jamaica, Queens, hold a procession venerating a replica of the "Black Christ of Esquipulas," a four-hundred-year-old statue of Jesus, believed to have healing powers. The Archbishop of Guatemala City has come to officiate, and St. Patrick's Cathedral has hosted masses honoring the Black Christ.

What Are Their Lives Like?

"Many Guatemalans would like to return home, but so much has changed, it would be too hard. It's really just a dream," said Rosita. Life is challenging for Guatemalans in Metro New York. Many are separated from family, and they work long hours at low-wage jobs. Most have limited education and English skills, making it difficult to find better-paying work. The majority of Amerindians are non-literate and twenty-seven percent speak no Spanish, although some say this helps them learn English more quickly than those who can fall back on Spanish![6] The goal for most is to earn as much as they can to send back home. In 2008, $4 billion in remittances was sent by Guatemalans in the US.[7]

How Can I Pray?

✳ As evidenced by the Guatemalan devotion to the "Black Christ," Christianity for many is simply an expedient measure to obtain personal blessing. Pray that Guatemalans would realize that true blessing in Christ comes not from the fulfillment of self-centered desires but God's.

The Garifuna, an ethnic group of mixed ancestry, primarily come from Honduras, Guatemala, and Belize.

Garifuna

QUICK FACTS:

Place of Origin:
Coastline of Honduras, Belize, Guatemala

Significant Subgroups:
Garifuna from Honduras (75%); Belize (15%); Guatemala (10%)

Location in Metro New York:
Harlem, South Bronx, Brooklyn (East New York)

Population in Metro New York:
100,000 (Community Estimate)

Primary Religion:
Christianity (Roman Catholic)

Secondary Religions:
Traditional Afro-Indian religious beliefs (often syncretized with Catholicism); Christianity (evangelical)

Status of Christian Witness:
Those from Honduras: Greater than or equal to 10% evangelical. Those from Belize and Guatemala: Less than 2% evangelical. Some evangelical resources available, but no active church planting within the past two years.[4]

Primary Languages:
Garifuna, Spanish, English

Registry of Peoples Code:
101510

Significant Notes:
❋ Although "Garifuna" has become commonly used as both singular and plural, the word "Garinagu" is plural for Garifuna.
❋ One of the most devastating fires in New York City in the 20th century happened in 1990 at the Happy Land social club in the Bronx. Out of the 87 people killed, over 70% were Garifuna.
❋ The Garifuna are renowned for their punta rock music, which is an adaptation of punta music used in sacred rituals.
❋ Garifuna from Honduras and Guatemala speak Spanish, while those from Belize speak English.

With dark-skinned men wearing "Garifuna Celebrity" T-shirts, a variety of hand drums providing the event's soundtrack instead of brass instruments, and Garifuna yellow, black, and white flags largely replacing the blue and white of Honduras, Bronx's annual Honduran and Central American Parade is somewhat of a misnomer—considering the celebration is almost exclusively a display of Garifuna presence. As a reminder of her heritage, a Honduran woman marching in the parade carries a miniature ship with the word "Garifuna" on its side. In 1635, two Spanish ships carrying West African slaves shipwrecked off the coast of St. Vincent. The Africans escaped, swam to shore, and were sheltered by the island's inhabitants, a mixed race of Arawaks and Caribs known as Island Caribs. Over the coming years, the Africans intermarried with the Island Caribs, and the blend of ancestry, language, religion, and traditions created a new people called the Garifuna.[1] The Garifuna pride themselves on having never been enslaved although they were forced off St. Vincent by the British in 1797. At first settling in Roatan off the coast of Honduras, the Garifuna soon ventured to the coastland of Honduras, Belize, Guatemala, and Nicaragua, where they remain today as minorities in their respective countries. In Metro New York, however, a majority of the Hondurans are Garifuna, and out of all of the Garifuna in the city, roughly seventy-five percent

are from Honduras, fifteen percent from Belize, and ten percent from Guatemala.[2] Most Garifuna community leaders estimate their population to number over 100 thousand in Metro New York.[3]

When Did They Come To New York?

Due to a crippled banana industry and America's need for sailors during World War II, many Garifuna men signed up as merchant marines, taking them to great port cities such as New York City. Allowing their unemployed friends on board as stowaways, adventurous Garifuna clandestinely made their way to live and work in New York. After Hurricane Hattie wreaked destruction on the coastline of Central America in 1961, America opened its doors to refugees, and a great number of Garifuna joined and strengthened their community in New York City. After the 1960s, migration has largely consisted of Garifuna reuniting with families or overstaying visas.

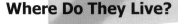

Where Do They Live?

Although Garifuna move in and out of the African-American and Hispanic-Caribbean populations in Harlem and the South Bronx, they have established their own cultural spaces in the neighborhoods with their own restaurants, community centers, dance clubs, and even parks, such as Trujillano Park on Southern Boulevard in the Bronx, which is actually named after a town in Honduras.

What Do They Believe?

While the majority of Garifuna are Roman Catholic, traditional Afro-Indian beliefs remain a strong part of Garifuna religious life. The weeklong Dugu (Feasting of the Dead) is the most important of three ancestral rites and involves a great amount of food, beverage, music, chanting, and dancing. Although it is a joyous time for the Garifuna who join together in celebration, its purpose is to appease an ancestral spirit, who is communicated with through a shaman, and to gain guidance for the present and future. Sometimes even a Catholic Mass will be included in the proceedings. In the Bronx, a traditional Garifuna Mass is celebrated on the third Sunday of each month at St. Anthony of Padua Catholic Church. There is also a strong evangelical community, with over ten Garifuna churches currently in New York City.

What Are Their Lives Like?

"Am I Hispanic, or am I African-American? Or neither one?" These are the questions that often go through the minds of younger Garifuna in New York. As a result, much effort has been made by the Garifuna community to promote their history, culture, language, and identity. Although the Garifuna work a variety of jobs in New York, many are educators or involved in health care.

How Can I Pray?

✴ The Honduran Garifuna have responded to the gospel much more than the Belizean and Guatemalan. Pray that God would reveal His power over evil spirits and call Garifuna to Himself.

The Garifuna trace their ancestry back to two West African slave ships that crashed in the Caribbean. Ghana was one of the major areas from which slaves were shipped.

157

Ghanaians

QUICK FACTS:

Place of Origin:
Ghana (primarily Kumasi and Accra)

Significant Subgroups:
Akan (50%); Ga, Ewe, Hausa (the next three largest)

Location in Metro New York:
Bronx (Morris Heights, Highbridge, Tracey Towers, Parkchester); Queens (Lefrak City); New Jersey (Newark); Brooklyn (Flatbush)

Population in Metro New York:
100,000 (Community Estimate); 33,750 (ACS 2008 Total Ancestry Reported); 35,227 (ACS 2008 Born in Ghana)[5]

Population in New York City:
24,015 (ACS 2008 Total Ancestry Reported); 23,723 (ACS 2008 Born in Ghana)

Primary Religion:
Christianity (evangelical)

Secondary Religion:
Islam

Status of Christian Witness:
Greater than or equal to 10% evangelical.

Primary Languages:
Twi, Ewe, Ga, Hausa

Secondary Language:
English

Registry of Peoples Codes:
100179, 103095, 102974

Significant Notes:
❉ More Ghanaians live in Metro New York than any other metropolitan area in the United States. The only other metro area in the US with a comparable number of Ghanaians is around Washington, DC, which, according to the 2008 American Community Survey, has 19,199 people born in Ghana.

❉ According to the CIA *World Factbook*, around 70% of Ghanaians in Ghana claim to be Christian. This number is most likely larger in Metro New York, as most emigration took place from highly Christianized south Ghana.

As "the royal party" paraded into the rented gathering place in the Bronx, the boisterous chatter of pastors and leaders of Ghanaian churches from across the country died down. The occasion was an annual conference of Ghanaian churches in America, and due to the high percentage of Christian Ghanaians, such an event served as an important cultural marker for the people. Perhaps as much as any immigrant group in New York, the Ghanaians retain their traditional ways in America, and the arrival at the conference of the Asantefuohene (the chief of the Ashanti tribe in New York) certainly put these traditions on display. After the first members of the procession passed through, a man carrying an oversized, pink umbrella adorned with orange fringe signaled the arrival of the Asantefuohene, who wore a loose-fitting *kente* cloth robe draped over one shoulder with the other left bare.[1] Unlike Ghana, where the chiefs and kings primarily come from traditional royal families, the chiefs in America are elected every few years, often not from royal lineage. Nevertheless, they are treated as royalty and certainly have responsibilities that mimic the roles of chiefs and kings in Ghana. The elected Asantefuohene, apart from their day jobs in New York, are expected to help preserve Ashanti language and culture among the second generation, as well as settle disputes between adults. Whether it be divorce or criminal cases, many Ashanti are encouraged to settle their disputes with the Asantefuohene instead of placing themselves at the mercy of the American judicial system.[2] The Ashanti, who are part of the larger Akan ethnic grouping, are the largest Ghanaian ethnic group in Metro New York, and the Akan make up one-half of the over 35 thousand Ghana-born in Metro New York (ACS 2008). However, Ghanaians are incredibly diverse, and there are up to one hundred Ghanaian ethnic groups represented in the city, with the Ga, Ewe, and Hausa being the next largest.

When Did They Come To New York?

Declaring independence from Britain in 1957, Ghana subsequently went through several military governments and periodic economic hardships. As schooling was a focus of Ghana's early development, many educated Ghanaian professionals and merchants immigrated to New York in the 1960s and '70s.[3] The Ghanaian population has increased exponentially since the 1980s up until the present time by taking advantage of reunification, diversity, and tourist visas.

Where Do They Live?

The concentration of Ghanaian restaurants, businesses, and churches in the West Bronx provides evidence that Ghanaians have developed a small enclave in the Morris Heights and Highbridge neighborhoods. Ghanaians also

have a sizeable population in large New York City housing complexes such as Tracey Towers and Parkchester, as well as in Newark, New Jersey.

What Do They Believe?

An enthusiastic Ghanaian pastor claimed, "It is easy to start churches among Ghanaians. Almost everyone is already Christian. You just have a contact in a new place and you start a meeting." There is no lack of Ghanaian churches in Metro New York, and denominations from Ghana are regularly starting branches in New York City. While charismatic and Pentecostal churches are the majority, the Seventh-day Adventists also have a large representation among the community. About sixteen percent of Ghanaians in Ghana are Muslim, but this number is somewhat lower in New York, as most emigration has occurred from the "Christian" south.[4]

What Are Their Lives Like?

From the illegal service worker to the former Secretary General of the UN, Kofi Annan, Ghanaians have found work in a variety of occupations. Most envision returning home to live in a house built with New York money. Ghanaians mainly organize and socialize along ethnic lines.

How Can I Pray?

✴ Although an overwhelming number of Ghanaians regularly attend church and claim to be Christian, there is little outreach done among other ethnic groups, such as the Muslim Hausa, and ethnocentricity is the source of much conflict. Pray for humility, unity, and a sense of mission.

Ghanaians and Nigerians are known for their vibrant Christian faith and for starting many churches throughout Metro New York.

Nigerians

QUICK FACTS:

Place of Origin:
Nigeria (primarily the south)

Significant Subgroups:
Yoruba (small majority); Igbo (large minority); Hausa (very small minority)

Location in Metro New York:
Staten Island (Concord, Fox Hills); New Jersey (Unionburg, Newark Heights, Irvington); Brooklyn (East New York)

Population in Metro New York:
36,953 (ACS 2008 Born in Nigeria)

Population in New York City:
22,865 (ACS 2008 Born in Nigeria)

Primary Religion:
Christianity (Roman Catholic, evangelical)

Secondary Religions:
Islam, traditional religions

Status of Christian Witness:
Greater than or equal to 10% evangelical.

Primary Languages:
Yoruba, Igbo, Hausa, other Nigerian tribal languages

Secondary Languages:
English, Nigerian Pidgin English

Registry of Peoples Codes:
111095, 103963, 103733

Significant Notes:
- One out of every seven Africans in Africa is Nigerian, and close to one out of every five sub-Saharan Africans in Africa is Nigerian.
- Most Nigerians will move back to Nigeria when they are too old to work.

Growing up in America, some kids dream of being a prince or princess. Growing up in Nigeria, some princes dream of being American. Such was the case with Ali, a Nigerian prince who was next in line to be king.[1] When his father died, Ali refused the crown, preferring to raise his family in New York where he could receive more education and see the world. On the whole, Nigerians in New York have pedigrees similar to Ali's, with an overwhelming number coming from the middle and upper class. Despite being born with status, over 37 thousand Nigerians (ACS 2008) have left their country and currently reside in Metro New York. Amazingly, living in New York—at least for a few—is better than being king. While Nigeria is made up of over 250 ethnic groups, the most populous groups (the Yoruba, Igbo, and Hausa) are those mainly represented in Metro New York. The Yoruba make up the majority of Nigerians in the city and are from the southwestern area of Nigeria, which includes the capital Lagos. The Igbo make up the majority of other Nigerians in Metro New York and hail from the southeastern part of the country. The Hausa are from the northern part of Nigeria. Due to their prominent political status, military positions, and relative success, they have not desired to immigrate to America as much as the other two groups.

When Did They Come To New York?

With the discovery of oil in the 1970s, Nigeria quickly became one of the wealthiest African countries. During this time, many students came to America for education. In the 1970s and '80s, Nigeria was even among the top six countries that sent students to America.[2] Following plummeting oil prices in the late 1970s and a stream of corrupt military rule that continued into the 1990s, many

bright students sought out the education, employment, and political security that America offered. With the end of military rule in 1999 and the Nigerian economy booming once again, the same Nigerian professionals that opted to stay in America are beginning to look at career options in their home country. Lured by a chance to help Nigeria—not to mention the possibility of benefits like housing, maids, vehicles, and drivers—living as "a king" in Nigeria is resonating with Nigerian Americans much more now than it did in previous decades.[3] Even if waiting until retirement is necessary, most Nigerians plan on moving back to their country.

Where Do They Live?

Most West Africans in Metro New York cluster together in the same neighborhoods with their compatriots. Nigerians, on the other hand, are much more spread out, as they prefer to buy homes wherever they get the best deal and can live most comfortably. Nevertheless, there are three main Nigerian clusters in the Metro area, including the Unionburg-Newark Heights area of New Jersey, East New York in Brooklyn, and Concord-Fox Hills in Staten Island.

What Do They Believe?

With a history of civil war and friction between the mainly Muslim north and mainly Christian south of Nigeria, one would think that religious and ethnic

tension would spill over into America. Instead, the common thread of being Nigerian keeps people from different groups closely connected. Over half of the Yoruba in the city identify themselves as Christian, and slightly less than half are Muslim. Almost all of the Igbo are Catholic Christians, and there are even a couple of weekly Igbo Masses in Queens. In direct contrast, almost all of the Hausa are Muslim.

What Are Their Lives Like?

Whether working as a cab driver even though one has a master's degree, or going to school all over again even though one is a doctor, Nigerians have been willing to persevere through difficult circumstances to obtain success in America. Most Nigerians carry on with the same line of work as they did back home. The Yoruba, for instance, strongly value education and often have jobs in the law, medical, or education industries. The Igbo are known for their entrepreneurial ability and often start their own African shops and restaurants throughout the city. The Hausa are heavily involved in the military and politics and make up a bulk of the Nigerian Consulate's employees.

How Can I Pray?

✳ Due to religious friction in their country, many Nigerian Christians are reluctant to share the gospel with their Muslim friends. Pray that they would lovingly and boldly share their faith.

✳ Pray that Nigerian churches would focus on the glory of God in all circumstances and not just in "health and wealth."

Many Nigerians and Liberians are concentrated together in Newark, New Jersey, as well as Staten Island.

Liberians

QUICK FACTS:

Place of Origin:
Liberia

Significant Subgroups:
Kpelle, Bassa, Mandingo, Vai, Kru, other tribal groups

Location in Metro New York:
Staten Island (Park Hill-Clifton, Stapleton, Concord); New Jersey (Newark)

Population in Metro New York:
35,000 (Community Estimate); 10,583 (ACS 2008 Born in Liberia)

Population in New York City:
4,873 (ACS 2008 Born in Liberia)

Primary Religion:
Christianity (evangelical, Roman Catholic, mainline Protestant)

Secondary Religions:
Islam (Sunni), traditional African religions

Status of Christian Witness:
Greater than or equal to 10% evangelical.

Primary Languages:
English, various tribal languages

Significant Notes:
✦ The US government offered Temporary Protected Status (TPS) to thousands of Liberians who escaped the civil war. Liberians who are under TPS cannot obtain permanent US residency (a green card) and are expected to return home once conditions improve. Unless they are granted permanent residency, enforced departure (i.e., deportation) could begin in March 2010.
✦ If a deportation edict is given, community leaders expect thousands of Liberians to remain in Metro New York illegally rather than return to Liberia.
✦ There are approximately 20 Liberian churches in Staten Island.

Imagine passing a young man on a New York City street who looks vaguely familiar. Suddenly, you have a terrifying flashback: His face appears among the gang of teenagers who dragged you from your bed, murdered your father before your eyes, and raped your mother and sisters. Many Liberians in Metro New York have experienced similar horrors. Atrocities abounded during Liberia's two civil wars (1989-2004), killing more than 250 thousand people.[1] Most notable was the conscription of child soldiers, forced to torture and kill in order to survive. Liberians find it very painful to talk about the war. Many feel such discussions are too risky, since perpetrators and victims live side by side, often worshipping at the same churches. Most want to forget the past and focus on Liberia's future. Today, an estimated 35 thousand Liberians live in the New York Metro area, including a large concentration of former child soldiers.[2] These traumatized young men typically deny their identity for fear of rejection and retaliation. Additionally, thousands of Liberians live under a cloud of uncertainty. When their Temporary Protected Status from the US government expires in March 2010, they may have to return to Liberia—leaving jobs and family behind—or risk remaining here illegally.[3]

When Did They Come To New York?

Despite its history as Africa's oldest republic—founded by freed American slaves in 1847—Liberia plunged into chaos in the 1980s. Over the next two decades, 1.5 million people were displaced.[4] Many remain in refugee camps in West Africa. Thousands resettled or sought asylum in the US. Before then, only a trickle of Liberians came to America. Almost all Liberians in the New York Metro area arrived during the two worst periods of conflict: 1989-1996 and 1999-2003.

Where Do They Live?

Metro New York is home to the largest concentration of Liberians outside of Africa, with the most populous communities in Staten Island and Newark, New Jersey. "Little Liberia" in Staten Island centers around the Park Hill Apartments, a group of twelve run-down high-rise apartment buildings primarily populated by Liberians. This former public housing project, which hosts makeshift African markets in the warmer weather, is a stark contrast to the surrounding suburban homes that mark the mostly white, middle-class enclave of Staten Island. Liberian businesses in Staten Island are most concentrated along Targee Street from the neighborhood of Clifton into the adjoining neighborhood of Stapleton.

What Do They Believe?

Liberia has strong historic ties to Christianity; its American-born founders established it as a Christian republic and actively sought to convert the indigenous tribes. While much of the coastal population became Christian, the interior tribes retained traditional African religions or Islam. In the New York Metro area, ethnic Mandingoes and Vais, who are Muslim, have a presence, but the vast majority of Liberians (ninety-five percent) are Christian.

Several Liberian churches and ministries are active in Staten Island and Newark, representing Baptist, Lutheran, Episcopalian, Methodist, Catholic, and various Pentecostal denominations.

What Are Their Lives Like?

Dealing with the past is difficult for all Liberians, who desperately seek healing and peace. While the primarily urban-professional Liberians who arrived during the first civil war successfully adjusted to life in the US, later arrivals have faced more challenges. Most had lived in refugee camps for years, where they experienced repeated violence, family breakdown, lack of education, and unemployment. The Park Hill neighborhood—home to most recent arrivals—is now plagued by drugs and gang violence, and families are often headed by single mothers or grandparents. Those with financial resources typically support family members in Liberia or refugee camps. In an effort to bring closure, the Liberian Truth and Reconciliation Commission is collecting war stories to document atrocities; however, many people do not want to relive the past. They want to move forward.

How Can I Pray?

✹ Most Liberians have experienced brutal violence, often at the hands of neighbors or friends. Pray for healing, forgiveness, and reconciliation and that Christians will lead the way in this process.

✹ Pray that former child soldiers come to live transformed lives through the power of the gospel.

Many Liberians and Burmese came to Metro New York due to the civil wars that have plagued their countries.

Burmese

QUICK FACTS:

Place of Origin:
Myanmar (formerly called Burma)

Significant Subgroups:
Burman (65%); Chin (10%); Rakhine (10%); Karen (5%); Mon (5%); Kachin (5%)

Location in Metro New York:
Queens (Jackson Heights, Sunnyside, Woodside, Elmhurst); Brooklyn (Homecrest, Sunset Park)

Population in Metro New York:
12,000 (Community Estimate)

Primary Religion:
Theravada Buddhism

Secondary Religion:
Christianity (evangelical)

Status of Christian Witness:
Greater than or equal to 10% evangelical.

Primary Language:
Burmese

Secondary Languages:
Chin, Karen, Mon, Jingpho/Kachin, Arakanese/Rakhine

Registry of Peoples Codes:
101776, 106013, 108886, 104372, 200170

Significant Notes:

❋ The military junta changed the country's name from Burma to Myanmar in 1989. Although the name change has sparked political reactions, "Burma" is essentially just a colloquial form of "Myanmar," with both referring to Burmans, the largest ethnic group in the country.

❋ A common sight at rallies for Burma are flags bearing the likeness of Burmese pro-democracy leader Aung San Suu Kyi, who has spent 11 of the last 20 years under house arrest.[6]

❋ Myanmar Baptist Church in Queens holds an ethnic "Fun Fair" every August, which receives a lot of publicity.

Noted author Salman Rushdie was among several prize-winning writers who stood alongside Burmese monks in September 2008, addressing a crowd of 650 New Yorkers gathered to mark the anniversary of the Saffron Revolution—an uprising in Myanmar (formerly known as Burma), named for the color of the monks' robes.[1] Since 1962, after a century of British colonial rule and wartime occupation by the Japanese, Myanmar has been controlled by oppressive socialist military regimes, which have impoverished the once-prosperous nation. In September 2007, distressed by the government's decision to burden its people with an astronomical hike in the price of fuel, Burmese monks began protesting with a simple act: Turning over their alms bowls, they denied military leaders the opportunity to give offerings and gain the blessing of Buddha. Soon after, the monks took to the streets, joined by thousands of Burmese citizens. The standoff lasted for nine days until the military opened fire, killing several people. Although Metro New York's Burmese community is not large—around 12 thousand people—it has well-organized associations and support from celebrities who keep Myanmar's struggle for democracy in the public eye.[2] Rallies and protests at the United Nations occur several times a year. Myanmar is one of the world's most ethnically diverse countries, with eight main groups and 130 subgroups. Metro New York's Burmese population consists of Burmans (the majority group), Rakhine, and Mon, who originate in Myanmar's lowlands, along with Karen, Chin, and Kachin from the hill areas.

When Did They Come To New York?

A few Burmese students, professors, and professionals came to Metro New York following the military takeover in 1962. However, the majority are refugees who have come since the late 1990s after spending many years in refugee camps in Thailand and Malaysia. Recent US policy changes led to a wave of arrivals in 2006 that is expected to continue for several years.

Where Do They Live?

As newcomers to Metro New York, Burmese have yet to form a distinct ethnic neighborhood. Rather, they are clustered in neighboring communities in Queens, including Jackson Heights, Sunnyside, Woodside, and Elmhurst, as well as Homecrest and Sunset Park in Brooklyn.[3] "Because of the high cost of living, many refugees who initially resettled in New York leave after a few months," explained Reverend Maw, a Burmese pastor in Queens. "They go to Burmese enclaves around the country like Rochester, New York; Indianapolis, Indiana; and Amarillo, Texas."

What Do They Believe?

"Buddhism is deeply rooted in the Burmese people," said Reverend Maw. In fact, Burmese pro-democracy leader Aung San Suu Kyi referred to Theravada Buddhism as "the single greatest factor affecting Burmese culture and civilization."[4] Theravada is the world's oldest surviving Buddhist sect and the main Buddhist sect in Southeast Asia. It emphasizes the individual's ability and responsibility to end the wearisome cycle of cravings that lead to suffering and disappointment. It is

believed that suffering can be eliminated through the adjustment of one's mind, which can be done through obtaining wisdom, living ethically, and concentrating on Buddha's Eightfold Path, leading to Awakening. The religious affiliations of Burmese typically fall along ethnic lines. For example, Burmans, Rakhine, and Mon are almost exclusively Buddhist. Karen are approximately seventy percent Christian and thirty percent Buddhist or animist. As a result of strong missionary outreach in the early 1900s, almost all Chin and most Kachin are evangelical Christians.[5] Currently, Queens has two evangelical churches led by Burmese pastors. There are also several Theravada Buddhist temples in Queens, in addition to the American Burma Buddhist Association meditation centers in Brooklyn and New Jersey.

What Are Their Lives Like?

"I tell new arrivals the faster they learn to speak English, the quicker they'll get a job, and life in the US will be a lot easier," said Pastor Matu, whose church is active in refugee ministry in Queens. After spending years as refugees, most Burmese coming to Metro New York have little education, English skills, and work experience. Because of this, they receive assistance from refugee resettlement agencies, churches, and Buddhist temples to find housing and jobs.

How Can I Pray?

✳ Burmese Buddhists seek to eliminate suffering through good deeds to reach Awakening. Pray that Christians will point them to a Savior whose suffering assures believers of eternal life.

Burma—now called Myanmar—and Vietnam are two Southeast Asian countries with a history of civil wars.

Vietnamese

QUICK FACTS:

Place of Origin:
Vietnam (predominantly South Vietnam)

Significant Subgroups:
Vietnamese (small majority); Chinese-Vietnamese (large minority, mainly Cantonese and Teochew)

Location in Metro New York:
Queens (Flushing, Elmhurst, Jackson Heights); Bronx (University Heights, Fordham); New Jersey (Jersey City); Brooklyn (Sunset Park); Manhattan (Chinatown)

Population in Metro New York:
55,622 (ACS 2008 Vietnamese who selected Asian alone as race); 31,841 (ACS 2008 Born in Vietnam)

Population in New York City:
21,768 (ACS 2008 Vietnamese who selected Asian alone as race); 14,027 (ACS 2008 Born in Vietnam)

Primary Religion:
Buddhism

Secondary Religions:
Christianity (Roman Catholic, evangelical); Taoism; Hoa Hao; Cao Dai

Status of Christian Witness:
Greater than or equal to 10% evangelical.

Primary Languages:
Vietnamese, Chinese (Teochew or Cantonese)

Registry of Peoples Codes:
105018, 103701

Significant Notes:
❃ Most Vietnamese Americans identify with the former South Vietnam flag that is yellow with three horizontal red stripes and view the official Vietnam flag used today as a sign of communism.
❃ Tet, the Vietnamese New Year, is the most celebrated event of the year.
❃ The largest Vietnamese-American community is in Orange County, California.

After the United States realized that a decisive victory over North Vietnam in the Vietnam War would not be imminent, they began withdrawing troops and turning the war over to the South Vietnamese. Although the number of their artillery, tanks, and armored cars was far greater than their communist enemies', the South Vietnamese were easily defeated in 1975, and a mass exodus from the country took place. As a result, Vietnamese refugees and immigrants have become the largest Southeast Asian group represented in the United States. Metro New York is usually not a prime destination for refugee settlements, as refugees are typically placed in areas with a surplus of cheap housing stock. However, circumstances in Jersey City and the Bronx were favorable to the Vietnamese, and the Vietnamese soon established a sizeable community in Metro New York, which now numbers over 55 thousand (ACS 2008). As they still bear the scars of years of fighting, bloodshed, displacement, and loss, the Vietnamese community has struggled to form a cohesive identity, with ethnic, class, and religious differences still in play. The most obvious distinction is that between the ethnic Vietnamese and ethnic Chinese from Vietnam. The latter make up a significant portion of the Vietnamese

community in Metro New York, and they have settled alongside the large Chinese population in the city.

When Did They Come To New York?

Before 1975, there were hardly any Vietnamese in Metro New York. However, as the war situation became bleak in 1975, a US company

began relocating their Vietnamese employees to Jersey City.[1] When Saigon fell later that year, the first large wave of Vietnamese emigration ensued, with some joining the new community in Jersey City. This group consisted largely of educated urbanites with American connections, and many were Catholic. The second wave of Vietnamese immigrants, known as "boat people," started coming in the late 1970s and consisted primarily of less-educated farmers, fishermen, and coastal people with access to escape boats. At the same time, Vietnam and China went to war, causing anti-Chinese sentiment to escalate. As a result, many of the emigrants during this time were of Chinese extraction, usually either Teochew or Cantonese, even though they spoke Vietnamese fluently. These "boat people" had to live in refugee camps in Southeast Asia before being resettled in the United States, and sometimes their stay in the camps lasted up to fifteen years. In response to international pressure, the Vietnamese government facilitated emigration from Vietnam under the Orderly Departure Program, which legally brought tens of thousands of Vietnamese refugees to America throughout the 1980s and '90s.[2] While emigration continues from Vietnam in a variety of ways, Metro New York's Vietnamese population is also increasing due to internal immigration from elsewhere in the US.

Where Do They Live?

Jersey City and the area around University Avenue and Fordham Road in the Bronx were the first Vietnamese settlements in Metro New York, but the largest concentration today is found in Queens, particularly in Flushing, Elmhurst, and Jackson Heights. Although scattered "Saigon" or "Vietnamese" store sightings abound, there is no obvious Vietnamese enclave in the city.

What Do They Believe?

Thao, an elderly Buddhist "boat person" in Jersey City, attends an evangelical Vietnamese church every Sunday. Church members claim, "He comes because he wants his kids to learn Vietnamese." While half of Vietnamese Americans are Buddhist, Buddhism has not engaged the social lives of Vietnamese Americans like Christianity. Around twenty percent of Vietnamese Americans are Roman Catholic and thirteen percent, evangelical Christian.[3]

What Are Their Lives Like?

Thirty percent of Vietnamese in New York City live in poverty, and twenty-seven percent are at risk for depression.[4] Many Vietnamese, however, seek to erase the memories of the past through hard work. While there are many professionals, Vietnamese have found job niches at smoothie carts and Vietnamese restaurants. In fact, Vietnamese sandwiches (*bánh mì*) are becoming mainstream city fare.

How Can I Pray?

✵ The Christian church has played a prominent role in caring for Vietnamese refugees. Pray that God's love through His people will draw many Vietnamese to become followers of Christ.

Vietnam was colonized by France from the mid-nineteenth century to the mid-twentieth century.

French

QUICK FACTS:

Place of Origin:
France

Location in Metro New York:
Manhattan (Upper East Side); Westchester County (Larchmont, Mamaroneck)

Population in Metro New York:
59,911 (ACS 2008 Single Ancestry); 31,834 (ACS 2008 Born in France)

Population in New York City:
23,462 (ACS 2008 Single Ancestry); 19,744 (ACS 2008 Born in France)

Primary Religion:
Nonreligious

Secondary Religion:
Christianity (Roman Catholic, Protestant)

Status of Christian Witness:
Greater than or equal to 2% evangelical. Less than 5% evangelical.

Primary Language:
French

Registry of Peoples Code:
103059

Significant Notes:

✷ The first French-American Charter School in New York City is scheduled to open in Harlem in September 2010. The school will incorporate French and American educational practices, and classes will be taught in French and English.

✷ The French Institute de l'Alliance Française is the premiere French cultural organization in New York City, offering performing arts, literary, and culinary events. It has the largest French-language school in the country, with over 6,000 students. Its library is the most comprehensive private French library in the US.

"**I** came here the hard way! It took a lot of time and money to get my green card," exclaimed Katia, a young French woman who has lived in New York City since 2000. "Most of the French living here don't go through what I did because they're expats [expatriates] working for French companies. Their companies do everything—even pay for housing and private school," she explained. "But I'm glad I came the way I did. I learned a lot and assimilated quickly." Of the nearly 60 thousand people with a single French ancestry living in Metro New York (ACS 2008), the majority are expats who only stay a couple of years for work assignments. However, some French have chosen to make New York their permanent home—like Olivier, a shoe designer who left France twenty years ago. "In Paris, I had two little shoe stores, and I barely made enough to stay open, so I decided to come to the US," he explained. "I go back to Paris for business, but I'm very happy to be living here." Although French-American relations have been frosty in recent decades, there is a long history of goodwill between the two nations. Without the support of the French, it is unlikely the American colonies could have defeated the British in the Revolutionary War. A century later in 1884, France gave New York its most distinctive landmark, the Statue of Liberty. To return the favor, in the twentieth century, the US came to the aid of France in both world wars, helping the French defeat their enemies and keep Western Europe free from totalitarianism.

When Did They Come To New York?

The French were among the earliest settlers in New York. French Protestants, called Huguenots, first came in the early seventeenth century. A large wave arrived in the latter part of the seventeenth century after the Edict of Nantes was revoked and persecution against Protestants increased. During the French Revolution (1789-1799), thousands of Catholics fled France, shifting New York's French community from largely Protestant to Catholic.[1] Since then, French immigration has been steady without a major surge. Today, the majority come for work, marriage, education, or just to experience life in Metro New York.

Where Do They Live?

The towns of Larchmont and Mamaroneck in Westchester County are very popular with French expats because of their proximity to the French-American School of New York, a bilingual and bicultural school with over six hundred students. Similarly, the Upper East Side near the French Consulate and Lycée Français, a very exclusive school, also has a significant French presence. Non-expat French are more likely to assimilate into other parts of Metro New York.

What Do They Believe?

"I think the majority of French people do not believe in anything," said Reverend Massey, Rector of the L'Eglise Française du Saint Esprit in Manhattan, a French-speaking Episcopal church that traces its roots back to the Huguenots. "Of course, most will tell you they are Catholic, but maybe twenty-five percent adhere to it," he continued. French Catholics are known

to attend the St. Vincent de Paul Roman Catholic Church in Manhattan's Chelsea neighborhood, along with St. Augustine's in Larchmont, both of which hold French-language Masses. Up to five percent of the French in Metro New York are Protestants—mostly descendents of the Huguenots. Despite their small numbers, they have a strong voice in the French community. In France, although some regard evangelical churches as cults, the evangelical influence is growing. Close to 500 thousand French call themselves evangelicals, up from 50 thousand in the 1940s, and the number of churches has increased from eight hundred in 1970 to 2,200 in 2009.[2]

What Are Their Lives Like?

"Homesickness and adjusting to new ways are big issues, particularly for women," said Katia. "Since most wives of expats do not work, they get bored and lonely," she explained. Marie-Thérèse, an officer at the French Consulate, said, "Health care is the number one thing I deal with. The French don't understand the American system. It scares them." Reverend Massey sees a hunger for community among the French in Metro New York. "Events are great ways to reach out—the French love celebrations!" he said. "On Bastille Day, six hundred people came to our church."

How Can I Pray?

✳ France was once a strong Christian nation, producing passionate leaders such as Protestant Reformer John Calvin. Pray for a rekindling of desire for true biblical faith among the French.

The largest French-speaking population in Metro New York is Haitian.

Haitians

QUICK FACTS:

Place of Origin:
Haiti

Location in Metro New York:
Brooklyn (Flatbush, Flatlands-Canarsie); Queens (Alden Manor, North Valley Stream, Bellaire, Hollis); Rockland (Hillcrest, Spring Valley); New Jersey (Irvington); Nassau (New Cassel)

Population in Metro New York:
500,000 (Community Estimate); 252,922 (ACS 2008 Total Ancestry Reported); 171,859 (ACS 2008 Born in Haiti)

Population in New York City:
122,389 (ACS 2008 Total Ancestry Reported); 87,058 (ACS 2008 Born in Haiti)

Primary Religion:
Christianity (Roman Catholic, Catholicism syncretized with voodoo)

Secondary Religions:
Christianity (evangelical, Roman Catholic)

Status of Christian Witness:
Greater than or equal to 10% evangelical.

Primary Language:
Haitian Creole

Secondary Languages:
French, English

Registry of Peoples Code:
103642

Significant Notes:
☀ Over 30% of the Haiti-born in the United States live in the New York Metro area.
☀ The largest Haitian religious activity in North America takes place every year on July 15th and 16th as thousands of Haitians make a pilgrimage to Our Lady of Mt. Carmel (East Harlem) in honor of the "Miracle Virgin." Voodoo practices are also mixed in with the Catholic festivities.
☀ The Southern Baptist Convention (SBC) is the largest evangelical denomination in the United States, and the largest SBC church in New York City is the French Speaking Baptist Church of Brooklyn, which is Haitian.

Said to be inspired by voodoo and armed with magical weapons, an army of slaves revolted, won their independence from France in 1804, and made Haiti the first black-ruled country in the Americas.[1] A couple of centuries later, voodoo still retains an influence over Haiti and the Haitian diaspora. Among the estimated 500 thousand Haitians in Metro New York, hundreds of *manbos* (voodoo priestesses) and *houngans* (voodoo priests) service a community that longs for stability, financial success, health, luck, and happiness—all of which have been hard to come by in their home country of Haiti, as well as in America.[2] Through voodoo, many Haitians seek the protection and prosperity they long for by marrying themselves to spirits called Iwa. In a typical voodoo marriage ceremony, a small crowd gathers in an inconspicuous place like a Brooklyn townhome basement and offer food that pleases the "special guest" of the party as they conjure the Iwa through a mix of incantations, Catholic songs, and prayers. When the atmosphere is properly "heated up," an Iwa comes and possesses the *manbo*, *houngan*, or another guest. The Iwa then "rides" the human, taking over the person's voice, words, and behavior. In describing her marriage to the Iwa Danbala, ethnographer Karen Brown explains that Danbala chose to possess the *manbo's* young male relative. The young man fell to the ground, wiggling and hissing like a snake. After biting into an offering of raw egg, Danbala slid a coiled serpent wedding ring onto Brown's finger and, shortly

after, the two signed a marriage contract. Brown would honor Danbala, and Danbala would protect and guide Brown.[3] Although a vibrant evangelical Christian community certainly exists, many Haitians, in a city characterized by loneliness, have trusted in Iwa to provide security and companionship.

When Did They Come To New York?

Of the forty-nine countries listed by the UN as "least developed," Haiti is the only one located in the Western Hemisphere.[4] The chaos of government and economics in Haiti throughout the latter half of the twentieth century has literally brought "boatloads" of Haitians into America. From the professionals and politicians who arrived during the autocratic rule of François "Papa Doc" Duvalier (1957-1971), to the poorer "boat people" who arrived in Florida and then New York during the reign of "Baby Doc" Duvalier (1971-1986), Haitians have desperately "rowed" their way to economic and political respite. The 2010 earthquake that devastated Haiti will only increase Haitian immigration in the days ahead, legally or illegally.

Where Do They Live?

Beginning with the first large wave of Haitian immigrants to New York, the Caribbean neighborhood of Flatbush, Brooklyn, has been the heart of the Haitian community. Irvington-Orange, New Jersey, and the area northeast of JFK Airport also have large concentrations of Haitians.

What Do They Believe?

Concerning Haitian religion, a common joke claims that one hundred percent of Haitians have a Catholic or Protestant identity, but one hundred percent serve the voodoo spirits. Even in the *CIA World Factbook* entry on Haiti, Haitians are listed as eighty percent Catholic and 16 percent Protestant, yet a special note claims that "half of the population practices voodoo."[5] In New York, however, evangelicals are on the rise. Boasting some of the most successful church planting ministries in Metro New York, Haitian evangelicals have started churches throughout the Metro area and have led many of their people to place hope for security and companionship in Jesus Christ.

What Are Their Lives Like?

No matter where their religious loyalties lie, religion plays a vital role in Haitian life. Many first-generation nurses, nannies, store owners, taxi drivers, and professionals worry that their children are losing Haitian culture and identifying themselves more as African-Americans.

How Can I Pray?

✹ Practitioners of voodoo correlate Catholic saints with voodoo Iwa in a syncretistic Catholicism that pervades Haitian life. Pray that, instead, Haitians would wed themselves to truth in Christ.

Haitians and Afro-Guyanese are two of many groups that participate in the West Indian Day Parade along Brooklyn's Eastern Parkway, which is annually attended by over one million people.

Afro-Guyanese

QUICK FACTS:

Place of Origin:
Guyana

Location in Metro New York:
Brooklyn (East Flatbush, Flatbush, Brownsville, Crown Heights); Queens (Far Rockaway)

Population in Metro New York:
180,852 (ACS 2008 Born in Guyana); 157,846 (ACS 2008 Total Ancestry Reported)

Population in New York City:
150,130 (ACS 2008 Born in Guyana); 130,097 (ACS 2008 Total Ancestry Reported)

Primary Religion:
Christianity (evangelical)

Status of Christian Witness:
Greater than or equal to 10% evangelical.

Primary Languages:
Guyanese Creole, English

Registry of Peoples Code:
103602

Significant Notes:

⁂ 74% of people who report Guyanese ancestry in the US live in Metro New York (ACS 2008).

⁂ 83% of Guyanese in Metro New York live in New York City.

⁂ New York City has the 2nd-largest Guyanese population in the world and is not far behind the largest, which is Georgetown, Guyana's capital.

⁂ Guyana is larger in size than all of the English-speaking Caribbean islands put together.

⁂ Guyana entered the international spotlight in 1978 when over 900 Americans associated with the Peoples Temple cult, led by Jim Jones, committed mass suicide at their compound in the country.

In 1492, Christopher Columbus set sail to discover a westward route to "India," which would currently be identified as Asia. Upon the discovery of what is now the Bahamas, Columbus believed that he had reached the islands of the Indies. Instead, he had discovered a "New World," and this discovery launched a centuries-long battle of conquest and colonization by Western powers. Even though Columbus falsely labeled his discovery, the Caribbean became popularly known as the West Indies, and the original inhabitants of the new world as Indians—names that have remained until today. Whereas Guyana is located in South America on the northern coast, its people and culture are closely related to that of the English-speaking Caribbean islands. The Dutch were the first to colonize Guyana, but Britain gained firm control in 1814. After African slaves were granted freedom in 1834, the British recruited East Indians to work as indentured servants on their plantations. Instead of returning to India after a few years work, many stayed, and Guyana's population now has more people of East Indian descent than African (p. 74). In Metro New York, over 180 thousand people were born in Guyana (ACS 2008), and forty-three percent of these identify themselves as "black or African-American" (Census 2000). Afro-Guyanese are usually equally conversant in English and Guyanese Creole.

When Did They Come To New York?

Afro-Guyanese migrated to Metro New York throughout the twentieth century, but the 1950s and '60s saw the first large waves. Responding to a labor shortage among health care workers and maids and nannies in New York, Afro-Guyanese women were often the first to arrive. Once they were established, they made arrangements for their families to join them. When Guyana transitioned to a socialist government in the 1970s, unemployment and inflation skyrocketed, prompting the largest wave of Afro-Guyanese migration, which peaked in the 1980s.[1] Immigration has lessened since but still remains steady. Today, the Guyanese population in Metro New York is about one-quarter the size of its population in Guyana, and New York City's Guyanese population is only slightly less than Georgetown's, the capital and largest city in Guyana.[2]

Where Do They Live?

While Indo-Guyanese have established an enclave in Richmond Hill, Queens, the Afro-Guyanese prefer to settle in the neighborhoods east of Prospect Park in Brooklyn among other Caribbean people of African descent.

What Do They Believe?

"Oh, everyone is Christian," Grace claimed, discussing the Afro-Guyanese after a lively worship service in East Flatbush, Brooklyn. "A lot of people are Pentecostal, Anglican, Lutheran, Methodist, and Catholic. I haven't lived in Guyana in many years, but if things are the same, I would guess that around half the people that went to church in Guyana do here." When the Guyanese population exploded in the 1970s, they brought their faith with them, and many started independent churches throughout the city. Churches of a Pentecostal variety are among the most prevalent, and Lutherans are very active, even having a well-organized local ministry called MAG (Ministry Among Guyanese). Around ten to fifteen percent of the Afro-Guyanese have an affiliation with the Catholic Church, while almost all the rest have at least a nominal Protestant identity.

What Are Their Lives Like?

Discussing the customs of the Afro-Guyanese, Grace perked up when describing the *kwe-kwe*, a unique Guyanese celebration that takes place the night before a wedding. "All the family on both sides are there and there is plenty of food and drink," she explains. "It lasts late in the night, and they play games. It is like a bachelor and bachelorette party put together!" While these celebrations offer an occasional respite, most Afro-Guyanese spend long hours at work as nurses, nannies, teachers, security guards, shop owners, and construction workers. They usually marry other Guyanese or English-speaking Caribbeans.

How Can I Pray?

✳ Afro-Guyanese Christians are very active in their communities, and their churches are active in promoting social justice and meeting the needs of the poor. Pray that God would use these Christians to spread the "abundant life" in Christ throughout Brooklyn and the rest of the Metro area.

In 1991, after an Afro-Guyanese boy was killed by a Lubavitch Jew in a car accident, riots ensued for three days in Crown Heights, Brooklyn.

Lubavitch Jews

QUICK FACTS:

Place of Origin:
Russia (Lyubavichi)

Location in Metro New York:
Brooklyn (Crown Heights); New Jersey (Morristown)

Population in Metro New York:
15,000-20,000 (Community Estimate)

Primary Religion:
Judaism (Chabad-Lubavitch)

Status of Christian Witness:
Less than 2% evangelical. Some evangelical resources available, but no active church planting within the past two years.

Primary Language:
Yiddish

Secondary Language:
English

Significant Notes:

☀ The official Chabad-Lubavitch website is fascinating! See http://www.chabad.org.

☀ Rebbe Menachem Schneerson, the seventh Grand Rebbe, had no heirs and left no instructions regarding his successor, which fueled the belief that he was the Messiah. More than 15 years after his death, Chabad-Lubavitch has yet to name an eighth Grand Rebbe.

☀ *Shlichim* (Lubavitcher emissaries) are often the only Hasidic or Orthodox Jews in the communities where they live, yet they continue to maintain their distinct dress and traditions. They must be self-supporting after one year.

☀ Operating the Chabad empire costs approximately $800 million a year.[6]

The young man in the black fedora hat calls out to people on a crowded Manhattan street, "Excuse me, are you Jewish?" He is standing next to an imposing RV emblazoned with the phrases "Moshiach is Coming Now!" and "Do a Mitzvah." Known as a mitzvah tank, the vehicle is a signature feature of the Lubavitch movement, a Hasidic Jewish group headquartered in Crown Heights, Brooklyn. Since 1974, the tanks have been parked on the streets of Metro New York while their occupants, typically young Lubavitcher men, seek to engage any Jewish person in conversation. Their goal is to get every Jew to perform a mitzvah—one of the 613 commandments found in the Torah—and they have a supply of mitzvah materials and instructions at the ready. Driving their zeal is the Lubavitch belief that the arrival of Moshiach (the Messiah) can be hastened if all Jews return to God and follow His ways. Most mitzvah tanks are adorned with a picture of the late Rebbe Menachem Schneerson, beloved seventh Grand Rebbe of Lubavitch, who led the movement from 1950 until his death in 1994. Breaking with the other traditionally insular Hasidic groups, Rebbe Schneerson crafted an aggressive, outward-facing mission for the Lubavitch: to bring non-observant Jews back into the Orthodox fold. Also unlike other Hasids, the rebbe had no problem using the tools of the modern world, including television and the Internet, to spread the message. The Lubavitch movement, also called "Chabad" (an acronym of the Hebrew words for wisdom, comprehension, and knowledge) has the second-largest following among Hasidic groups in Metro New York, numbering approximately 15 thousand to 20 thousand.[1] Chabad has become a huge global phenomenon, with over 3,300 institutions. Crown Heights is its mecca, drawing thousands from around the world.

When Did They Come To New York?

In 1940 the sixth Lubavitcher rebbe came to Crown Heights after a US-orchestrated rescue from Nazi-occupied Poland, where the Lubavitchers had fled to escape the Soviets in the 1920s. In 1941, his son-in-law Rebbe Menachem Schneerson arrived from France. Thousands of Lubavitch survivors joined them after the war. In the late 1960s, due to rising crime, much of the white population was leaving Crown Heights. Rebbe Schneerson decided the Lubavitch would stay; they would not abandon their synagogues and fellow Jews who could not afford to move.[2]

Where Do They Live?

An elegant brick mansion at 770 Eastern Parkway in Brooklyn houses the Chabad-Lubavitch world headquarters. Even though the Lubavitchers are concentrated in Crown Heights, there are over 220 Chabad institutions throughout Metro New York, including schools, camps, and Chabad Houses, which are community centers offering Torah

classes and worship services.[3] These are led by *shlichim* (emissaries), couples sent into communities to teach secular Jews about living an Orthodox life.

What Do They Believe?

"Pick a mitzvah, any mitzvah!" Instead of focusing on the religious failures of non-observant Jews, Chabad has tried to make it easier to follow Jewish law. Rebbe Schneerson taught that even performing one mitzvah brought a Jew closer to God and the Messiah closer to earth. The Lubavitchers' great messianic fervor and devotion to Schneerson led many to believe that the rebbe himself was the Messiah, a claim he neither affirmed nor disputed. Although Chabad leadership denounces the "messianists" who have continued to promote this idea, the controversy has split the movement. Tensions have been so high at times that the police have stepped in.[4]

What Are Their Lives Like?

"One of my brothers has lived in Johannesburg for twelve years. The other is in Hollywood Hills. When I get married, I'll go somewhere too," explained Yakov.* Young Lubavitchers are excited to join the ranks of the *shlichim*, which numbers 3,800 and is growing. These husband-and-wife teams run Chabad Houses in forty-five US states, sixty-one countries, and on one hundred college campuses.[5]

How Can I Pray?

✴ Lubavitchers earnestly seek the Messiah and believe that following Jewish law will hasten his coming. Pray that they would see how Jesus fulfilled the Law and saved us through God's grace.

Lubavitch Jews consider themselves missionaries to nominal Jews, and many of the Russian Jews in Metro New York were non-practicing upon arrival.

Russians

QUICK FACTS:

Place of Origin:
Russia (primarily Moscow and St. Petersburg)

Significant Subgroups:
Russian ethnic Jews (70-90%); Russian non-Jews (10-30%)

Location in Metro New York:
Brooklyn (Brighton Beach, Bath Beach, Gravesend, Sheepshead Bay, Midwood, Starrett City, Bensonhurst, Bay Ridge, Borough Park, Williamsburg); Queens (Forest Hills, Rego Park); Manhattan (Washington Heights); Bronx (Co-op City); New Jersey (Fair Lawn); Staten Island (Great Kills)

Population in Metro New York:
110,000 (Community Estimate); 122,941 (ACS 2008 Born in Russia)

Population in New York City:
87,182 (ACS 2008 Born in Russia)

Primary Religion:
Judaism

Secondary Religions:
Nonreligious, Russian Orthodox

Status of Christian Witness:
Less than 2% evangelical. Initial (localized) church planting within the past two years.

Primary Language:
Russian

Registry of Peoples Codes:
108454, 108452

Significant Notes:
❈ Recent Jewish immigrants from the former Soviet Union now make up about 25% of New York City's Jewish population.
❈ Russian Jews in America form the largest Russian-speaking Jewish population in the world.

A local New Yorker gargled out questions to a Russian dentist as she worked on his teeth in a Harlem dentistry. "So, you don't live in Brooklyn?" he managed to mutter in response to her saying she first lived in Manhattan and now New Jersey. "Absolutely not!" she claimed, "Those Russians are trying to live in the past. They never get out and experience New York." The dentist's comments allude to the conflicting identities experienced by Russians in New York today. Coming off a heavy dose of communism, the new Russian immigrants have been uniquely positioned to form new identities in their adopted city. As a result, they have splintered into groups defined by being more Jewish, more Russian, more American, more Orthodox Christian, more atheist, more sophisticated, or even more open to other religions like evangelical Christianity. While religious identity has been muddled by the effects of communism, an estimated seventy to ninety percent of all Russians in New York City are ethnically Jews.[1] Without including Russian-speaking people from other former Soviet republics, there are around 110 thousand Russians in the New York Metro area.[2]

When Did They Come To New York?

Even though Russians have been immigrating to New York City since the 1800s, it is the large influx of immigrants in the last few decades that has made the word "Russian" synonymous with certain parts of New York City.[3] In the 1970s, many Soviet Jews were allowed to leave their country for Israel. This opened the way for many to come to America as well. More recently, policy changes under Mikhail Gorbachev allowed Russians to more freely leave the country and, in 1989, the United States Congress

from being swept away by Christian missionaries in Jewish disguise. According to a 2000 survey of Russian-speakers in New York, forty-one percent identify their religion as Judaism within their first three years in America, but this increases to sixty-four percent for those who have been in America nine years or more.[5] Having lived under a communist system that suppressed belief in God for decades, many Russian Jews in New York have awakened their faith by becoming members of Orthodox synagogues. However, as the Brooklyn signs indicate, a growing minority have converted to evangelical Christianity. At least ten percent of Russians in Metro New York belong to the Russian Orthodox Church.

designated Soviet Jews as eligible to receive refugee status if they could prove they had a credible fear of persecution.[4] As a result, the 1990s witnessed an influx of more Soviet Jews to New York City than any other immigrant group. While economics was the main motivation for migration, religious persecution in Russia provided strong motivation as well.

Where Do They Live?

Unlike the Harlem dentist who sees herself on the "more sophisticated" side of Russian identity, sixty-two percent of Russians in New York City live in Brooklyn (ACS 2008). In particular, the south Brooklyn neighborhoods of Brighton Beach, Bath Beach, Gravesend, Sheepshead Bay, Bensonhurst, Starrett City, and Midwood have a strong Russian flavor.

What Do They Believe?

Periodically along streets in Jewish neighborhoods in Brooklyn, plastered signs appear that appeal to the Orthodox Jewish community to save their Russian Jewish brothers

What Are Their Lives Like?

If one were to stroll down Brighton Beach Avenue in winter, one would notice an abundance of women extravagantly promenading in fur coats. Russians love fashion, classical music, plays, ballroom dancing, and the sophisticated lifestyle. While some have realistically entered that world, for others it is a false veneer that hides the psychological trauma of adjusting to America and being a highly educated professional forced to work a lower-level job.

How Can I Pray?

❋ Pray for the continued success of evangelical church plants focused on reaching Russian Jews and that Russian Christians would have confidence in Christ in the midst of persecution.

❋ Russians have one of the highest suicide rates in the city. Pray that they would find hope, worth, and meaning in Christ.

Whereas Russian Jews are most often Ashkenazi, the form of Judaism associated with Eastern Europe, Bukharan Jews are Sephardic, the form of Judaism associated with Jews from Spain and the Maghreb.

Bukharan Jews

QUICK FACTS:

Place of Origin:
Uzbekistan (primarily Tashkent, Bukhara, and Samarkand); Tajikistan (Dushanbe); Kazakhstan; Kyrgyzstan

Significant Subgroups:
Mainly religious: Orthodox (20%); traditional (60%); unaffiliated (20%)

Location in Metro New York:
Queens (Forest Hills, Rego Park, Lefrak City)

Population in Metro New York:
50,000 (Community Estimate)

Primary Religion:
Judaism (Sephardic)

Status of Christian Witness:
Less than 2% evangelical. Some evangelical resources available, but no active church planting within the past two years.

Primary Language:
Russian

Secondary Languages:
Bukhori, English

Registry of Peoples Code:
104244

Significant Notes:
✦ By far the most visible Bukharan adherent to Orthodox Judaism is Lubavitcher Lev Leviev, a diamond cutter who is one of the world's wealthiest Jews and biggest philanthropists, donating millions to Chabad Lubavitch (p. 174) and Bukharan causes.

✦ Many Bukharan Jews are more comfortable in Russian than they are Bukhori, which leads people to confuse them with "Russian Jews."

✦ The language of Bukhori is having a small revival in Queens, where a Bukharan theater regularly performs plays in Bukhori.

"We hate the word 'melting pot,'" Aron Aronov claimed, reflecting on his people's disposition regarding American assimilation. Aronov, who is often called the Mayor of Queensistan, has received the unusual moniker because of his arduous activism for preserving the culture, language, and heritage of his people, the Bukharan Jews, who have migrated en masse to Queens from Uzbekistan, Tajikistan, Kazakhstan, and Kyrgyzstan.[1] The Bukharan Jews, also known as Bukharian and Bukharic Jews, are believed to be descendants of Israelites who were exiled to Babylonia in 586 BC. Having later come under the influence of the Persians, Bukharan Jews today speak a language called Bukhori, which is similar to Tajik Persian, with a trace of Hebrew and Russian. For over two thousand years, Bukharan Jews were one of the most isolated Jewish groups in the world. Eventually settling in the region of Bukhara in Central Asia due to, among other reasons, commercial opportunities along the Silk Road, Jews from this region came to be known as "Bukharan Jews." While only a few hundred are left in Central Asia today, an estimated 50 thousand now call Metro New York home, making it the largest concentration of Bukharan Jews in the world and home to one-fourth of the world's Bukharan Jewish population.[2]

When Did They Come To New York?

The biblical exile led the Bukharan Jews to settle along the great commercial route called the Silk Road; the new exile has led them to one of the greatest commercial centers in the world—New York City. The immigration primarily started in the 1960s, and the first Bukharan Jewish synagogue in Queens was founded in 1965.[3] Bukharan Jewish immigration continued sporadically until the disintegration of the Soviet Union. In newly formed countries such as Uzbekistan and Tajikistan, increased nationalism, xenophobia, and Islamic fundamentalism led to a mass exodus throughout the 1990s of most Bukharan Jews still in Central Asia. During the different waves of immigration to New York, some Bukharan Jews came directly from Central Asia, while others came via Israel.

Where Do They Live?

With such a concentration of Bukharan Jews along 108th Street in Forest Hills, the street has been dubbed "Bukharan Broadway," and neighboring Rego Park has been dubbed "Regostan," both, of course, part of "Queensistan." The Bukharan Jews are so concentrated in the borough that Queens College actually started a Bukharan Jewish history and culture class in 2010.

What Do They Believe?

Now that freedom to practice their religion has been realized, many Bukharan Jews have used the opportunity not only to embrace their distinct religious identity but also to gain knowledge of Orthodox traditions normally associated with the Ashkenazi branch of Judaism. As the Bukharan Jewish community's chief rabbi explains, "About twenty percent of the community are Orthodox, sixty percent are traditional but not necessarily observant, and twenty percent are unaffiliated."[4] Despite the influence of Ashkenazi Orthodoxy in Queens, Bukharans (while being

Mizrahi like many other Jews from Central Asia) still practice Sephardic Judaism. Most Bukharan Jews are very superstitious and do not question their rabbis, which is one reason why their distinct religious rites and customs have been preserved. Although evangelistic Bible studies are occurring with Bukharan Jews—some of whom have become believers—there is still no Bukharan Christian church or messianic synagogue in Metro New York.

What Are Their Lives Like?

Almost nightly, the Bukharan restaurants in Queens convert into party halls, usually celebrating someone's birthday, wedding, bar mitzvah, or a Jewish holiday. If a Bukharan family is wealthy enough, these parties take place in their large mansions, which house multiple generations of families under one roof. While the Bukharan community has its share of unemployed people with limited English skills, a super-wealthy class has emerged as well, primarily from working in the jewelry industry.

How Can I Pray?

✳ Although Queens is the most strategic place in the world to share the gospel with Bukharan Jews, there are only a couple of workers among them. Pray that God would send laborers.

✳ Pray for the first church or messianic synagogue to be started among the Bukharan Jews.

Endnotes
In alphabetical order

Afghans

1 The estimate of 20,000 Afghans in Metro New York is quoted in almost every journalistic piece on Afghans in Metro New York. See Robert Worth, "Back to Kabul, With a Queens Accent," *The New York Times*, November 3, 2003, http://www.nytimes.com/2e003/11/03/nyregion/back-kabul-with-queens-accent-many-immigrants-returning-remade-afghanistan-some.html (accessed October 22, 2009). The Afghan Communicator, the largest nonreligious Afghan association in Metro New York, estimates 25,000 Afghans in New York. See *The Afghan Communicator*, http://www.afghancommunicator.com/AfghanHeritageDay.asp (accessed July 16, 2008).

2 Corey Kilgannon, "Mosque Remains Divided, Despite Ruling From Court," *The New York Times*, August 7, 2004, http://query.nytimes.com/gst/fullpage.html?res=9407EEDF103CF934A3575BC0A9629C8B63 (accessed July 26, 2008).

3 Sarah Garland, "Hindus Flee Afghanistan, Flourish in New York," *New York Sun*, March 31, 2008, http://www.nysun.com/new-york/hindus-flee-afghanistan-flourish-in-new-york/73886/ (accessed July 5, 2008).

4 Reuven Fenton, "Afghan Seder Saver," *New York Post*, April 8, 2009, http://www.nypost.com/p/news/international/afghan_seder_saver_OebYgVJISTgYo-7AMW2xLbO (accessed October 22, 2009).

Afro-Guyanese

1 Jacqueline A. McLeod, "Guyanese Americans," in Robert Dassanowsky and Jeffrey Lehman, eds., *Gale Encyclopedia of Multicultural America*, vol. 2 (Farmington Hills, MI: Gale Group, 2000), 786.

2 Central Intelligence Agency, "Guyana," *The World Factbook*, https://www.cia.gov/library/publications/the-world-factbook/geos/gy.html (accessed February 4, 2010). The website currently lists the population of Guyana as 752,940, and the 2008 American Community Survey estimates 180,852 people in Metro New York were born in Guyana. If subsequent generations were counted, this number would be even higher.

Afro-Trinidadians

1 West Indian American Day Carnival Association, "Guide to Carnival," http://www.wiadca.com/index.php?option=com_content&view=article&id=39&Itemid=28 (accessed January 26, 2010).

2 In personal interviews, the Consul General estimated 400,000 people from Trinidad and Tobago live in Metro New York, while other community leaders estimated around 300,000, 70 percent of which is 210,000.

3 New York City Department of City Planning, *The Newest New Yorkers 2000* (New York: New York Department of City Planning Population Division, 2004), 102.

4 Central Intelligence Agency, "Trinidad and Tobago," *The World Factbook*, https://www.cia.gov/library/publications/the-world-factbook/geos/td.html (accessed January 26, 2010).

Albanians

1 This estimated number is often quoted by Albanian organizations and was given to the author by a Christian worker among Albanians in Metro New York. An article on the Albanian diaspora also gives an estimate of 200,000. See "War in Yugoslavia: KLA and Albanian Diaspora," *Traces* 5 (March 1999), http://www.transcomm.ox.ac.uk/traces/issue5.htm (accessed November 24, 2009).

2 Malesia E. Madhe, comment on "Explain the Dif between Serbs, Kosovo, Albanians," Topix, comment posted December 17, 2006, http://www.topix.com/forum/world/serbia/TGUOSI8E8U6E4565B/p2 (accessed November 27, 2007).

3 Personal interview with a Christian worker among Albanians in Metro New York.

Argentines

1 Estimate from the Argentina Observatory. Quoted in Alejandra Davidzuik and Alys Willman-Navarro, "Discovering the Diaspora: Los Argentinos in New York City" (New York: The Argentina Observatory, 2006).

2 Julio Rodriguez, "Argentinean Americans," in Robert Dassanowsky and Jeffrey Lehman, eds., *Gale Encyclopedia of Multicultural America*, vol. 1 (Farmington Hills, MI: Gale Group, 2000), 125.

3 Carlos G. Fernandez Valdovinas, "Growth, Poverty and Social Equity in Argentina," *En Breve* 82 (November 2005), http://siteresources.worldbank.org/INTENBREVE/Newsletters/20847679/82-NOV05-AR_Growth.pdf (accessed August 3, 2009).

4 Seth Kugel, "Neighborhood Report: Elmhurst; In Little Argentina, Transplants Watch as their Homeland Unravels," *New York Times*, December 30, 2001, http://www.nytimes.com/2001/12/30/nyregion/neighborhood-report-elmhurst-little-argentina-transplants-watch-their-homeland.html (accessed August 9, 2009).

5 Central Intelligence Agency, "Argentina," *The World Factbook*, https://www.cia.gov/library/publications/the-world-factbook/geos/ar.html (accessed August 9, 2009).

6 "Cuts of Meat in Argentina," *Cooking with Teresita*, http://www.try2cook.com/cuts-of-meat-in-Argenitna.html (accessed August 10, 2009).

7 "History of the Jews of Argentina," Wikipedia, http://en.wikipedia.org/wiki/History_of_the_Jews_of_Argentina (accessed August 9, 2009).

Bangladeshis

1 Interview with Biju Matthew, *Social Justice Movements*, http://socialjustice.ccnmtl.columbia.edu/index.php/The_Alliance (accessed November 12, 2009).

2 Michael Luo, "Study of Taxi Drivers Finds More Immigrants at Wheel," *The New York Times*, July 7, 2004, http://www.nytimes.com/2004/07/07/nyregion/study-of-taxi-drivers-finds-more-immigrants-at-wheel.html (accessed November 11, 2009).

3 Number quoted by Akhter Hossain, the President of the Bangladesh Society, in Martin Mbugua, "Bangladeshis Build New Life in New York," *Daily News*, May 27, 1998, http://www.nydailynews.com/archives/ny_local/1998/05/27/1998-05-27_bangladeshis_build_new_life_.html (accessed November 12, 2009) and in Sarah Kershaw, "Queens to Detroit: A Bangladeshi Passage," *The New York Times*, March 8, 2001, http://www.nytimes.com/2001/03/08/nyregion/queens-to-detroit-a-bangladeshi-passage.html (accessed November 12, 2009).

Barbadians

1 Isabel Fonseca, "Barbados: This Earth, This Realm, This Little England," *Condé Nast Traveler*, July 2009, http://www.concierge.com/cntraveler/articles/500991?pageNumber=1 (accessed January 28, 2010).

2 Personal interview.

3 Central Intelligence Agency, "Barbados," *The World Factbook*, https://www.cia.gov/library/publications/the-world-factbook/geos/bb.html (accessed January 28, 2010).

4 Lloyd E. Mulraine, "Barbadian Americans," *Gale Encyclopedia of Multicultural America*, vol. 1 (Farmington Hills, MI: Gale Group, 2000), 198.

5 Ibid., 199.

Belarusians

1 Condoleezza Rice, "Opening Statement before the Senate Foreign Relations Committee," January 18, 2005, US Senate Committee on Foreign Relations, http://foreign.senate.gov/testimony/2005/RiceTestimony050118.pdf (accessed January 23, 2010). The other countries mentioned were Cuba, Burma, North Korea, Iran, and Zimbabwe.

2 Research Institute of New Americans (RINA), "Russian Jewish Immigrants in New York City: Status, Identity, and Integration" (New York: American Jewish Committee, 2000), estimates 400,000 Russian-speaking Jews live in Metro New York. Surveys, including ones done by RINA, indicate that 70-90 percent of Russian-speakers in Metro New York are ethnic Jews. If this range is averaged out to 80 percent, then 100,000 non-Jewish Russian-speakers also live in Metro New York. In RINA, "Russian-Jewish Opinion Survey 2004," American Jewish Committee, http://www.ajc.org/site/apps/nlnet/content3.aspx?c=ijITI2PHKoG&b=846741&ct=1030151 (accessed January 16, 2010), 11 percent of Russian-speakers interviewed identified themselves as immigrants from the Byelorussian Republic of the former Soviet Union. Eleven percent of 400,000 is 44,000, and 11 percent of 100,000 is 11,000. In a personal interview, Dr. Kipel expressed similar estimates of 10,000 Belarusians and 50,000 Belarusian Jews in Metro New York.

3 Vitaut Kipel, "Belarusan Americans," in Robert Dassanowsky and Jeffrey Lehman, eds., *Gale Encyclopedia of Multicultural America*, vol. 1 (Farmington Hills, MI: Gale Group, 2000), 222.

Bobover Jews

1 Public Broadcasting Service, "A Brief Introduction to Hasidism," A Life Apart: Hasidism in America, http://www.pbs.org/alifeapart/intro.html (accessed September 14, 2009).

2 Stephen Harlan Norwood and Eunice G. Pollack, eds., *Encyclopedia of American Jewish History*, vol. 2 (Santa Barbara: ABC-CLIO, 2007), 102.

3 Jack Wertheimer, "Low Fertility and High Intermarriage are Pushing American Jewry to Extinction," http://www.aish.com/jw/s/48899452.html (accessed September 10, 2009).

Bosniaks

1 "The Bosnian War," Wikipedia, http://en.wikipedia.org/wiki/Bosnian_War (accessed October 26, 2009).

2 Estimate derived from interviews with community members as well as in Barbara Franz, *Uprooted and Unwanted: Bosnian Refugees in Austria and the United States* (College Station: Texas A&M UP, 2005), 161.

3 "Local Bosnians Still Struggle with Post-traumatic Stress More Than a Decade after Fleeing Their Home," *St. Louis Beacon*, August 20, 2009, http://www.stlbeacon.org/content/view/11006/219/ (accessed February 24, 2010).

4 "The Bosnian War."

5 "Srebrenica Massacre," Wikipedia, http://en.wikipedia.org/wiki/Srebrenica_massacre (accessed October 27, 2009).

Brazilians

1 Gary Duffy, "Brazilians Shun 'American Dream,'" *BBC News*, March 25, 2008, http://news.bbc.co.uk/2/hi/business/7312408.stm (accessed July 1, 2009) and Fernanda Santos, "A Brazilian Outpost in Westchester," *The New York Times*, June 26, 2006, http://query.nytimes.com/gst/fullpage.html?res=940DEEDF1730F935A15755C0A9609C8B63 (accessed July 1, 2009).

2 Diana Jean Schemo, "Tense Times on the Front Line of Brazil's Battle on Hyperinflation: Empty Shops," *The New York Times*, January 20, 1999, http://www.nytimes.com/1999/01/20/world/tense-times-on-front-line-of-brazil-s-battle-on-hyperinflation-empty-shops.html (accessed July 17, 2009).

3 "Editorial: Boa vinda a Framingham!" *The Boston Globe*, July 31, 2006, http://www.boston.com/news/globe/editorial_opinion/editorials/articles/2006/07/31/boa_vinda_a_framingham (accessed July 16, 2009).

4 Santos.

5 Tony Carnes, email to the author, November 21, 2009. According to Carnes, anthropologist Donizete Rodrigues has counted 45 such churches.

6 Estimates based on personal research and samples by Maxine L. Margolis, *Little Brazil* (Princeton: Princeton UP, 1994), 92.

7 Community estimate is from the Washington-based Brazil Information Center. See "History of the Brazilian Day in NY," Brazilian Day in New York: 2009, http://www.brazilianday.com/2009/eng/historia.html (accessed July 18, 2009).

British

1 Lucas Mann, "Brits Retreat, Plan New Street-sign Campaign," *The Villager 77, no. 8* (July 25-31, 2007), http://www.thevillager.com/villager_221/britsretreatplannew.html (accessed September 29, 2009).

2 *American Community Survey 2008* (US Census Bureau, 2008). Composite figure of people claiming the following ancestries: British, English, Scotch-Irish, Scottish, and Welsh.

3 "Don't Call Us British, We're from England," *London Evening Standard*, January 23, 2007, http://www.thisislondon.co.uk/news/article-23382833-dont-call-us-british-were-from-england.do;jsessionid=1E4D9A822A0DAE3635810A959C1A0254 (accessed September 29, 2009).

4 Personal interviews conducted with British business owners and a representative from the St. George's Society of New York.

Bukharan Jews

1 Edith Honan, "The Bukharian Jewish Community of Queens: Jews Rebuild Homeland in NY Enclave," *Matzav Network*, October 21, 2009, http://matzav.com/the-bukharian-jewish-community-of-queens-jews-rebuild-homeland-in-ny-enclave (accessed November 17, 2009).

2 Fifty thousand is the number most often quoted concerning the population of Bukharan Jews in Metro New York, and the world's Bukharan Jewish population is often estimated to be around 200,000. See "History of Bukharian Jews," *Beth Gavriel: World Center of Bukharian Jews*, http://bethgavrielcenter.com/content/History-Of-Bukharian-Jews.html (accessed November 18, 2009).

3 Rahel Musleah, "Bukharian Jews: Preserving Identity," *Hadassah Magazine* 90.1 (2008), http://www.hadassah.org/news/content/per_hadassah/archive/2008/08_sep/feature_1.asp (accessed November 18, 2009).

4 Ibid.

Burmese

1 "Writers Commemorate Burmese Uprisings; Rally for Jailed Writers," PEN American Center, September 24, 2008, http://www.pen.org/viewmedia.php?prmMID/2842/prmID/1331 (accessed January 15, 2010).

2 Population estimate derived from interviews with local Burmese pastors. A representative from the Myanmar American Association gave a much higher, and probably inflated, estimate of 35,000 in Metro New York.

3 Fernanda Santos, "Fearing for Many at Home, City's Burmese Unite to Aid Cyclone Victims," *The New York Times*, May 11, 2008, http://www.nytimes.com/2008/05/11/nyregion/11burmese.html (accessed January 19, 2010).

4 Amy Cooper, "Burmese Americans," in Robert Dassanowsky and Jeffrey Lehman, eds., *Gale Encyclopedia of Multicultural America*, vol. 1 (Farmington Hills, MI: Gale Group, 2000), 303.

5 Donald A. Ranard and Sandy Barron, eds., *Refugees from Burma: Their Backgrounds and Refugee Experiences* (Washington, DC: Center for Applied Linguistics, 2007), 9, 31, 52, 62, 63.

6 British Broadcasting Corporation, "Profile: Aung San Suu Kyi," http://news.bbc.co.uk/2/hi/asia-pacific/1950505.stm (accessed January 15, 2010).

Canadians

1 "Religions in Canada," Statistics Canada, http://www12.statcan.ca/english/census01/Products/Analytic/companion/rel/canada.cfm (accessed December 7, 2009).

2 John Longhurst, "The Future of the Evangelical Movement," *Winnipeg Free Press*, March 22, 2009, http://www.winnipegfreepress.com/life/faith/the-future-of-the-evangelical-movement-41647397.html?viewAllComments=y (accessed December 7, 2009).

3 "Unreached People: The Québecois," Pray for Québec, http://www.prayforquebec.com/wordpress/?page_id=3 (accessed December 18, 2009).

4 Leigh Kamping-Carder, "Canadians Among US!" *The New York Observer*, July 31, 2008, http://www.observer.com/2008/real-estate/canadians-among-us# (accessed December 7, 2009).

5 "National Hockey League," Wikipedia, http://en.wikipedia.org/wiki/National_Hockey_League (accessed December 16, 2009).

Colombians

1 Colombia Migration Project, http://colombiamigrationproject.net (accessed February 23, 2008).

2 Pamela Sturner, "Colombian Americans," *Gale Encyclopedia of Multicultural America*, vol. 1 (Farmington Hills, MI: Gale Group, 2000), 419-420.

3 Colombia Migration Project, http://colombiamigrationproject.net (accessed February 23, 2008).

Croats

1 "Croatian War of Independence," Wikipedia, http://en.wikipedia.org/wiki/Croatian_War_of_Independence (accessed October 23, 2009).

2 Estimate derived from conversations with community leaders and representatives at the Croatian Consulate in New York.

3 "St. Jerome, Doctor of the Church," *Catholic Online*, http://www.catholic.org/saints/saint.php?saint_id=10 (accessed October 24, 2009).

Cubans

1 Mark E. Reisinger, "Latinos in America: Historical and Contemporary Settlement Patterns," in John W. Frazier and Eugene Tetley-Fio, eds., *Race, Ethnicity, and Place in a Changing America* (Binghamton: Global Academic Publishing, 2006), 191.

2 Max Pizzaro, "Menedez to Christie: Cuba is a State Issue," http://www.politickernj.com/max/29255/menendez-christie-cuba-state-issue (accessed August 6, 2009).

3 Personal conversation with Pastor Paul Flores of the Nazareth Baptist Church in West New York, New Jersey.

4 "Bergenline Avenue," Wikipedia, http://en.wikipedia.org/wiki/Bergenline_Avenue (accessed August 6, 2009).

Dominicans

1 Pamela M. Graham, "Political Incorporation and Re-Incorporation: Simultaneity in the Dominican Migrant Experience," in Héctor R. Cordero-Guzmán, Robert C. Smith, and Ramón Grosfoguel, eds., *Migration, Transnationalization, and Race in a Changing New York* (Philadelphia: Temple UP, 2001), 87.

2 Ibid., 88.

3 Nancy Foner, *New Immigrants in New York: Completely Revised and Updated Edition* (New York: Columbia UP, 2001), 3.

4 Unpublished survey data from the Pew Research Center Survey on Latino Religious Belief in America, 2007.

Ecuadorians

1 Dustin Brown, "Nueva Dorians: Most Consider New York Andean Nation's Third-Largest City," *Ecuador Travel*, http://www.ecuador.us/news/archives/ecuadorians_in_new_york/ (accessed September 6, 2008).

2 Ana C. Melo, *Transnationalism in New York City: A Study of Remittance Sending by Ecuadorian Migrants* (MA in Law and Diplomacy Thesis, The Fletcher School of Tufts University, May 2006), 18-20.

3 Jeremy Mumford, "Ecuadoran Americans" in Robert Dassanowsky and Jeffrey Lehman, eds., *Gale Encyclopedia of Multicultural America*, vol. 1. (Farmington Hills, MI: Gale Group, 2000), 562.

4 Melo, 23.

Egyptians

1 Andrea Elliott, "A Bloody Crime in New Jersey Divides Egyptians," *New York Times*, January 21, 2005, http://www.nytimes.com/2005/01/21/nyregion/21rift.html (accessed September 03, 2008).

2 According to ACS 2008, 26.2% of the Egypt-born in America are in Metro New York. An estimate of 420,000 Egyptians in the United States was used to derive the community estimate for Metro New York. See "Egyptian Copts Warn against Congressional Pressure," *Washington Report on Middle East Affairs*, September 1998, http://www.wrmea.com/backissues/0998/9809071.html (accessed September 9, 2008).

Ethiopians

1 Estimate provided by Abyanesh Asrat, an Ethiopian community leader and philanthropist, in a personal interview on August 8, 2009.

2 Jennifer Bleyer, "The Next Wave: Scenes; First the Mass, Then the Fellowship," *The New York Times*, November 21, 2004, http://query.nytimes.com/gst/fullpage.html?res=9B07E7D8113FF932A15752C1A9629C8B63 (accessed January 9, 2010).

3 Central Intelligence Agency, "Ethiopia," *The World Factbook*, https://www.cia.gov/library/publications/the-world-factbook/geos/et.html (accessed January 10, 2010).

4 Israel Association for Ethiopian Jews, "Ethiopian Jewry," History, http://www.iaej.co.il/pages/history_in_the_beginning.htm (accessed January 11, 2010).

Filipinos

1 Dilip Ratha and Zhimei Xu, *Migration and Remittances Factbook 2008*, World Bank, http://siteresources.worldbank.org/INTPROSPECTS/Resources/334934-119980.

2 Robert Burgess and Vikram Haksar, *Migration and Foreign Remittances in the Philippines* (International Monetary Fund, 2005), 3, http://www.imf.org/external/pubs/ft/wp/2005/wp05111.pdf (accessed October 3, 2008).

3 Nancy Foner, *From Ellis Island to JFK: New York's Two Great Waves of Immigration* (London: Yale UP, 2000), 92.

French

1 "New York's French Colony," *The New York Times*, June 1, 1902, http://query.nytimes.com/mem/archive-free/pdf?_r=1&res=940DE2DD113DEE32A25752C0A9609C946397D6CF (accessed February 1, 2010).

2 Lizzie Davies, "Rise of French Evangelicals Puts Secularism in a Spin," The Age, November 8, 2009, http://www.theage.com.au/world/rise-of-french-evangelicals-puts-secularism-in-a-spin-20091107-i2te.html (accessed February 1, 2010).

3 "New York's French Colony."

Fuzhounese

1 Kenneth J. Guest, *God in Chinatown* (New York: New York UP, 2003), 15, 28, 47. Although Guest claims the going rate for being smuggled into the US in 2002 was $50,000-$60,000, the amount of $30,000-$35,000 is common.

2 Guest, "Liminal Youth among Fuzhou Chinese Undocumented Workers," in Tony Carnes and Fenggang Yang, eds., *Asian American Religions* (New York: New York UP, 2004), 60-61.

3 Zai Liang and Wenzhen Ye, "From Fujian to New York: Understanding the New Chinese Immigration," in David Kyle and Rey Koslowski, eds., *Global Human Smuggling* (Baltimore: John Hopkins UP, 2001), 202.

4 Guest, "Liminal Youth among Fuzhou Chinese Undocumented Workers," 67-68.

Garifuna

1 Liz Swain, "Garifuna Americans," in Robert Dassanowsky and Jeffrey Lehman, eds., *Gale Encyclopedia of Multicultural America*, vol. 1 (Farmington Hills, MI: Gale, 2000), 687.

2 Percentages derived from personal interview with Andrew Nuñez, Garifuna church pastor, community leader, and President of the Evangelical Garifuna Council of Churches.

3 Garifuna American Heritage Foundation, "Garinagu Seek to Preserve Their Ancestral Language," *Bronx Beat*, May 7, 2007, https://cranberry.cc.columbia.edu/cs/ContentServer?childpagename=Bronxbeat%2FJRN_Content_C%2FBBArticleDetail&c=JRN_Content_C&p=1165426883227&pagename=JRN%2FBBWrapper&cid=1175372036306 (accessed November 19, 2009) and Jesse Hardman, "Garifuna Ethnic Group Seeks Voice in New York City," *National Public Radio*, November 15, 2009, http://www.npr.org/templates/story/story.php?storyId=120381718 (accessed November 19, 2009).

4 Personal interview with Andrew Nuñez.

Germans

1 "The General Slocum and Little Germany," New-York Historical Society, https://www.nyhistory.org/web/default.php?section=exhibits_collections&page=exhibit_detail&id=3216444 (accessed December 2, 2009).

2 "Alphabet City: Early History," Wikipedia, http://en.wikipedia.org/wiki/Alphabet_City,_Manhattan (accessed December 2, 2009).

3 Comparison of Census 2000 and ACS 2008 data.

4 Willi Adams, "Why the Germans Left Home," in *The German Americans: An Ethnic Experience,* Lavern Rippley and Eberhard Reichmann, trans., http://www-lib.iupui.edu/kade/adams/author.html (accessed December 3, 2009).

5 Joseph Berger, "The Germans Came, Now They Are Us: An Ethnic Queens Neighborhood is Melting Away into America," *New York Times*, October 25, 2003, http://www.nytimes.com/2003/10/25/nyregion/germans-came-now-they-are-us-ethnic-queens-neighborhood-melting-away-into.html (accessed December 17, 2009).

Ghanaians

1 "First North American Baptist Convention," GhanaWeb, http://www.ghanaweb.com/GhanaHomePage/religion/photo.day.php?ID=125012 (accessed December 19, 2008).

2 James Dao, "Ghanaians Hail a Surrogate King," *The New York Times*, May 25, 1992, http://query.nytimes.com/gst/fullpage.html?res=9E0CE5DD103AF936A15756C0A964958260&n=Top/Reference/Times%20Topics/People/D/Dao,%20James (December 19, 2008).

3 Joseph Berger, *The World in a City* (New York: Ballantine Books, 2007), 161.

4 Central Intelligence Agency, "Ghana," *The World Factbook*, https://www.cia.gov/library/publications/the-world-factbook/geos/gh.html (accessed December 19, 2008).

5 Community estimate derived from interviews with Ghanaian association leaders and pastors.

Gorsky-Kavkazi Jews

1 "You Know You're Gorsky When," Facebook, http://www.facebook.com/topic.php?uid=2212825577&topic=2069 (accessed November 13, 2009).

2 Estimate derived from personal interviews with staff at the Gorsky-Kavkazi Cultural Center on May 30 and 31, 2009.

3 Norman Finkelshteyn, "The Mountain Jews of Brooklyn," *Hadassah* 89, no. 5 (January 2008), http://www.hadassah.org/news/content/per_hadassah/archive/2008/08_JAN/feature_1.asp (accessed November 16, 2009).

4 "Jewish Tat," *Joshua Project*, http://www.global-prayer-digest.org/dailydata/getdaily.asp?which=chosenday&whichyear=2008&whichmonth=12&whichday=14 (accessed November 13, 2009).

5 "Mizrahi Jews," Wikipedia, http://en.wikipedia.org/wiki/Mizrahi_Jews (accessed November 14, 2009).

6 "Mountain Jews," *The Red Book of the Peoples of the Russian Empire*, http://www.eki.ee/books/redbook/mountain_jews.shtml (accessed November 14, 2009).

Greeks

1 Ivar Ekman, "Neighborhood Report: Astoria; Less a Greek Neighborhood, More a Greek Destination," *The New York Times*, July 7, 2002, http://www.nytimes.com/2002/07/07/nyregion/neighborhood-report-astoria-less-a-greek-neighborhood-more-a-greek-destination.html?pagewanted=1 (accessed February 26, 2010).

2 Jane Jurgens, "Greek Americans," in Robert Dassanowsky and Jeffrey Lehman, eds., *Gale Encyclopedia of Multicultural America*, vol. 2 (Farmington Hills, MI: Gale Group, 2000), 735.

Guatemalans

1 Maria Hong, "Guatemalan Americans," in Robert Dassanowsky and Jeffrey Lehman, eds., *Gale Encyclopedia of Multicultural America*, vol. 2 (Farmington Hills, MI: Gale Group, 2000), 764.

2 United Nations Refugee Agency, "State of the World's Minorities and Indigenous Peoples 2009: Guatemala," *Refworld*, http://www.unhcr.org/refworld/topic,463af2212,469f2e812,4a66d9b550,0.html (accessed November 28, 2009).

3 "Guatemalan Civil War," Wikipedia, http://en.wikipedia.org/wiki/Guatemalan_Civil_War (accessed November 27, 2009).

4 "Indigenous Peoples, Poverty, and Human Development in Latin America: 1994-2004," World Bank, http://web.worldbank.org (accessed December 3, 2009).

5 Public Broadcasting Service, "Guatemala: A Rising Faith," *Religion and Ethics Weekly,* May 6, 2005, http://www.pbs.org/wnet/religionandethics/week836/cover.html (accessed November 28, 2009).

6 Guatemala Human Rights Commission, "USA Fact Sheet," http://www.ghrc-usa.org/Programs/Immigration_Trade/factsheet_immigration.pdf (accessed November 27, 2009).

7 Ibid.

Gujaratis

1 Hiral Dholakhia-Dave, "42% of US Hotel Business is Gujarati," http://timesofindia.indiatimes.com/NEWS/World/US/42-of-US-hotel-business-is-Gujarati/articleshow/2191584.cms (accessed August 17, 2009).

2 Lavina Melwani, "The Gujaratis," http://www.littleindia.com/february2002/The%20Gujaratis.htm (accessed September 27, 2009). Estimate of 110,000 is 20% of the total number of Asian Indians in Metro New York (547,539) as per ACS 2008.

3 "Large Numbers, Rapid Growth, Recent Immigration and Queens Hub Characterize New York City's Indian American Community," http://www.aafny.org/proom/pr/pr20040210.asp (accessed August 18, 2009).

4 Steve Raymer, "Indian Doctors Help Fill US Health Care Needs," http://yaleglobal.yale.edu/display.article?id=3340&page=1 (accessed August 17, 2009).

5 "Asian Indian Communities in the US," ePodunk: The Power of Place, http://www.epodunk.com/ancestry/Asian-Indian.html (accessed August 14, 2009).

6 "New Jersey's Asian American Population is Nation's Fifth-largest After Nearly Doubling in a Decade," Asian American Federation, http://www.aafny.org/proom/pr/pr20040520.asp (accessed August 18, 2009).

Haitians

1 Elizabeth McAlister, "The Madonna of 115th Street Revisited," in R. Stephen Warner and Judith G. Wittner, eds., *Gatherings in Diaspora* (Philadelphia: Temple UP, 1998), 147.

2 Josh Getlin, "Haitians Feel Under Siege in Brooklyn," *The Los Angeles Times*, April 2, 2000, http://www.commondreams.org/views/040200-105.htm (accessed December 20, 2008). Getlin claims 500,000 Haitians live in the New York area. See also Karen McCarthy Brown, *Mama Lola: A Vodou Priestess in Brooklyn*, updated and expanded ed. (Berkeley: U of California P, 2001), 4. Brown claims there are approximately 450,000 Haitians in New York City.

3 Brown, 306-307. Marriage to an *Iwa* does not normally exclude a human from marrying another human. However, the human who marries the Iwa is often required to devote one night a week to their Iwa spouse and must refrain from sexual relations with humans on that night.

4 United Nations Conference on Trade and Development, *The Least Developed Countries Report 2008*, http://www.unctad.org/en/docs/ldc2008_en.pdf (accessed December 24, 2008).

5 Central Intelligence Agency, "Haiti," *The World Factbook*, https://www.cia.gov/library/publications/the-world-factbook/geos/ha.html (accessed December 24, 2008).

Hong Kongese

1 Pei-te Lien and Tony Carnes, "The Religious Demography of Asian American Boundary Crossing," in Tony Carnes and Fenggang Yang, eds., Asian American Religions (New York, New York UP, 2004), 44.

Indo-Caribbeans

1 Odeen Ishmael, *The Guyana Story*, chapters 50 and 99, 2005, http://www.guyana.org/features/guyanastory/guyana_story.html (accessed May 14, 2008).

2 Central Intelligence Agency, *The World Factbook*, https://www.cia.gov/library/publications/the-world-factbook/index.html (accessed May 14, 2008).

3 Of the few estimates published, 300,000 appears most frequently, but this number seems high. See "Indo-Caribbean Issues Discussed at St. John's University," *India Abroad* (April 9, 1999), http://www.highbeam.com/doc/1P1-23662828.html (accessed November 25, 2009) and Nina Bernstein, "From Asia to the Caribbean to New York, Appetite Intact," *New York Times* (April 20, 2007), http://www.nytimes.com/2007/04/20/nyregion/20immigrants.html?_r=1 (accessed November 25, 2009).

Indonesians

1 Ashutosh Varshney, Rizal Panggabean, and Mohammad Zulfan Tadjoeddin, "Patterns of Collective Violence in Indonesia (1990-2003)," UN Support Facility for Indonesian Recovery, July 2004, http://www.conflictrecovery.org/.../Patterns_of_collective_violence_July04.pdf (accessed October 14, 2009).

2 The Indonesian Consul General estimates 8,000 to 15,000 Indonesians live in Metro New York.

3 Numbers given by Indonesian Consulate General Official Harbangan Napitupulu. See Putut Widjanarko, "Indonesian Muslims in New York City: A Transnational Community in the Making?" Salaam Institute for Peace and Justice, April 2006, http://www.salaminstitute.org/Putut.pdf (accessed October 11, 2009).

4 Ibid.

5 Widjanarko.

Iranians

1 Population estimate derived from personal interviews with community members.

2 Christopher Lewis, "It's Primetime in Iran," *Christianity Today*, September 28, 2008, http://www.christianitytoday.com/ct/2008/september/34.70.html (accessed October 8, 2009).

3 "The Holy Trifecta of Career Choices," http://stuffpersianslike.com/blog/category/health/medicine/ (accessed October 16, 2009).

Irish

1 Brendan A. Rapple, "Irish Americans," in Robert Dassanowsky and Jeffrey Lehman, eds., *Gale Encyclopedia of Multicultural America*, vol. 2 (Farmington Hills, MI: Gale Group, 2000), 938-940.

2 Nina Bernstein, "Back Home in Ireland, Greener Pastures," *The New York Times*, November 10, 2004, http://www.nytimes.com/2004/11/10/nyregion/10irish.html (accessed February 26, 2010).

3 In Census 2000, 52,672 people in Metro New York were counted as born in Ireland and 30,411 in New York City.

Israelis

1 Roi Ben-Yehuda, "Next Year in Jerusalem: Israelis in America, Temporarily," *Presentense Magazine: Jewish Life Here and Now* 5, http://www.presentensemagazine.org/mag/?page_id=325 (accessed May 22, 2008).

2 Rachel Soren, "Reaching Israel from New York City," *Jews for Jesus*, September 1, 2006, http://jewsforjesus.org/publications/newsletter/2006_09/israel (accessed February 27, 2010).

3 Laura C. Rudolph, "Israeli Americans," *Countries and Their Cultures*, http://www.everyculture.com/multi/Ha-La/Israeli-Americans.html (accessed May 22, 2008).

Italians

1 Billy Kounatsos and Casey Mesick, "The Italian Community in New York City," *Voices of New York*, New York University, http://www.nyu.edu/classes/blake.map2001/italy.html (accessed November 6, 2008).

2 George Pozzetta, "Italian Americans," *Countries and Their Cultures*, http://

www.everyculture.com/multi/Ha-La/Italian-Americans.html (accessed November 6, 2008).

Jamaicans

1 N. Samuel Murrell, "Jamaican Americans," in Robert Dassanowsky and Jeffrey Lehman, eds., *Gale Encyclopedia of Multicultural America*, vol. 2, (Farmington Hills, MI: Gale Group, 2000), 1002.

2 Randal L. Hepner, "The House That Rasta Built: Church-Building and Fundamentalism among New York Rastafarians," in Stephen Warner and Judith Wittner, eds., *Gatherings in Diaspora* (Philadelphia: Temple UP, 1998), 198.

3 Murrell, 1001.

Japanese

1 Jiro Adachi, "How Q Found Her Groove," *The New York Times*, January 30, 2005, http://www.nytimes.com/2005/01/30/nyregion/thecity/30feat.html (accessed October 18, 2008).

2 John McQuaid, "A View of Religion in Japan," *US-Japan Foundation Media Fellows Program*, 2001, Japan Society, http://www.japansociety.org/a_view_of_religion_in_japan (accessed October 18, 2008).

Jordanians

1 Estimate provided in personal interview with Mr. Haddad, former President of the Arab-American Foundation and Jordanian community leader in Yonkers. See also United Nations Relief and Works Agency for Palestinian Refugees (UN-WRA), http://www.un.org/unrwa/publications/index.html (accessed January 5, 2009).

2 Anan Ameri and Dawn Ramey, eds., *Arab-American Encyclopedia* (Detroit: UXL/Gale Group, 2000), 50.

3 Jeffrey Fleishman, "For Christian Enclave in Jordan, Tribal Lands are Sacred," *The Los Angeles Times*, May 10, 2009, http://www.latimes.com/news/nation-world/world/la-fg-tribal-catholic10-2009may10,0,6480090.story (accessed December 29, 2009).

Keralites

1 Estimate provided by the Kerala Center during a phone interview. The center's website is http://keralacenter.tripod.com/Center_Intro.htm.

2 Estimates of church affiliation derived through interviews with Keralite clergy and Mr. Tenney Thomas, editor of *Yearbook of American and Canadian Churches* and student of Keralite Christian culture.

3 Estimates derived from figures provided in interviews with Keralite clergy, Kerala Hindu Association, and FOKANA (Federation of Kerala Associations in North America).

4 "St. Thomas Christians and Other Christian Sects in Kerala History," Kerala Café, http://www.kerala.cc/keralahistory/index36.htm (accessed September 4, 2009).

Korean-Chinese

1 Estimates come from the Korean-Chinese Association of USA and the Korean-Chinese Association of New York. Quoted in Jong Sik Kong, "More Korean-Chinese Choose New York," http://english.donga.com/srv/service.php3?biid=2006012794428&path_dir=20060127 (accessed August 29, 2009).

2 Ibid.

3 Kim Chong-Hoon, "Make room for the Korean-Chinese in Flushing," *Korea Daily News*, January 5, 2005, http://www.indypressny.org/nycma/voices/152/news/news_1/ (accessed July 23, 2009).

Koreans

1 Rebecca Y. Kim, *God's New Whiz Kids: Korean American Evangelicals on Campus* (New York: New York UP, 2006), 35.

2 In a phone interview, the Council of Korean Churches of Greater New York claimed that 500 churches partner with them but that there are well over 1,000 churches in the area with a primarily-Korean membership.

3 Asian American Federation, "Recent Immigration, Limited English and Elderly Poverty Common Among Korean New Yorkers, Census Data Shows," http://www.aafny.org/proom/pr/pr20040421.asp (accessed July 24, 2009).

4 Ibid.

5 "11363 Zip Code Detailed Profile (Douglaston, Queens)," http://www.city-data.com/zips/11363.html (accessed July 28, 2009); US Census Data, 2000. See "Palisades Park, New Jersey," Wikipedia, http://en.wikipedia.org/wiki/Palisades_Park,_New_Jersey (accessed July 28, 2009).

Liberians

1 British Broadcasting Corporation, "Country Profile: Liberia," http://news.bbc.co.uk/2/hi/africa/country_profiles/1043500.stm (accessed June 9, 2009).

2 Ken R. Wells, "Liberian Americans," in Robert Dassanowsky and Jeffrey Lehman, eds., *Gale Encyclopedia of Multicultural America*, vol. 2 (Detroit: Gale Group, 2000), 1129.

3 Kirk Semple, "Liberians in New York, 'Jubilant' at Expulsion Reprieve," *The New York Times*, March 22, 2009, http://www.nytimes.com/2009/03/22/nyregion/22liberians.html?_r=2&ref=world (accessed June 9, 2009).

4 Joel Frushone, "World Refugee Survey, 2004: Africa," US Committee for Refugees, http://www.refugees.org/article.aspx?id=1158 (accessed June 9, 2009).

Lubavitch Jews

1 Population estimate derived from source suggesting that 6-8 percent of approximately 200,000 Crown Heights residents are Lubavitchers. See Henry Goldschmidt, *Race and Religion among the Chosen People of Crown Heights* (New Brunswick, NJ: Rutgers UP, 2006), 6, and Tricia Andryszewski, *Communities of the Faithful: American Religious Movements Outside the Mainstream* (Brookfield, CT: Millbrook Press, 1997), 95.

2 Edward S. Shapiro, *Crown Heights: Blacks, Jews and the 1991 Brooklyn Riot* (Lebanon, NH: UPNE, 2006), 74.

3 "Search for Chabad Lubavitch Centers," Chabad, http://www.chabad.org/centers/default_cdo/jewish/Centers.htm (accessed September 24, 2009).

4 Elizabeth Dwoskin, "The Crown Heights Lubavitchers: Ecstatic Jews, a Messiah Proclaimed, and the Consequential Divisions," *Village Voice*, August 27, 2008, http://www.villagevoice.com/content/printVersion/586011 (accessed September 24, 2009).

5 Review of *The Rebbe's Army: Inside the World of Chabad-Lubavitch*, by Sue Fishkoff, Amazon, http://www.amazon.com/Rebbes-Army-Inside-World-Chabad-Lubavitch/dp/product-description/0805211381 (accessed September 25, 2009).

6 Ibid.

Macedonians

1 "Albanians in the Republic of Macedonia," Wikipedia, http://en.wikipedia.org/wiki/Albanians_in_the_Republic_of_Macedonia (accessed November 10, 2009).

2 "Insurgency in the Republic of Macedonia," Wikipedia, http://en.wikipedia.org/wiki/Insurgency_in_the_Republic_of_Macedonia (accessed November 16, 2009).

3 Estimate derived from interviews with Macedonian community members, including the Honorary Consul for Macedonia in New Jersey, Slavco Madzarov.

4 "Lawmakers Delay Macedonia Envoy Vote over Greece Flap," *USA Today*, July 19, 2008, http://www.usatoday.com/news/washington/2008-07-19-macedonia-envoy_N.htm (accessed November 10, 2009).

Mainland Cantonese

1 Peter Kwong, *The New Chinatown*, revised ed., (New York: Hill and Wang, 1996), 97-100.

Mainland Han

1 In a personal interview, a representative of the largest umbrella Chinese Christian association in New York estimated that 10% of Chinese in Metro New York are Han Mandarin. In a survey done in the 1990s with 200 Chinese in Metro New York, 10% selected Mandarin as their first language. See Shiwen Pan, "Chinese in New York," in Ofelia Garcia and Joshua Fishman, eds., *The Multilingual Apple* (Berlin: Mouton de Gruyter, 2002), 241.

2 Kirk Semple, "In Chinatown, Sound of the Future is Mandarin," *New York Times*, October 21, 2009, http://www.nytimes.com/2009/10/22/nyregion/22chinese.html?pagewanted=2&_r=1&th&emc=th (accessed November 7, 2009).

3 Peter Kwong, *The New Chinatown*, revised ed. (New York: Hill and Wang, 1996), 5.

Malaysians

1 Maybank, "Small Entrepreneur Guarantee Scheme: Bumiputra 100% Guarantee," http://www.maybank2u.com.my/mbb_info/m2u/public/personalDetail04.do?channelId=LOA-Loans&cntTypeId=0&programId=LOA11-SolePropProfessionalFinancing&cntKey=BFIN05.09&chCatId=/mbb/Personal/LOA-Loans (accessed January 21, 2010).

2 Estimate derived from interviews with a local pastor and leaders at the Malaysian American Association and the Malaysian Tourism Promotion Board.

3 Asian American Federation of New York, "Census Profile: New York City's Asian American Population," 2004, http://www.aafny.org/cic/briefs/newyorkbrief.pdf (accessed January 21, 2010).

4 "Constitution of Malaysia," Wikipedia, http://en.wikisource.org/wiki/Constitution_of_Malaysia (accessed February 3, 2010).

5 "Malaysian Christians Stand Firm on the use of 'Allah,'" *The New York Times*, January 12, 2010, http://www.nytimes.com/aponline/2010/01/12/world/AP-AS-Malaysia-Allah-Ban.html (accessed January 24, 2010).

Mexicans

1 These are my own estimates based on different figures seen and current trends of migration. See Robert Courtney Smith, *Mexican New York: Transnational Lives of New Immigrants* (Berkeley: U of California P, 2006), 15, 23.

2 Lawrence E. Harrison, *Who Prospers: How Cultural Values Shape Economic and Political Success* (New York: BasicBooks, 1992), 178.

3 Smith, 204.

Nepalis

1 ABC News, "Sherpas in the City," *World News with Diane Sawyer*, December 2, 2007, http://www.abcnews.go.com/WN/story?id=3943658&page=2 (accessed November 24, 2009).

2 Ibid.

3 In personal interviews with five different Nepali community leaders, an estimate of 35,000 was average, with the most conservative estimate being 30,000. We used the latter estimate here, as it is also quoted in Jeff van Dam, "For a People Overlooked, A Lens at Last," *New York Times*, April 29, 2007, http://query.nytimes.com/gst/fullpage.html?res=9D07E3DA123EF93AA15757C0A9619C8B63 (accessed November 25, 2009).

4 United Nations High Commissioner for Refugees, "Over 20,000 Bhutanese Refugees Resettled from Nepal," *UNHCR Briefing Notes*, September 8, 2009, http://www.unhcr.org/4aa641446.html (accessed December 1, 2009).

Nigerians

1 Although Nigeria has a modern democratic government with a structure much like the United States', there are hundreds of kings that serve as leaders over small "kingdoms," which are usually towns or cities.

2 Kwasi Sarkodie-Mensah, "Nigerian Americans," *Countries and Their Cultures*, http://www.everyculture.com/multi/Le-Pa/Nigerian-Americans.html (accessed September 30, 2008).

3 Katy Pownall, "Nigeria Sees Boom in Brain Gain: Many Return to Oil-Rich Nation for High-Paying Jobs," *Houston Chronicle*, September 20, 2008, http://www.chron.com/disp/story.mpl/headline/world/6012534.html (accessed September 30, 2008).

Pakistanis

1 "Special Registration," Wikipedia, http://en.wikipedia.org/wiki/Special_Registration (accessed November 11, 2009).

2 Joe Spring, "Pakistan Earthquake Rumbles Through South Brooklyn," *Colombia Journalist,* November 2005, http://www.columbiajournalist.org/article.asp?subj=city&course=rw1_hancock&id=616 (accessed October 18, 2008).

3 Robert Polner, "A Neighborhood in a Fishbowl," *Newsweek*, August 1, 2005, http://www.newsday.com/news/a-neighborhood-in-a-fishbowl-1.559231 (accessed November 11, 2009).

4 Adil Najam, *Portrait of a Giving Community: Philanthropy by the Pakistani-American Diaspora* (Cambridge: Harvard UP, 2007), 62, and *Aminah Mohammad-Arif, Salaam America: South Asian Muslims in New York* (London: Anthem Press, 2002), 35-36.

Palestinians

1 Randa Serhan, "Second Generation Palestinian-Americans: At the Intersection of Ethnicity and Nationalism" (paper presented at the annual meeting for the American Sociological Association, Montreal, Quebec, Canada, August 10, 2006), http://www.allacademic.com/meta/p105183_index.html (accessed May 6, 2009).

2 Anemona Hartocollis, "From Jerusalem to Paterson," *New York Times*, April 24, 2005, http://query.nytimes.com/gst/fullpage.html?res=9B0DE5D81731F937A15757C0A9639C8B63&sec=&spon=&pagewanted=1 (accessed May 5, 2009).

Panamanians

1 Central Intelligence Agency, "Panama," *The World Factbook*, https://www.cia.gov/library/publications/the-world-factbook/geos/pm.html (accessed November 12, 2008).

2 Personal conversation with Dr. Marco Mason, CEO of the Panamanian Council of New York.

3 Ibid.

4 Personal interview with Archbishop Wilbert McKinley of Elim International Fellowship.

Persian Jews

1 Sanford J. Ungar, "'We Know Who We Are': The Mashadi," in Ungar, ed., *Fresh Blood: The New American Immigrants* (Urbana: U of Illinois P, 1998), 305-308; Bernard Livi, "Mashadi Jewish Community History: Anussim of Mashad," Mashadi Rabbi, http://mashadirabbi.com/history.php (accessed November 9, 2009).

2 The number 11,000 is derived from the oft-quoted 15,000 Persian-Jewish and the 4,000 Mashadi-Jewish populations of Metro New York. See Karmel Melamed, "Iranian Jews in New York Still Keeping a Low Profile," *Jewish Journal*, February 3, 2008, http://www.jewishjournal.com/iranianamericanjews/item/iranian_jews_in_new_york_still_keeping_a_low_profile/ (accessed November 9, 2009) and Ungar, 328.

Peruvians

1 Eric Asimov, "Peruvian Cuisine Takes on the World," *The New York Times*, May 26, 1999, http://query.nytimes.com/gst/fullpage.html?res=9E05E7D91331F935A15756C0A96F958260 (accessed October 23, 2008).

2 Rodolfo F. Acuña, *US Latino Issues* (Greenwood Publishing Group, 2003), 13-14.

3 John Packel, "Peruvian Americans," *Countries and Their Cultures*, http://www.everyculture.com/multi/Pa-Sp/Peruvian-Americans.html (accessed October 24, 2008).

4 Guy D. Garcia, Laura Lopez, and Sharon Stevenson, "Peru Lurching toward Anarchy," TIME Magazine, March 27, 1989, http://www.time.com/time/magazine/article/0,9171,957331-1,00.html (accessed October 24, 2008).

Poles

1 Jeff Vandam, "Neighborhood Report: Staten Island Up Close; A New Miss Polonia Reigns Over a Growing Polish Stronghold," *The New York Times*, May 30, 2004, http://www.nytimes.com/2004/05/30/nyregion/neighborhood-report-staten-island-up-close-new-miss-polonia-reigns-over-growing.html (accessed June 23, 2009).

2 *Census 2000*, http://factfinder.census.gov/servlet/QTTable?_bm=y&geo_id=16000US3476490&-qr_name=DEC_2000_SF3_U_DP2&-ds_name=DEC_2000_SF3_U&-_lang=en&-_sse=on (accessed June 26, 2009).

3 Kirk Semple, "A Land of Opportunity Lures Poles Back Home," *The New York Times*, September 20, 2008, http://www.nytimes.com/2008/09/21/nyregion/21poles.html (accessed June 23, 2009).

4 For community estimate, see "Centers of Polish Immigration in the World: USA and Germany," *Polish Culture*, http://culture.polishsite.us/articles/art90fr.htm (accessed 21 February 2010).

Portuguese

1 "History of the Sport Club Portugués," Sport Club Portugués, http://scportugues.org/main/index.php?option=com_content&task=view&id=12&Itemid=26 (accessed September 18, 2008).

2 Estimate provided by Fernando Santos, Senior News Editor of the Luso Americano Newspaper, in a personal interview.

3 Ernest E. Norden, "Portuguese Americans," *Countries and Their Cultures*, http://www.everyculture.com/multi/Pa-Sp/Portuguese-Americans.html (accessed September 18, 2008).

Puerto Ricans

1 Dominicans and Mexicans are the major candidates for surpassing Puerto Ricans' population numbers. See Ramona Hernandez and Francisco L. Rivera-Batiz, *Dominicans in the United States: A Socioeconomic Profile, 2000* (CUNY Dominican Studies Institute, 2003), http://www.earth.columbia.edu/cgsd/advising/documents/rivera_batiz.pdf (accessed August 15, 2008) and Eric Pape, "So Far From God, So Close to Ground Zero," *The Los Angeles Times*, August 3, 2003, http://articles.latimes.com/2003/aug/03/magazine/tm-nymex31 (accessed August 15, 2008).

2 Derek Green, "Puerto Rican Americans," *Countries and Their Cultures*, http://everyculture.com/multi/Pa-Sp/Puerto-Rican-Americans.html (accessed

August 18, 2008).

3 Pew Forum on Religion and Public Life, "Changing Faiths: Latinos and the Transformation of American Religion," *Pew Hispanic Center*, April 25, 2007, http://pewhispanic.org/reports/report.php?ReportID=75 (accessed August 18, 2008).

Punjabis

1 "Sikhism," Encarta, http://encarta.msn.com/encyclopedia_761566784_2/sikhism.html (accessed October 21, 2009).

2 "Sikh," Wikipedia, http://en.wikipedia.org/wiki/Sikh (accessed October 19, 2009).

3 "Sikh American Leaders Meet with White House Officials," SikhNet, September 29, 2008, http://fateh.sikhnet.com/s/SikhsMeetWhiteHouse (accessed October 18, 2009).

4 Estimate derived from interview with Mohinder Singh, President of the Baba Makhan Shah Lobana Sikh Center in Richmond Hill, and 2008 American Community Survey data indicating there are 547,539 Asian Indians in Metro New York.

Quichua

1 Jeremy Mumford, "Ecuadoran Americans," in Robert Dassanowsky and Jeffrey Lehman, eds., *Gale Encyclopedia of Multicultural America*, vol. 1 (Farmington Hills, MI: Gale Group, 2000), 560.

2 Estimate comes from personal interviews with Quichuan pastors.

3 Jason Pribilsky, as quoted in Leah Rae, "Indigenous South American Tongues a Challenge," *The Journal News*, November 29, 2005, http://www.alipac.us/ftopicp-60969.html (accessed February 12, 2010).

4 Pribilsky, *La Chulla Vida: Gender, Migration, and the Family in Andean Ecuador and New York City* (Syracuse: Syracuse UP, 2007), 11-12.

Romanians

1 Daniel Soyer, *Jewish Immigrant Associations and American Identity in New York, 1880-1939: Jewish 'Landsmanshaftn' in American Culture* (Detroit: Wayne State UP, 2002), 50.

2 Vladimir Werstman, "Romanians," *Encyclopedia of New York City* (New Haven: Yale UP, 1995), 1018.

Russians

1 In a Research Institute of New Americans (RINA) study titled, "Russian Jewish Immigrants in New York City: Status, Identity, and Integration" (New York: American Jewish Committee, 2000), 71 percent of Russian speakers interviewed were Jewish. In a 2004 survey by RINA, 91 percent of Russian speakers identified themselves as definitely having a Jewish identity. See RINA, "Russian-Jewish Opinion Survey 2004," American Jewish Committee, http://www.ajc.org/site/apps/nlnet/content3.aspx?c=ijITI2PHKoG&b=846741&ct=1030151 (accessed January 16, 2010).

2 RINA's "Russian Jewish Immigrants in New York City" estimates 400,000 Russian-speaking Jews living in Metro New York. Surveys, including those by RINA, indicate that 70-90 percent of Russian speakers in Metro New York are ethnically Jewish. If this range is averaged out to 80 percent, then 100,000 non-Jewish Russian-speakers also live in Metro New York. In "Russian-Jewish Opinion Survey 2004," 22 percent of Russian-speakers interviewed identified themselves as immigrants from the Russian Republic of the former Soviet Union. Twenty-two percent of 500,000 is 110,000.

3 The first three major waves of Russian migration occurred from the 1880s to 1914, the 1920s through the 1930s, and the few years following the Second World War. However, the subsequent generations of these immigrants more readily identify themselves as Americans and are generally not included when talking about the Russians of New York.

4 Samuel Kliger, "The Religion of New York Jews from the Former Soviet Union," in Tony Carnes, Anna Karpathakis, eds., *New York Glory: Religion in the City* (New York: New York UP, 2001), 149.

5 RINA, "Russian Jewish Immigrants in New York City."

Salvadorans

1 Kirk Semple, "Market for Day Laborers Sours with the US Economy," *The New York Times*, October 20, 2008, http://www.nytimes.com/2008/10/20/world/americas/20iht-20laborers.17089577.html?pagewanted=all (accessed June 25, 2009).

2 US Department of State, "Background Note: El Salvador," http://www.state.

gov/r/pa/ei/bgn/2033.htm (accessed June 24, 2009).

3 Sarah J. Mahler, "Suburban Transnational Migrants: Long Island's Salvadorans," in Héctor R. Cordero-Guzmán, Robert C. Smith, and Ramón Grosfoguel, eds., *Migration, Transnationalization, and Race in a Changing New York* (Philadelphia: Temple University Press, 2001) 111.

4 Deann Alford, "El Salvador's Values Voters," *Christianity Today*, April 21, 2009, http://www.ctlibrary.com/ct/2009/may/7.18.html (accessed June 26, 2009).

5 E. J. Tamara, "US Salvadorans Make Opinion Count in Election," *ABC News*, March 14, 2009, http://abcnews.go.com/US/wireStory?id=7082155 (accessed June 25, 2009).

6 Jeremy Mumford, "Salvadoran Americans," in Robert Dassanowsky and Jeffrey Lehman, eds., *Gale Encyclopedia of Multicultural America*, vol. 1 (Farmington Hills, MI: Gale Group, 2000), 1538.

Satmar Jews

1 Jack Wertheimer, *Imagining the American Jewish Community* (Lebanon, NH: UPNE, 2006), 168.

2 "Religious Authorities Announce New Satmar Hasidim Leader," *Associated Press*, April 12, 2006, http://web.israelinsider.com/Articles/Briefs/8333.htm (accessed September 17, 2009).

3 Wertheimer, 159.

4 Ibid, 158.

5 Matt King, "KJ Highest US Poverty Rate, Census Says," *Times-Herald-Record*, January 30, 2009, http://www.recordonline.com/apps/pbcs.dll/article?AID=/20090130/NEWS/901300361 (accessed September 18, 2009).

6 Sewall Chan and Jo Craven McGinty, "Explosive Growth Since 2000 in State's Hasidic Enclaves," *The New York Times*, June 29, 2007, http://www.nytimes.com/2007/06/29/nyregion/29census.html (accessed September 19, 2009).

Senegalese

1 The Senegalese Consulate is quoted as estimating that 30,000 Senegalese live in Metro New York in Dan Kois, "Waiting for the Youssou N'Dour Concert," *New York Times*, Aug. 22, 2004, http://www.nytimes.com/2004/08/22/nyregion/thecity/22sene.html (accessed Oct 6, 2009). In personal interviews with the Senegalese Consul General and the Secretary of the Senegalese Association of America in 2007, the Consul General said that out of 9,700 Senegalese registered to vote with the Senegalese Consulate, an estimated 7,000 are Wolof. He estimated the actual population to be ten times this number, but the Senegalese Association of America estimated that there are only 20,000 Senegalese in Metro New York.

Serbs

1 This estimate comes from personal interviews with Djokan Majstorovic, the Father of the Serbian St. Sava Cathedral in New York City, and "Serbs in New York City," *Slavs of New York*, March 9, 2006, http://www.slavsofnewyork.com/2006/03/serbs-in-new-york-city.html (accessed October 30, 2008).

2 "Vidovdan," Wikipedia, http://en.wikipedia.org/wiki/Vidovdan (accessed October 30, 2008).

3 Marc Ferris, "Serbs," in Kenneth T. Jackson, ed., *The Encyclopedia of New York City*, (New Haven: Yale UP, 1995), 1059.

Syrian Jews

1 Sarina, Roffe, "Syrian Jews in New York," in M. Avrum Ehrlich, ed., *Encyclopedia of the Jewish Diaspora: Origins, Experiences, and Culture* (Santa Barbara: ABC-CLIO, 2009), 619.

2 Larry Cohler-Esses, "An Inside Look at a Syrian-Jewish Enclave," *Jewish Daily Forward*, July 28, 2009, http://www.forward.com/articles/110943/ (accessed November 10, 2009).

3 Seventy-five thousand is the number almost always quoted as the number of Syrian Jews in Metro New York. See Cohler-Esses as well as Paul Vitello, "Brooklyn Blogs Buzzing with Talk about Rabbis," *The New York Times*, July 24, 2009, http://www.nytimes.com/2009/07/25/nyregion/25syrians.html (accessed November 10, 2009).

4 Bob Cullinane, "A Money Tree Grows in Brooklyn," *Asbury Park Press*, August 21, 2006, http://www.app.com/article/99999999/DWEK02/399990093 (accessed November 10, 2009).

Syrio-Lebanese Christians

1 Estimate based on two-thirds of ACS 2008 Total Ancestry Reported figures, as suggested by the Gale Encyclopedia. See Significant Notes.

2 J. Sydney Jones, "Syrian Americans," in Robert Dassanowsky and Jeffrey Lehman, eds., *Gale Encyclopedia of Multicultural America*, vol. 3 (Farmington Hills, MI: Gale Group, 2000), 1717.

3 Anan Ameri and Dawn Ramey, eds., *Arab-American Encyclopedia* (Detroit: UXL/Gale Group, 2000), 60.

4 Paula Hajar and J. Sydney Jones, "Lebanese Americans," in *Gale Encyclopedia of Multicultural America*, vol. 2 (Farmington Hills, MI: Gale Group, 2000), 1116.

5 "Background: Lebanon's Confessional Political System," *Lebanon Wire*, June 2, 2009, http://www.lebanonwire.com/0906MLN/09060214DP.asp (accessed December 11, 2009).

Syrio-Lebanese Muslims

1 Estimate derived from ACS 2008 data on individuals reporting their place of birth as Lebanon or Syria. According to the *Arab-American Encyclopedia*, since 1965 between 60-90 percent of immigrants from these countries are Muslim. See Anan Ameri and Dawn Ramey, eds., *Arab-American Encyclopedia* (Detroit: UXL/Gale Group, 2000) 47, 104.

2 Public Broadcasting Service, "Caught in the Crossfire: Arab Americans," http://www.pbs.org/itvs/caughtinthecrossfire/arab_americans.html (accessed December 15, 2009).

3 Global Security, "Lebanon: Civil War, 1975-1991," *Military*, http://www.globalsecurity.org/military/world/war/lebanon.htm (accessed December 17, 2009).

4 Susan Sachs, "Assad Patronage Puts a Small Sect on Top in Syria," *The New York Times*, June 22, 2000, http://www.nytimes.com/library/world/mideast/062200syria-assad.html (accessed December 15, 2009).

5 "Contestant No. 2," *PBS Wide Angle*, July 29, 2009, http://www.pbs.org/wnet/wideangle/episodes/contestant-no-2/slideshow-who-are-the-druze/5255/ (accessed December 15, 2009).

Taiwanese

1 Mainland Affairs Council, Executive Yuan, *Across the Taiwan Strait* (Taipei: Panray International Enterprise, 2004), 11-12.

2 In a personal interview, Dr. Lai estimated that in Metro New York, 20-30 percent of native Taiwanese and 30-40 percent of ex-mainlanders are Christian. For similar statistics, see also Carolyn Chen, *Getting Saved in America* (Princeton: Princeton UP, 2008), 2. She claims Taiwanese Americans are 20-25 percent Christian.

Thai

1 Todd LeRoy Perreira, "*Sasana Sakon* and the New Asian American," in T. Carnes and F. Yang, eds., *Asian American Religions: The Making and Remaking of Borders and Boundaries* (New York: New York UP, 2004), 313.

2 Perreria, "New Cosmopolitans in Buddhist America: Transcultural Dynamics and the Thai Community" (paper presented at the annual conference for the Asian Pacific Americans and Religions Research Initiative, Claremont, California, August 6-8, 2009), http://pana.psr.edu/new-cosmopolitans-buddhist-america-transcultural-dynamics-and-thai-community (accessed January 26, 2010).

3 Estimate derived from conversations with community members and leaders at the Wat Thai in Elmhurst, New York, in July 2009.

4 Megan Ratner, "Thai Americans," in Robert Dassanowsky and Jeffrey Lehman, eds., *Gale Encyclopedia of Multicultural America*, vol. 3 (Farmington Hills, MI: Gale Group, 2000), 1743-1744.

5 Perreira, "*Sasana Sakon*," 336.

6 Patrick Winn, "Thailand: The War You've Never Heard," *Global Post*, March 12, 2009, http://www.globalpost.com/dispatch/thailand/090311/thailand-the-war-youve-never-heard?page=0,1 (accessed January 28, 2010).

Tibetans

1 The Office of Tibet in New York in 2008 estimated 9,000 Tibetans live in America. In the same article, 3,000 of these were said to live in New York. Seonaigh MacPherson, Anne-Sophie Bentz, and Dawa Bhuti Ghoso, "Global Nomads: The Emergence of the Tibetan Diaspora (Part 1)," *Migration Information Source* (September 2008), http://www.migrationinformation.org/USFocus/display.cfm?ID=693 (accessed November 25, 2009).

2 MacPherson, Bentz, and Ghoso.

Turks

1 Estimate derived from personal interviews with leaders in the Turkish community and outreach groups working with Turks in Metro New York.

2 Yelda Bektas, Ayhan Demir, and Randall Bowden, "Psychological Adaptations of Turkish Students at US Campuses," *International Journal for the Advancement of Counseling* 31, no. 2 (June 2009), http://www.springerlink.com/content/y0607q43jv7n365w/ (accessed November 18, 2009).

Ukrainians

1 Research Institute of New Americans (RINA) estimates 400,000 Russian-speaking Jews live in Metro New York. Surveys, including ones done by RINA, indicate that 70-90 percent of Russian-speakers in Metro New York are ethnic Jews. If this range is averaged out to 80 percent, then 100,000 non-Jewish Russian-speakers also live in Metro New York. Thirty-six percent of Russian-speakers who were interviewed identify themselves as immigrants from the Ukrainian Republic of the former Soviet Union. Thirty-six percent of 500,000 is 180,000, and 36 percent of 100,000 is 36,000. See RINA, "Russian Jewish Immigrants in New York City: Status, Identity, and Integration" (New York: American Jewish Committee, 2000) and "Russian-Jewish Opinion Survey 2004," *American Jewish Committee*, http://www.ajc.org/site/apps/nlnet/content3.aspx?c=ijITI2PHKoG&b=846741&ct=1030151 (accessed January 16, 2010).

2 Personal interview with Lubow Wolynetz, Librarian and Museum Curator at the Ukrainian Museum, December 2007.

3 Ibid. Other community leaders gave the same figures that 75 percent of non-Jewish Ukrainian immigrants come from west Ukraine and 25 percent from the east.

4 Annelise Orleck, "Soviet Jews: The City's Newest Immigrants Transform New York Jewish Life," in Nancy Foner, ed., *New Immigrants in New York*, revised edition (New York: Columbia UP, 2001), 113.

Vietnamese

1 Adelaida Reyes, *Music and the Vietnamese Refugee Experience: Songs of the Caged, Songs of the Free* (Philadelphia: Temple UP, 1999), 76.

2 Carl L. Bankston, III, "Vietnamese Americans," in Robert Dassanowsky and Jeffrey Lehman, eds., *Gale Multicultural Encyclopedia*, vol. 3 (Farmington Hills, MI: Gale Group, 2000), 1850-1851.

3 Pei-te Lien and Tony Carnes, "The Religious Demography of Asian American Boundary Crossing," in Tony Carnes and Fenggang Yang, eds., *Asian American Religions* (New York: New York UP, 2004), 48.

4 C. Ngo, D. Le, N. Abesamis-Mendoza, H. Ho-Asjoe, and M. J. Rey, *Community Health Needs and Resource Assessment: An Exploratory Study of Vietnamese in NYC* (New York: NYU Center for the Study of Asian American Health, 2007).

Wenzhounese

1 Kate Xiao Zhou, *China's Long March to Freedom: Grassroots Modernization* (New Brunswick: Transaction Publishers, 2009), 83-84.

2 In 2003, the director of the Wenzhou Office of Chinese Overseas Affairs estimated that 100,000 Wenzhounese live in America. Around one-half of these are believed to live in Metro New York, which would bring the number to 50,000. Many Wenzhounese community leaders in New York estimate their population to be over 100,000, but this seems way too high. See John T. Ma and Him Mark Lai, "The Wenzhounese Community in New York City," *Chinese America: History and Perspectives 18* (2004).

3 Ma and Lai.

4 Nicholas Kristof, "Christianity is Booming in China Despite Rifts," *The New York Times*, February 7, 1993, http://www.nytimes.com/1993/02/07/world/christianity-is-booming-in-china-despite-rifts.html?pagewanted=1 (accessed December 19, 2009).

Yemenis

1 "1994 Civil War in Yemen," Wikipedia, http://en.wikipedia.org/wiki/1994_civil_war_in_Yemen (accessed December 22, 2009).

2 Estimate based on 200,145 Arabs in Metro New York (ACS 2008) and calculated according to the Arab American Association of New York's records, indicating that 10% of those they come into contact with are Yemeni.

3 Anan Ameri and Dawn Ramey, eds., *Arab-American Encyclopedia*, 1st ed. (Detroit: UXL/Gale Group, 2000), 53.

4 Mohammed Jamjoom, "UN: Yemen's Civil War Spreads to Saudi Arabia," CNN, November 14, 2009, http://edition.cnn.com/2009/WORLD/africa/11/14/yemen.fighting/index.html (accessed December 22, 2009).

5 Central Intelligence Agency, "Yemen," *The World Factbook*, https://www.cia.gov/library/publications/the-world-factbook/geos/ym.html (accessed December 22, 2009).

Photo Credits
In alphabetical order

All maps throughout the book were done by Jonathan Blazs.

Front Cover
TL-Bolivian woman at 45th Annual Hispanic Day Parade, 5th Avenue, Manhattan © Kristine Endsley; TR-9/11 demonstrator, Financial District, Manhattan © Kristine Endsley; ML-African Day Parade, Harlem, Manhattan © Kristine Endsley; MR-Upper West Side, Manhattan © Joanna Johnson; BL-Deepavali Festival, South Street Seaport, Manhattan © Kristine Endsley; BM-Midtown, Manhattan © Joanna Johnson; BR-Little India, Jackson Heights, Queens © Joanna Johnson

Back Cover
TR-Arab American Festival, Brooklyn © Clara Kim; BL-Muslim Day Parade, Manhattan © Kristine Endsley; BR-Hindu Temple, Flushing, Queens © Joanna Johnson

Afghans
FG: LTR-Afghan Crown Fried Chicken owner in Jamaica, Queens © Leah Gonzalez; LMR-Kennedy Fried Chicken, Harlem, Manhattan © Leah Gonzalez; RTM and RM-Majid Hazrat Abubakr Islamic Center, Flushing, Queens © Chris Clayman; RBL-Afghan Kebab House, Upper East Side, Manhattan © Chris Clayman; BG: Majid Hazrat Abubakr Islamic Center, Flushing, Queens © Chris Clayman

Afro-Guyanese
FG: LTR and RBL-West Indian Parade, Brooklyn © Kristine Endsley; Resurrection Temple, East Flatbush, Brooklyn © Bridget Covell; RMR-Epiphany Church Recreation Center, Crown Heights, Brooklyn © Bridget Covell; BG: LMR-Eastern Parkway and Nostrand Avenue, Crown Heights, Brooklyn © Bridget Covell

Afro-Trinidadians
FG: LTR, LBR, RTL, RTR, RM, and RBL-West Indian Parade © Kristine Endsley; BG: West Indian Parade © Kristine Endsley

Albanians
FG: LTR-Turkish Festival in Central Park, Manhattan © Kristine Endsley; LBR and RMR-Immigrants Parade, Manhattan © Leah Gonzalez; RTL-Broadway and 50th Street, Manhattan © Leah Gonzalez; RBL-Mulberry Street, Little Italy, Manhattan © Joanna Johnson; BG: RMR-Immigrants Parade, Manhattan © Leah Gonzalez

Argentines
FG: LTR and LBM-45th Annual Hispanic Day Parade on 5th Avenue, Manhattan © Kristine Endsley; LBL, RTL, RTR, and RBM- Jackson Heights, Queens © Joanna Johnson; BG: Jackson Heights, Queens © Joanna Johnson

Bangladeshis
FG: LTR, LBR, RTM, RBL, and RBR-Bangladesh Festival, Queens © Joanna Johnson; BG: RTM-Bangladesh Festival, Queens © Joanna Johnson

Barbadians
FG: LTR, LBM, RTL, RBL, and RMR-West Indian Parade, Brooklyn © Kristine Endsley; BG: RTM-West Indian Parade, Brooklyn © Kristine Endsley

Belarusians
FG: LTR-Belarusian Festival, Whitehead, South River, New Jersey © Heather Bowshier; LBM and RBL-Belarusian Festival, Whitehead, South River, New Jersey © Leah Gonzalez; RTM-Russian Orthodox Church, South River, New Jersey © Heather Bowshi-er; BG: Russian Orthodox Church, South River, New Jersey © Heather Bowshier

Bobover Jews
FG: LTR, LB, and RTM-15th Avenue, Borough Park, Brooklyn © Leah Gonzalez; RM-Bobov Promenade, Borough Park, Brooklyn © Jonathan Blazs; RBL-Torah Animal World in Borough Park, Brooklyn © Leah Gonzalez; RBR-Bobover Yeshiva (School) in Borough Park, Brooklyn © Jonathan Blazs

Bosniaks
FG: LTR, RBL, and RBR-Turkish Festival, Central Park © Kristine Endsley; RTM-Black Bull Mini Market, Astoria, Queens © Kristine Endsley; RM-Astoria, Queens © Brian Smith; BG: LBR-Astoria, Queens © Brian Smith

Brazilians
FG: LTR, LM, LBL, and RBR-Brazilian Day Festival on 6th Avenue, Manhattan © Kristine Endsley; RBL-Astoria, Queens © Joanna Johnson; RT-Midtown, Manhattan © Kristine Endsley; BG: RBL-Newark, New Jersey © Joanna Johnson

British
FG: LTR and LBR-A Salt & Battery in Chelsea, Manhattan © Leah Gonzalez; RTM and RM-Tea & Sympathy in Chelsea, Manhattan © Leah Gonzalez; RBM-Tea & Sympathy in Chelsea, Manhattan © Heather Bowshier; BG: A Salt & Battery in Chelsea, Manhattan © Leah Gonzalez

Bukharan Jews
FG: LTR, RTR, RBL, and RBR-Forest Hills, Queens © Joanna Johnson; BG: LBR and RMR, Forest Hills, Queens © Joanna Johnson

Burmese
FG: LTR, LBR, RTL, and RBL-Dag Hammarskjold Plaza, Midtown, Manhattan © Kristine Endsley; RTR-Cafe Mingala, Upper East Side, Manhattan © Chris Clayman; RBR-Burmese New Year's Water Festival, Manhattan © Leah Gonzalez

Canadians
FG: LTR, RTR, and RML-Tim Hortons, Midtown, Manhattan © Jamy McMahan; RBM-Consulate General of Canada, Manhattan © Bridget Covell; BG: RBR-Consulate General of Canada, Manhattan © Bridget Covell

Colombians
FG: LTR, LBR, RBL, and RBR-45th Annual Hispanic Day Parade on 5th Avenue, Manhattan © Kristine Endsley; LBL-Colombian Independence Day, Flushing Meadows Park, Queens © Joanna Johnson; RTM-Colombian dancing couple at Immigrant Day Parade, Manhattan © Leah Gonzalez; BG: 82nd Street and Roosevelt Avenue, Queens © Travis Pace

Croats
FG: LTR, LBR, RTM, and RBR-Astoria, Queens © Joanna Johnson; RML-Croatian Roman Catholic Church, Midtown, Manhattan © Nichole Clayman

Cubans
FG: LTR, RTL, and RMR-Main Street, Union City, New Jersey © Joanna Johnson; LBM and RBM-Cuban Parade, Union City, New Jersey © Leah Gonzalez

Dominicans
FG: LTR, RTR, RBL, and RBR-Dominican Day Parade, 6th Avenue, Manhattan © Kristine Endsley; LBM-Dominican Day Parade, 6th Avenue, Manhattan © Joanna Johnson; BG: Dominican Day Parade, 6th Avenue, Manhattan © Joanna Johnson

Ecuadorians
FG: LTR and LB-Ecuadorian Festival, Jersey City, New Jersey © Joanna Johnson; RTL and RBM-45th Annual Hispanic Day Parade on 5th Avenue, Manhattan © Kristine Endsley; RMR-Roosevelt Avenue, Corona, Queens © Joanna Johnson; LTM-45th Annual Hispanic Day Parade on 5th Avenue, Manhattan © Kristine Endsley; RML-Roosevelt Avenue and 102nd Street, Corona, Queens © Joanna Johnson

Egyptians
FG: LTR and RBR-Arab American Festival, Brooklyn © Clara Kim; LBL and LBM-Coptic Orthodox Church of St. Mark, Jersey City, New Jersey © Kristine Endsley; RML-"Little Egypt" on Steinway Street, Astoria, Queens © Joanna Johnson; RTR-Arab American North African Street Festival, Brooklyn © Leah Gonzalez; BG: RBL-Arab American Festival, Bay Ridge, Brooklyn © Joanna Johnson; RTR-"Little Egypt" on Steinway Street, Astoria, Queens © Joanna Johnson

Ethiopians
FG: LTR and RBL-Emmanuel Worship Center, Bronx © Leah Gonzalez; LMR and RBR-Ethiopian Orthodox Church, Morningside Heights, Manhattan © Jonathan Blazs; RTM-African Day Parade © Kristine Endsley

Filipinos
FG: LTR, LB, RBL, and RMR-Filipino Independence Day Parade, Manhattan © Joanna Johnson; RTL-Phil-Am Food Mart, Woodside, Queens © Joanna Johnson; BG: RBM-Filipino Independence Day Parade, Manhattan © Joanna Johnson

French
FG: LTR, RTM, RMR, RBL, and RBR-Bastille Day Festival, Midtown, Manhattan © Joanna Johnson; BG: Bastille Day Festival, Midtown, Manhattan © Joanna Johnson

Fuzhounese
FG: LTR-Chinatown, Manhattan © Joanna Johnson; LMR-Lin Ze Xu Statue in Chatham Square, Chinatown, Manhattan © Nichole Clayman; LBM-Church of Grace to Fujianese, Chinatown, Manhattan © Nichole Clayman; RTM-East Broadway Street, Chinatown, Manhattan © Leah Gonzalez; RM-Southern Heaven Gate and School Of Taoism, Sunset Park, Brooklyn © Heather Bowshier; RBL-Elmhurst, Queens © Joanna Johnson; RBR-Sincere Employment Agency, Chinatown, Manhattan © Joanna Johnson; BG: RTM-East Broadway, Manhattan © Leah Gonzalez

Garifuna
FG: LTR, RTL, and RBR-African Day Parade, Harlem, Manhattan © Kristine Endsley; LBR, RTM, and RBL-Honduran Parade, Bronx © Kristine Endsley; BG: Honduran Parade, Bronx © Kristine Endsley

Germans
FG: LTR, RTL, RM, RBL, and RBR-German-American Steuben Parade, Manhattan © Kristine Endsley; BG: LBR-German-American Steuben Parade, Manhattan © Kristine Endsley

Ghanaians
FG: LTR and RBL-African United Day Parade, Claremont Park, Bronx © Joanna Johnson; LBM and RBR-African Day Parade, Harlem, Manhattan © Kristine Endsley; RTM and RM-African Market, Morris Heights, Bronx © Joanna Johnson

Gorsky-Kavkazi Jews
FG: LTR-Brooklyn © Kristine Endsley; LBM and

RBL-Gorsky-Kavkazi Synagogue and Cultural Center, Flatbush, Brooklyn © Kate Stanley; RTM-Gorsky-Kavkazi Synagogue and Cultural Center, Flatbush, Brooklyn © Bridget Covell; RM and RBR-Flatbush, Brooklyn © Kate Stanley; **BG:** Ocean Parkway and Avenue C, Brooklyn © Bridget Covell

Greeks
FG: LTR, LBL, RTL, and RTR-Astoria, Queens © Joanna Johnson; RBL and RBR-Greek Parade, Midtown, Manhattan © Clara Kim; **BG:** Greek Parade, Midtown, Manhattan © Clara Kim

Guatemalans
FG: LTR, LBR, RTM, RBL, and RMR-Annual Hispanic Day Parade, Manhattan © Kristine Endsley

Gujaratis
FG: LTR-At Patel Brothers, Jackson Heights, Queens © Leah Gonzalez; LBM-2008 Indian Parade on Madison Avenue, Manhattan © Kristine Endsley; RTL-Newsstand at 5th Avenue and 23rd Street, Manhattan; RMR and RB-Flushing, Queens © Joanna Johnson; **BG:** Patel Brothers, Jackson Heights, Queens © Leah Gonzalez

Haitians
FG: LTR-West Indian Parade, Brooklyn © Kristine Endsley; LBR, RTM, RM, RBL, RBM, and RBR-Our Lady Of Mt. Carmel Pilgrimage, East Harlem, Manhattan © Joanna Johnson

Hong Kongese
FG: LTR-Chinatown, Manhattan © Tim Kelly; RTL-Oversea Chinese Mission Fun Day, Chinatown, Manhattan © Heather Bowshier; RTM-Hong Kong Supermarket, Sunset Park, Brooklyn © Heather Bowshier; RMR-Chinatown, Manhattan © Heather Bowshier; RBL-Hong Kong Boat Festival, Flushing Meadows, Queens © Joanna Johnson; **BG:** LBR-Hong Kong Boat Festival, Flushing Meadows, Queens © Joanna Johnson

Indo-Caribbeans
FG: LTR-Phagwah Parade, Richmond Hill, Queens © Chris Clayman; LBL, RBL, and RBR-Phagwah Parade, Richmond Hill, Queens © Matt Gillis; RTR-Liberty Avenue, Richmond Hill, Queens © Chris Clayman

Indonesians
FG: LTR, LBR, and RM-Minangasli Indonesian Restaurant, Elmhurst, Queens © Joanna Johnson; RTR-Muslim Parade, Manhattan © Kristine Endsley; RBL and RBM-Elmhurst Baptist Church, Elmhurst, Queens © Joanna Johnson; RBR-Elmhurst, Queens © Joanna Johnson; **BG:** RTM-Goldfish © Joanna Johnson

Iranians
FG: LTR and RBL-Silent Vigil in Union Square, Manhattan © Leah Gonzalez; LBM, RTR, and RBR-Persian Parade © Chris Clayman; RM-Upper East Side, Manhattan © Chris Clayman

Irish
FG: LTR, LBL, RTL, and RMR-Woodside, Queens © Joanna Johnson; LBM, RML, and RBL-Irish Parade, Manhattan © Chris Clayman; **BG:** LTM-Woodside, Queens © Joanna Johnson

Israelis
FG: LTR, LMR, RT, and RBR-East Village, Manhattan © Joanna Johnson; LBL and RM-Salute to Israel Parade, Manhattan © Joanna Johnson; RBL-Around Coney Island Avenue and Ocean Parkway, Brooklyn © Joanna Johnson; **BG:** LTR-East Village, Manhattan © Joanna Johnson

Italians
FG: LTR, RTL, and RMR-Little Italy, Manhattan © Kristine Endsley; LBM-Columbus Day Parade, Manhattan © Kristine Endsley; RBL-Italian Festival in Hoboken, New Jersey © Joanna Johnson; **BG:** Italian Festival in Hoboken, New Jersey © Joanna Johnson

Jamaicans
FG: LTR, RTL, and RTR-West Indian Parade, Brooklyn © Kristine Endsley; RBM-Harlem, Manhattan; **BG:** West Indian Parade, Brooklyn © Kristine Endsley

Japanese
FG: LTR, LBL, RTL, RTR, and RBR-Obon Festival, Bryant Park, Manhattan © Clara Kim; LBR-Battery Park, Manhattan © Joanna Johnson; RBM-Manhattan © Joanna Johnson; **BG:** RTM and RBL-Obon Festival, Bryant Park, Manhattan © Clara Kim

Jordanians
FG: LTR-Arab-American Festival, Brooklyn © Clara Kim; RTM-Yonkers © Chris Clayman; RBL-Immaculate Conception of St. Mary, Yonkers © Chris Clayman; **BG:** RM-Yonkers © Chris Clayman

Keralites
FG: LTR-Keralite Church Pastor in Queens © Leah Gonzalez; LB and RBR-St. Mary's Orthodox Church of India, Bronx © Bridget Covell; RTL, RTM, and RBL-Indian Parade on Madison Avenue, Manhattan © Kristine Endsley; **BG:** St. Mary's Orthodox Church of India, Bronx © Bridget Covell

Korean-Chinese
FG: LTR and RTR-Mani 1 Restaurant, Flushing, Queens © Leah Gonzalez; LMR-Il Bok Restaurant, Flushing, Queens © Leah Gonzalez; LBM and RM-H-Mart, Flushing, Queens © Heather Bowshier; RTR-Mani 1 Restaurant, Flushing, Queens © Heather Bowshier; RBM-Korean-Chinese Association of New York, Flushing, Queens © Leah Gonzalez; **BG:** Chinese Consulate, Manhattan © Bridget Covell

Koreans
FG: LTR, LBM, and RBL-Korean Day Parade on Broadway, Manhattan © Kristine Endsley; LMR-Korean Church of Queens Mural © Chris Clayman; RTM-Korean Pastor, Flushing, Queens © Chris Clayman; RTR-Full Gospel Calvary Korean Assembly of God, Flushing, Queens © Chris Clayman; RBR-Little Korea, West 32nd Street, Manhattan © Kristine Endsley

Liberians
FG: LTR, LBM, RTM, RMR, and RBL-Park Hill-Clinton, Staten Island © Kristine Endsley; **BG:** Park Hill-Clinton, Staten Island © Kristine Endsley

Lubavitch Jews
FG: LTR-Lubavitch man on subway © Leah Gonzalez; LBM-Picture of Rebbe Menachem Schneerson on converted taxi, Rego Park, Queens © Chris Clayman; RTM and RBR-Brooklyn © Joanna Johnson; RBL-Lubavitch Headquarters, Crown Heights, Brooklyn © Leah Gonzalez

Macedonians
FG: LTR © Kristine Endsley; RTM-Macedonian Orthodox Church, Cedar Grove, New Jersey © Bridget Covell; RBL- Aleksandria Macedonian Cultural Center, Totowa, New Jersey © Bridget Covell; RMR-Deja-Vu Cafe, Garfield, New Jersey © Bridget Covell; **BG:** Macedonian Orthodox Church, Cedar Grove, New Jersey © Bridget Covell

Mainland Cantonese
FG: LTR and RTL-Chinatown, Manhattan © Joanna Johnson; RTR and RBM-Chinese New Year Parade, Chinatown, Manhattan © Clara Kim; RBL-Cantonese Restaurant, Chinatown, Manhattan © Nichole Clayman; **BG:** LBR-Chinatown, Manhattan © Nichole Clayman

Mainland Han
FG: LTR-Flushing, Queens © Kristine Endsley; LBR-Flushing, Queens © Joanna Johnson; RTL and

RTM-Mahayana Buddhist Temple, Chinatown, Manhattan © Nichole Clayman; RMR-Confucius Statue, Chinatown, Manhattan © Nichole Clayman; RBL and RBM-Chinatown, Manhattan © Joanna Johnson

Malaysians
FG: LTR-Asian American Coalition Extravaganza, Flushing, Queens © Leah Gonzalez; RM-Malaysian Market, Flushing, Queens © Leah Gonzalez; RBL-Sentosa Restaurant, Flushing, Queens © Leah Gonzalez; **BG:** Asian American Coalition Extravaganza, Flushing, Queens © Leah Gonzalez

Mexicans
FG: LTR, LBM, and RM-Mexican Parade on Madison Avenue, Manhattan © Kristine Endsley; RTM-Mexican performers on the subway © Joanna Johnson; RBL-Around Roosevelt Avenue, Jackson Heights, Queens © Joanna Johnson; RBM-Mexican man and child at Bangladesh Festival, Queens © Joanna Johnson; RBR-Our Lady of Guadalupe Festival, Manhattan © Chris Clayman; **BG:** Around Roosevelt Avenue, Jackson Heights, Queens © Joanna Johnson

Nepalis
FG: LTR, RTL, and RBL-Jackson Heights, Queens © Joanna Johnson; LBM and RMR-Asian American Coalition Extravaganza, Flushing, Queens © Leah Gonzalez

Nigerians
FG: LTR-African United Day Parade, Claremont Park, Bronx © Joanna Johnson; LBL, RTR and RBM-Nigerian Parade, Manhattan © Kristine Endsley; RTL-African Day Parade, Harlem, Manhattan © Kristine Endsley; **BG:** Nigerian Parade, Manhattan © Kristine Endsley

Pakistanis
FG: LTR-Jackson Heights, Queens © Joanna Johnson; LBR, RTL, and RBL-Pakistan Parade in Manhattan © Kristine Endsley; RM-Pakistani Restaurant in Jackson Heights, Queens © Joanna Johnson

Palestinians
FG: LTR, LBR, and RM-Arab Festival, Brooklyn © Clara Kim; LM and RBR-Arab American Festival, Bay Ridge, Brooklyn © Joanna Johnson; RBL-Steinway Street, Astoria, Queens © Joanna Johnson; **BG:** Steinway Street, Astoria, Queens © Joanna Johnson

Panamanians
FG: LTR-Roosevelt Avenue, Jackson Heights, Queens © Joanna Johnson; LB-Honduran Parade on Southern Boulevard, Bronx © Kristine Endsley; RTM and RBL-Nigerian Parade, Manhattan © Kristine Endsley; RBR-West Indian Parade, Brooklyn © Kristine Endsley; **BG:** West Indian Parade, Brooklyn © Kristine Endsley

Persian Jews
FG: LTR, LBR, RTR, and RBL-Great Neck, Long Island © Kristine Endsley; **BG:** Great Neck, Long Island © Kristine Endsley

Peruvians
FG: LTR and RTR-Hispanic Day Parade, Manhattan © Kristine Endsley; LBL, RBL, and RBR-Peruvian Parade, Paterson, New Jersey © Joanna Johnson; RTM-Upper West Side, Manhattan © Kristine Endsley

Poles
FG: LTR and RMR-Greenpoint, Brooklyn © Joanna Johnson; LBM, RTL, RML, and RBL-Polish Parade, Manhattan © Kristine Endsley; **BG:** RBR-Greenpoint, Brooklyn © Joanna Johnson

Portuguese
FG: LTR, LBL, RTL, RTM, RBL, and RBR-Newark, New Jersey © Joanna Johnson

Puerto Ricans
FG: LTR, LBL, LBR, RT, RM, and RBL-Puerto

189

Rican Parade, Manhattan © Joanna Johnson; RBR-Nuyorican Poets Café, Lower East Side, Manhattan © Chris Clayman; **BG:** RBL-Puerto Rican Parade, Manhattan © Joanna Johnson

Punjabis
FG: LTR-Sikh Day Parade, Manhattan © Patricia Pendergrass; LB-Richmond Hill, Queens © Chauntae Richardson; RTM, RM, RBL, and RBR-Sikh Day Parade, Manhattan © John Pringle

Quichua
FG: LTR-Thunderbird Pow-wow, Queens Farm Museum © Joanna Johnson; LBM-Times Square Subway Station, Manhattan © Bridget Covell; RTM and RM-Iglesia Evangelica Bautista Quichua "Piedra Viva," Bronx © Bridget Covell; RBL-Ecuadorian Parade, Queens © Joanna Johnson; **BG:** At Quichua church, Bronx © Bridget Covell

Romanians
FG: LTR, RMR, and RBM-Maranatha Romanian Baptist Church, Ridgewood, Queens © Kristine Endsley; LBM-Immigrants Day Parade, Manhattan © Leah Gonzalez; RTL-Astoria, Queens © Joanna Johnson; **BG:** 63rd Ave and Fresh Pond Road, Queens © Kristine Endsley

Russians
FG: LTR, LBL, and RBL-Brighton Beach, Brooklyn © Joanna Johnson; RTL, RTM, and RBR-Brooklyn © Joanna Johnson

Salvadorans
FG: LTR and RTM-Union City, New Jersey © Joanna Johnson; LBM and RBL-45th Annual Hispanic Day Parade on 5th Avenue, Manhattan © Kristine Endsley; **BG:** Main Street, Union City, New Jersey © Joanna Johnson

Satmar Jews
FG: LTR-Williamsburg, Brooklyn © Leah Gonzalez; LB, RTR, RM, and RBL-Kiryas Joel, New York © Leah Gonzalez; **BG:** Kiryas Joel, New York © Leah Gonzalez

Serbs
FG: LTR, LBL, RTL, RTM, RBL, and RBR-Serbian Orthodox Cathedral of St. Sava, Manhattan © Kristine Endsley; **BG:** Serbian Orthodox Cathedral of St. Sava, Manhattan © Kristine Endsley

Senegalese
FG: LTR, RTM, RML, and RBR-At the UN, Manhattan © Joanna Johnson; LB-Mouride Parade, Harlem, Manhattan © Leah Gonzalez; RTL-116th Street, Harlem, Manhattan © Barbara Thomas; RBM-Ahmadou Bamba Day Mouride Parade, Harlem, Manhattan © Leah Gonzalez

Syrian Jews
FG: LTR, LMR, and RTM-Flatbush, Brooklyn © Joanna Johnson; RTR, RML, RBL, and RBR-Flatbush, Brooklyn © Kristine Endsley; **BG:** LBR and RMR, Syrian and Lebanese Jewish Synagogues, Flatbush, Brooklyn © Kristine Endsley

Syrio-Lebanese Christians
FG: LTR-Arab-American Friendship Center, Brooklyn © Leah Gonzalez; LMR, RML, and RMR-Maronite church, Brooklyn © Kristine Endsley; RTR and RBL-Church of the Virgin Mary, 8th Avenue, Brooklyn © Heather Bowshier

Syrio-Lebanese Muslims
FG: LTR-Arab-American Friendship Center, Brooklyn © Leah Gonzalez; LBL and RBL-Astoria, Queens © Joanna Johnson; RTM-Arab-American Festival, Brooklyn © Joanna Johnson; **BG:** Astoria, Queens © Joanna Johnson; Arab American Festival, Brooklyn © Joanna Johnson

Taiwanese
FG: LTR, LBL, RTL, RM, RBL, and RBR-Taiwanese Rally, Times Square, Manhattan © Kristine Endsley; LMR-Taiwanese Tissue Package Distributed at Taiwanese Rally © Chris Clayman; **BG:** Taiwanese Rally, Times Square, Manhattan © Kristine Endsley

Thai
FG: LTR, LBR, and RM-Thai Temple, Elmhurst, Queens © Joanna Johnson; RTM- Immigrants Day Parade, Manhattan © Leah Gonzalez; RBL-International Cultures Parade © Joanna Johnson; **BG:** Thai Temple, Elmhurst, Queens © Joanna Johnson; Immigrants Parade, Manhattan © Leah Gonzalez

Tibetans
FG: LTR and LBL-National Tibetan Uprising Day, Manhattan © Chris Clayman; RTM and RM-Jackson Heights, Queens © Joanna Johnson; RBL-International Immigrants Foundation Parade, Manhattan © Joanna Johnson; RBR-Tibetan Festival, Queens © Clara Kim; **BG:** International Immigrants Foundation Parade, Manhattan © Joanna Johnson

Turks
FG: LTR, RTL, and RMR-Turkish Festival, Central Park, Manhattan © Kristine Endsley; RTR-Fatih Camii Mosque, Sunset Park, Brooklyn © Heather Bowshier; RBL and RBM-Paterson, New Jersey © Joanna Johnson; **BG:** Paterson, New Jersey © Joanna Johnson; Turkish Parade, Manhattan © Chris Clayman

Ukrainians
FG: LTR, LBR, RTM, RML, RBR-Brighton Beach, Brooklyn © Joanna Johnson; RBL-St. Michael's Ukrainian Catholic Church, Yonkers © Chris Clayman; **BG:** Brighton Beach, Brooklyn © Joanna Johnson

Vietnamese
FG: LTR, LBR, RTM, and RBR-International Cultures Parade © Joanna Johnson; RBL-Immigrants Day Parade, Manhattan © Leah Gonzalez; **BG:** Immigrants Day Parade, Manhattan © Leah Gonzalez

Wenzhounese
FG: LTR-Public Library, Flushing, Queens © Tim Kelly; LBR-Supermarket, Flushing, Queens © Megan Yates; RM-Canal Street, Chinatown, Manhattan © Mike LaPach; RBL-Faith Bible Church, Flushing, Queens © Megan Yates; **BG:** LBR-Supermarket, Flushing, Queens © Megan Yates; RTM-Canal Street, Chinatown, Manhattan © Mike LaPach

Yemenis
FG: LTR-Halal Deli Owner, Harlem, Manhattan © Leah Gonzalez; LBM-Arab American Festival in Bay Ridge, Queens © David Vining; RTM-Arab-American Festival, Brooklyn, Clara Kim; RM-Astoria, Queens © Joanna Johnson; RBL-Arab American Festival on Shore Road, Brooklyn © Joanna Johnson; RBR-Halal Deli, Harlem, Manhattan © Leah Gonzalez; **BG:** Arab American Festival in Bay Ridge, Queens © David Vining

Research and Writing Credits

Chris Clayman contributed writing and research on all profiles. Where Meredith Lee is credited as contributing writing, she was the primary writer for that profile. Brittni Pueppke and Tom Williams contributed editing on each profile. As there were no other contributors besides Chris Clayman on the Fuzhounese and Syrian Jews profiles, they are not listed below.

Afghans
Heather Town, Hillery Nyvall, June Chambliss, Sharon Ellison (research)

Afro-Guyanese
Jamy McMahan (research)

Afro-Trinidadians
Sarah Minott, Kyle Herrington (research)

Albanians
Peggy Itschner (research)

Argentines
Meredith Lee (research and writing); Brooke Keisling (research)

Bangladeshis
Brad Veitch (research)

Barbadians
Wilson Cowherd, Stephen Carl, Sarah Carl (research)

Belarusians
Susan Williams (research)

Bobover Jews
Meredith Lee (research and writing); Jonathan Blazs (research)

Bosniaks
Meredith Lee (research and writing); Evan Conrad, Brian M. Smith, Katrina Thomas (research)

Brazilians
Meredith Lee (research and writing); Jamy McMahan (research)

British
Meredith Lee (research and writing); Jamy McMahan (research)

Bukharan Jews
Steve Allen, Steve Able, Matthew Peterson (research)

Burmese
Meredith Lee (research and writing); Jonathan Blazs (research)

Canadians
Meredith Lee (research and writing); Jamy McMahan (research)

Colombians
Travis Pace, Becca Koe, Stacy Middelton (research)

Croats
Meredith Lee (research and writing); Jamy McMahan (research)

Cubans
Meredith Lee (research and writing); Brooke Keisling (research)

Dominicans
Donny Wadley, Matt Doane (research)

Ecuadorians
Alan Grissom, Caitlin Hawkins, Andrew Fultz (research)

Egyptians
Nate Staley, Kurt Osterloh (research)

Ethiopians
Meredith Lee (research and writing); Jonathan Blazs (research)

Filipinos
Jamy McMahan (research)

French
Meredith Lee (research and writing); Brooke Keisling (research)

Garifuna
Cory Murman, Kelly Carter, Jeremiah Pearson (research)

Germans
Meredith Lee (research and writing); Brooke Keisling (research)

Ghanaians
Jamy McMahan (research)

Gorsky-Kavkazi Jews
Meredith Lee (research and writing); Kate Stanley, Juliet Bleything (research)

Greeks
Stephanie Smith, Caleb Westbrook (research)

Guatemalans
Meredith Lee (research and writing); Brooke Keisling (research)

Gujaratis
Meredith Lee (research and writing); Kallie-Jo Wolf, Philip Martin, Michelle Brown, Brendan Austin (research)

Haitians
Theresa Jones, Dara Padilla, Kellen Cox, Emily Tebow, Jean Kim (research)

Hong Kongese
Heather Bowshier, Yiu Cheong Kung (research)

Indo-Caribbeans
Jeremy Pearson, Whitney Johnson (research)

Indonesians
Sharon Ellison (research)

Iranians
Meredith Lee (research and writing); Kallie-Jo Wolf (research)

Irish
Stephanie Smith, Caleb Westbrook (research)

Israelis
Mary Megan Yates, Thomas Summers (research)

Italians
Billy McMahan, Amy Armstrong (research)

Jamaicans
Amanda Gilmore, Britt Daugherty, Welby Jones (research)

Japanese
Megan Parris (research)

Jordanians
Meredith Lee (research and writing); David Vining (research)

Keralites
Meredith Lee (research and writing); Kallie-Jo Wolf (research)

Korean-Chinese
Meredith Lee (research and writing); Heather Bowshier (research)

Koreans
Meredith Lee (research and writing); Heather Bowshier, Eric K. Botts, Mike Tebow, Brea Daugherty, Abby Moenkhoff (research)

Liberians
Meredith Lee (research and writing); Anna Daniels, Rebecca LaChance, Zarah McPike (research)

Lubavitch Jews
Meredith Lee (research and writing); Jonathan Blazs (research)

Macedonians
Meredith Lee (research and writing); Justine Carter, Nichole Aragon, Michelle Scott (research)

Mainland Cantonese
Heather Bowshier, Yiu Cheong Kung (research)

Mainland Han
Megan Eubanks, Kyle Seaney, Megan Yates, Nathan Staley, Heather Bowshier (research)

Malaysians
Meredith Lee (research and writing); David Vining (research)

Mexicans
Jessica Vasquez, Sergio Su (research)

Nepalis
Meredith Lee (research and writing); Kallie-Jo Wolf (research)

Nigerians
Eileen Evind, Daniel Chacon (research)

Pakistanis
Haylee Wells, Carrie Nelson (research)

Palestinians
Meredith Lee (research and writing); Kelly Crosby, Andrew Denbow (research)

Panamanians
Erica Fronsoe, Rachael N. Smith

Persian Jews
Larry Strickland (research)

Peruvians
Brianne Jones, Elaine Smith, and Evan Lindauer (research)

Poles
Meredith Lee (research and writing); Megan Parris (research)

Portuguese
Jamy McMahan (research)

Puerto Ricans
Eric Smith, Andrew Boyd, Whitney Jennings (research)

Punjabis
Meredith Lee (research and writing); Chauntae Richardson, Rebekah Pearce, Tiana Murray (research)

Quichua
Steve Allen (research)

Romanians
Meredith Lee (research and writing); Megan Parris (research)

Russians
Kyle Seaney, Meagan Eubanks (research)

Salvadorans
Meredith Lee (research and writing); Kallie-Jo Wolf, David Hackney (research)

Satmar Jews
Meredith Lee (research and writing); Jonathan Blazs (research)

Serbs
Andrea Conway, Cassie Alexander, Nate Jones (research)

Senegalese
Sarah Rohrer, Andy Clark (research)

Syrio-Lebanese Christians
Meredith Lee (research and writing); Leah Gonzalez (research)

Syrio-Lebanese Muslims
Meredith Lee (research and writing); Leah Gonzalez (research)

Taiwanese
Kathy Haserick (research)

Thai
Meredith Lee (research and writing); Jeremiah Gallagher, Paul Pierce (research)

Tibetans
Kathy Haserick (research)

Turks
Meredith Lee (research and writing); Kallie-Jo Wolf, Kathy Haserick (research)

Ukrainians
Susan Williams, Kyle Seaney, Meagan Eubanks (research)

Vietnamese
Hannah Utley, Tim Jackson (research)

Wenzhounese
Megan Eubanks, Kyle Seaney, Megan Yates, Nathan Staley, Heather Bowshier, Jalin Liu (research)

Yemenis
Meredith Lee (research and writing); David Vining (research)

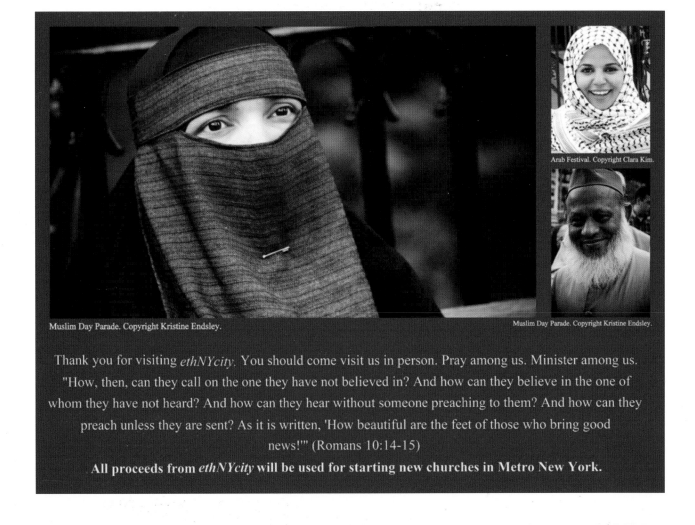

Arab Festival. Copyright Clara Kim.

Muslim Day Parade. Copyright Kristine Endsley.

Muslim Day Parade. Copyright Kristine Endsley.

Thank you for visiting *ethNYcity*. You should come visit us in person. Pray among us. Minister among us. "How, then, can they call on the one they have not believed in? And how can they believe in the one of whom they have not heard? And how can they hear without someone preaching to them? And how can they preach unless they are sent? As it is written, 'How beautiful are the feet of those who bring good news!'" (Romans 10:14-15)

All proceeds from *ethNYcity* will be used for starting new churches in Metro New York.